CAMBRIDGE
UNIVERSITY PRESS

Cambridge Lower Secondary
Mathematics

TEACHER'S RESOURCE 8

Lynn Byrd, Greg Byrd & Chris Pearce

CAMBRIDGE
UNIVERSITY PRESS

University Printing House, Cambridge CB2 8BS, United Kingdom

One Liberty Plaza, 20th Floor, New York, NY 10006, USA

477 Williamstown Road, Port Melbourne, VIC 3207, Australia

314–321, 3rd Floor, Plot 3, Splendor Forum, Jasola District Centre, New Delhi – 110025, India

103 Penang Road, #05-06/07, Visioncrest Commercial, Singapore 238467

Cambridge University Press is part of the University of Cambridge.

It furthers the University's mission by disseminating knowledge in the pursuit of education, learning and research at the highest international levels of excellence.

www.cambridge.org
Information on this title: www.cambridge.org/9781108771450

© Cambridge University Press 2021

First published 2014
Second edition 2021

20 19 18 17 16 15 14 13 12 11 10 9 8 7 6 5 4 3

Printed in Great Britain by CPI Group (UK) Ltd, Croydon CR0 4YY

A catalogue record for this publication is available from the British Library

ISBN 978-1-108-77145-0 Paperback with Digital Access

NOTICE TO TEACHERS IN THE UK

Disclaimer

Projects and their accompanying teacher guidance have been written by the NRICH Team. NRICH is an innovative collaboration between the Faculties of Mathematics and Education at the University of Cambridge, which focuses on problem solving and on creating opportunities for students to learn mathematics through exploration and discussion https://nrich.maths.org.

> Contents

Digital resources

The following items are available on Cambridge GO. For more information on how to access and use your digital resource, please see inside front cover.

Letter for parents – Introducing the Cambridge Primary and Lower Secondary resources

Active learning

Assessment for Learning

Developing learner language skills

Differentiation

Improving through questions

Language awareness

Metacognition

Skills for life

Lesson plan template and examples of completed lesson plans

Curriculum framework correlation

Scheme of work

Thinking and working mathematical questions

Diagnostic check and answers

Mid-point test and answers

End-of-year test and answers

Answers to Learner's Book questions

Answers to Workbook questions

Glossary

You can download the following resources for each unit:

Additional teaching ideas

Language worksheets and answers

Resource sheets

End-of-unit tests and answers

> Introduction

Welcome to the new edition of our very successful Cambridge Lower Secondary Mathematics series.

Since its launch, Cambridge Lower Secondary Mathematics has been used by teachers and children in over 100 countries around the world for teaching the Cambridge Lower Secondary Mathematics curriculum framework.

This exciting new edition has been designed by talking to Lower Secondary Mathematics teachers all over the world. We have worked hard to understand your needs and challenges, and then carefully designed and tested the best ways of meeting them. As a result, we've made some important changes to the series. This Teacher's Resource has been carefully redesigned to make it easier for you to plan and teach the course.

The series still has extensive digital and Online support, which lets you share books with your class. This Teacher's Resource also offers additional materials available to download from Cambridge GO. (For more information on how to access and use your digital resource, please see inside front cover.)

The series uses the most successful teaching approaches like active learning and metacognition and this Teacher's Resource gives you full guidance on how to integrate them into your classroom. Formative assessment opportunities help you to get to know your learners better, with clear learning intentions and success criteria as well as an array of assessment techniques, including advice on self and peer assessment. Clear, consistent differentiation ensures that all learners are able to progress in the course with tiered activities, differentiated worksheets and advice about supporting learners' different needs.

All our resources are written for teachers and learners who use English as a second or additional language. They help learners build core English skills with vocabulary and grammar support, as well as additional language worksheets.

We hope you enjoy using this course.

Eddie Rippeth

Head of Primary and Lower Secondary Publishing, Cambridge University Press

> About the authors

Lynn Byrd

Lynn gained an honours degree in mathematics at Southampton University in 1987 and then moved on to Swansea University to do her teacher training in Maths and P.E. in 1988.

She taught mathematics for all ability levels in two secondary schools in West Wales for 11 years, teaching across the range of age groups up to GCSE and Further Mathematics A level. During this time, she began work as an examiner. In 1999, she finished teaching and became a senior examiner, and focused on examining work and writing. She has written or co-authored a number of text books, homework books, work books and teacher resources for secondary mathematics qualifications.

Greg Byrd

After university and a year of travel and work, Greg started teaching in Pembrokeshire, Wales, in 1988. Teaching mathematics to all levels of ability, he was instrumental in helping his department to improve GCSE results. His innovative approaches led him to become chairman of the 'Pembrokeshire Project 2000', an initiative to change the starting point of every mathematics lesson for every pupil in the county. By this time he had already started writing. To date he has authored or co-authored over 60 text books, having his books sold in schools and colleges worldwide.

Chris Pearce

Chris has an MA from the University of Oxford where he read mathematics.

He has taught mathematics for over 30 years in secondary schools to students aged 11 to 18, and for the majority of that time he was head of the mathematics department.

After teaching he spent six years as a mathematics advisor for a local education authority working with schools to help them improve their teaching. He has also worked with teachers in other countries, including Qatar, China and Mongolia.

Chris is now a full-time writer of text books and teaching resources for students of secondary age. He creates books and other materials aimed at learners aged 11 to 18 for several publishers, including resources to support Cambridge Checkpoint, GCSE, IGCSE and A level. Chris has also been an examiner.

> How to use this series

All of the components in the series are designed to work together.

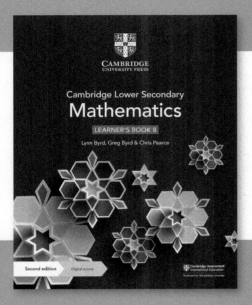

The Learner's Book is designed for students to use in class with guidance from the teacher. It contains fifteen units which offer complete coverage of the curriculum framework. A variety of investigations, activities, questions and images motivate students and help them to develop the necessary mathematical skills. Each unit contains opportunities for formative assessment, differentiation and reflection so you can support your learners' needs and help them progress.

The Teacher's Resource is the foundation of this series and you'll find everything you need to deliver the course in here, including suggestions for differentiation, formative assessment and language support, teaching ideas, answers, unit and progress tests and extra worksheets. Each Teacher's Resource includes:

- A **print book** with detailed teaching notes for each topic
- **Digital Access** with all the material from the book in digital form plus editable planning documents, extra guidance, worksheets and more.

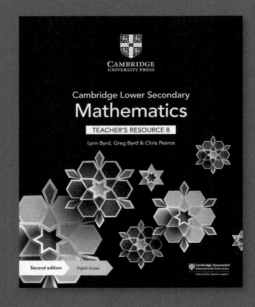

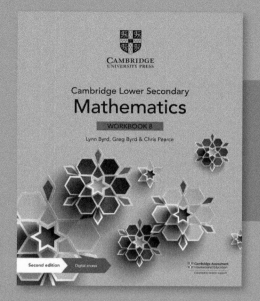

The skills-focused Workbook provides further practice for all the topics in the Learner's Book and is ideal for use in class or as homework. A three-tier, scaffolded approach to skills development promotes visible progress and enables independent learning, ensuring that every learner is supported.

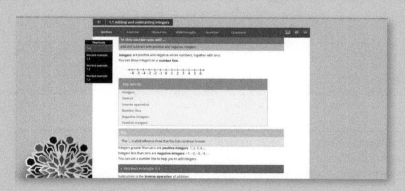

Access to **Cambridge Online Mathematics** is provided with the Learner's Book. A Teacher account can be set up for you to create online classes. The platform enables you to set activities, tasks and quizzes for individuals or an entire class with the ability to compile reports on learners progress and performance. Learners will see a digital edition of their Learner's Book with additional walkthroughs, automarked practice questions, quickfire quizzes and more.

 A letter to parents, explaining the course, is available to download from Cambridge GO (as part of this Teacher's Resource).

> How to use this Teacher's Resource

This Teacher's Resource contains both general guidance and teaching notes that help you to deliver the content in our Cambridge Lower Secondary Mathematics resources. Some of the material is provided as downloadable files, available on **Cambridge GO**. (For more information about how to access and use your digital resource, please see inside front cover.) See the Contents page for details of all the material available to you, both in this book and through Cambridge GO.

Teaching notes

This book provides **teaching notes** for each unit of the Learner's Book and Workbook. Each set of teaching notes contains the following features to help you deliver the unit.

The **Unit plan** summarises the topics covered in the unit, including the number of learning hours recommended for the topic, an outline of the learning content and the Cambridge resources that can be used to deliver the topic.

Topic	Approximate number of learning hours	Outline of learning content	Resources
Introduction and Getting Started	10–15 minutes		Learner's Book
1.1 Factors, multiples and primes	3	Understand factors, multiples, prime factors, highest common factors and lowest common multiples.	Learner's Book Section 1.1 Workbook Section 1.1 ⬇ Additional teaching ideas Section 1.1
Cross-unit resources ⬇ Language worksheet 1.1–1.4 ⬇ Diagnostic check ⬇ End of Unit 1 test			

The **Background knowledge** feature explains prior knowledge required to access the unit and gives suggestions for addressing any gaps in your learners' prior knowledge.

Learners' prior knowledge can be informally assessed through the **Getting started** feature in the Learner's Book.

BACKGROUND KNOWLEDGE

Before teaching unit 1, you may want to use diagnostic check activity to assess whether the learners are ready to begin Stage 8. This diagnostic check can assist you as the teacher to identify gaps in the learner's understanding which you can use to address before teaching this unit.

The **Teaching skills focus** feature covers a teaching skill and suggests how to implement it in the unit.

TEACHING SKILLS FOCUS

Active learning

It is important learners are given the chance to explore new mathematical situations for themselves so that they can look for patterns and make conjectures.

Reflecting the Learner's Book, each unit consists of multiple sections. A section covers a learning topic.

At the start of each section, the **Learning plan** table includes the framework codes, learning objectives and success criteria that are covered in the section.

It can be helpful to share learning intentions and success criteria with your learners at the start of a lesson so that they can begin to take responsibility for their own learning

LEARNING PLAN

Framework codes	Learning objectives	Success criteria
8Ni.03	• Understand factors, multiples, prime factors, highest common factors and lowest common multiples.	• Use a factor tree to write a composite number over 100 as a product of prime numbers, e.g. 135 or 280.

There are often **common misconceptions** associated with particular learning topics. These are listed, along with suggestions for identifying evidence of the misconceptions in your class and suggestions for how to overcome them.

Misconception	How to identify	How to overcome
Learners sometimes put '1' on one of the branches of a factor tree.	Give them a number and ask 'how can we start?' So 20 could start with 2 and 10 or 4 and 5 but not with 1 and 20.	Emphasise that they should not see 1 on any branch. Ask 'what would happen if we did allow 1?' (You would split 1 as 1 and 1; then split each of those as 1 and 1; it never stops!)

For each topic, there is a selection of **starter ideas**, **main teaching ideas** and **plenary ideas**. You can pick out individual ideas and mix and match them depending on the needs of your class. The activities include suggestions for how they can be differentiated or used for assessment. **Homework ideas** are also provided.

Starter idea

Prior knowledge (10 minutes)

Resources: 'Getting started' questions in the Learner's Book

Description: Give the learners a few minutes to try the questions.

Main teaching idea

Factor trees (30 minutes)

Learning intention: Investigating the properties of factor trees.

Resources: Learner's Book Exercise 1.1, Question 1

The **Language support** feature contains suggestions for how to support learners with English as an additional language. The vocabulary terms and definitions from the Learner's Book are also collected here.

LANGUAGE SUPPORT

Factor tree: a method of finding prime factors

HCF: an abbreviation for highest common factor

The **Cross-curricular links** feature provides suggestions for linking to other subject areas.

CROSS-CURRICULAR LINKS

Many of the key words in this unit and in the Learner's Book will be used in different types of businesses, in economics, engineering and science.

Thinking and working mathematically skills are woven throughout the questions in the Learner's Book and Workbook. These questions, indicated by ◁, incorporate specific characteristics that encourage mathematical thinking. The teaching notes for each unit identify all of these questions and their characteristics. The **Guidance on selected Thinking and working mathematically questions** section then looks at one of the questions in detail and provides more guidance about developing the skill that it supports.

Additional teaching notes are provided for the six **NRICH projects** in the Learner's Book, to help you make the most of them.

Guidance on selected *Thinking and working mathematically* questions

Specialising and generalising

Learner's Book Exercise 1.4, Question 15

For part **a** of Question 15, learners need to do more than say 'yes' or 'they are the same'. The best answer will be to write $(5^2)^3$ as the product of three terms $(5^2 \times 5^2 \times 5^2)$ giving 5^6 and then do something similar with $(5^3)^2$.

Digital resources to download

This Teacher's Resource includes a range of digital materials that you can download from Cambridge GO. (For more information about how to access and use your digital resource, please see inside front cover.) This icon ⬇ indicates material that is available from Cambridge GO.

Helpful documents for planning include:

- **Letter for parents – Introducing the Cambridge Primary and Lower Secondary resources:** a template letter for parents, introducing the Cambridge Primary Mathematics resources.
- **Lesson plan template:** a Word document that you can use for planning your lessons. Examples of completed lesson plans are also provided.
- **Curriculum framework correlation:** a table showing how the Cambridge Primary Mathematics resources map to the Cambridge Primary Mathematics curriculum framework.
- **Scheme of work:** a suggested scheme of work that you can use to plan teaching throughout the year.

Each unit includes:

- **Language worksheets:** these worksheets provide language support and can be particularly helpful for learners with English as an additional language. Answers sheets are provided.
- **Resource sheets:** these include templates and any other materials that support activities described in the teaching notes.
- **End-of-unit tests:** these provide quick checks of the learner's understanding of the concepts covered in the unit. Answers are provided. Advice on using these tests formatively is given in the Assessment for Learning section of this Teacher's Resource.

Additionally, the Teacher's Resource includes:

- **Diagnostic check and answers:** a test to use at the beginning of the year to discover the level that learners are working at. The results of this test can inform your planning.
- **Mid-point test and answers:** a test to use after learners have studied half the units in the Learner's Book. You can use this test to check whether there are areas that you need to go over again.
- **End-of-year test and answers:** a test to use after learners have studied all units in the Learner's Book. You can use this test to check whether there are areas that you need to go over again, and to help inform your planning for the next year.
- **Additional teaching ideas**
- **Answers to Learner's Book questions**
- **Answers to Workbook questions**
- **Glossary**

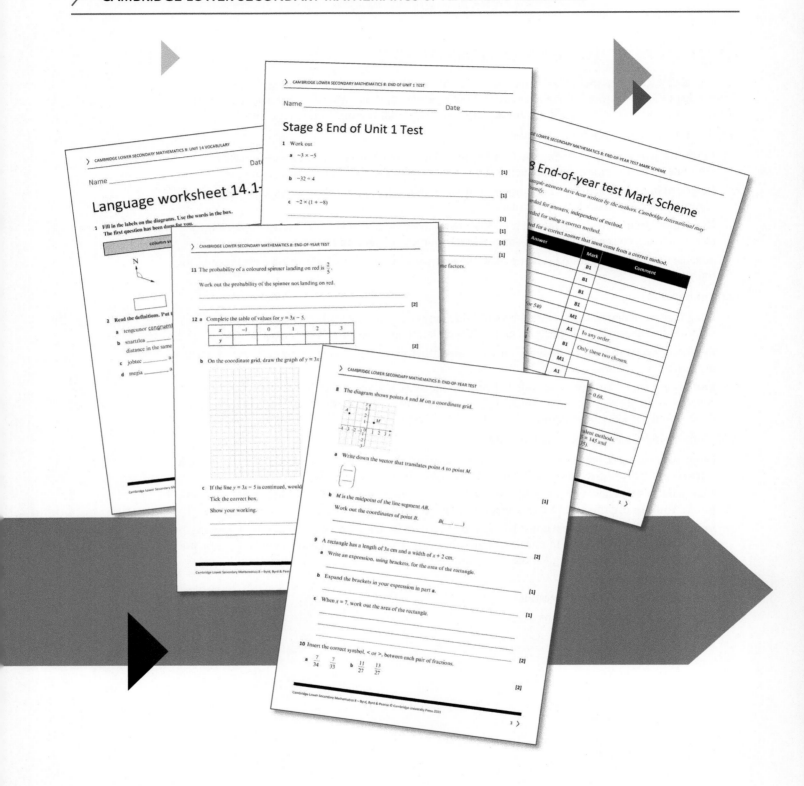

> CAMBRIDGE LOWER SECONDARY MATHEMATICS 8: UNIT 14 VOCABULARY

Name _____ Date _____

Language worksheet 14.1–

1 Fill in the labels on the diagrams. Use the words in the box.
   The first question has been done for you.

column vec...

N

2 Read the definitions. Put t...

   a tengcunor _congruen..._

   b snartilca _____
      distance in the same...

   c jobtec _____ a

   d megia _____ a

Cambridge Lower Secondary M...

> CAMBRIDGE LOWER SECONDARY MATHEMATICS 8: END-OF-YEAR TEST

11 The probability of a coloured spinner landing on red is $\frac{2}{5}$.

    Work out the probability of the spinner not landing on red.

    _____ [2]

12 a Complete the table of values for $y = 3x - 5$.

x	–1	0	1	2	3
y					

                                          [2]

   b On the coordinate grid, draw the graph of $y = 3x$

   c If the line $y = 3x - 5$ is continued, would...
      Tick the correct box.
      Show your working.

Cambridge Lower Secondary Mathematics 8 – Byrd, Byrd & Pea...

> CAMBRIDGE LOWER SECONDARY MATHEMATICS 8: END OF UNIT 1 TEST

Name _____ Date _____

Stage 8 End of Unit 1 Test

1 Work out

   a -3×-5

                                          [1]

   b $-32 \div 4$

                                          [1]

   c $-2 \times (1 + -8)$

                                          [1]
                                          [1]
                                          [1]
                                          [1]
                                          [1]

                                ...e factors.

> CAMBRIDGE LOWER SECONDARY MATHEMATICS 8: END-OF-YEAR TEST

8 The diagram shows points A and M on a coordinate grid.

   a Write down the vector that translates point A to point M.

      $\begin{pmatrix} \\ \end{pmatrix}$

   b M is the midpoint of the line segment AB.   [1]
      Work out the coordinates of point B.   B(___ , ___)

                                                          [2]

9 A rectangle has a length of $3x$ cm and a width of $x + 2$ cm.
   a Write an expression, using brackets, for the area of the rectangle.

                                                          [1]

   b Expand the brackets in your expression in part a.

                                                          [1]

   c When $x = 7$, work out the area of the rectangle.

10 Insert the correct symbol, < or >, between each pair of fractions.

   a $\frac{7}{34}$ $\frac{7}{33}$ b $\frac{11}{27}$ $\frac{13}{27}$ [2]

                                                          [2]

Cambridge Lower Secondary Mathematics 8 – Byrd, Byrd & Pearce © Cambridge University Press 2021

                                                          3 >

> CAMBRIDGE LOWER SECONDARY MATHEMATICS 8: END-OF-YEAR TEST MARK SCHEME

8 End-of-year test Mark Scheme

...ample answers have been written by the authors. Cambridge International may
...rently.

...rded for answers, independent of method.
...rded for using a correct method.
...ed for a correct answer that must come from a correct method.

Answer		Mark	Comment
		B1	
		B1	
		B1	
...or 540		B1	
		M1	
		A1	In any order.
		B1	Only these two chosen.
		M1	
		A1	

... ≈ 0.68.

...alent methods.
... = 145 and
...35).

1 >

> About the curriculum framework

The information in this section is based on the Cambridge Lower Secondary Mathematics (0862) curriculum framework from 2020. You should always refer to the appropriate curriculum framework document for the year of your learners' examination to confirm the details and for more information. Visit www.cambridgeinternational.org/lowersecondary to find out more.

The Cambridge Lower Secondary Mathematics curriculum framework (0862) from 2020 has been designed to encourage the development of mathematical fluency and ensure a deep understanding of key mathematical concepts. There is an emphasis on key skills and strategies for solving mathematical problems and encouraging the communication of mathematical knowledge in written form and through discussion.

At the Lower Secondary level, the framework is divided into three major strands:

- Number
- Geometry and Measure
- Statistics and Probability.

Algebra is introduced as a further strand in the Lower Secondary framework.

Underpinning all of these strands is a set of *Thinking and working mathematically* characteristics that will encourage students to interact with concepts and questions. These characteristics are present in questions, activities and projects in this series. For more information, see the *Thinking and working mathematically* section in this resource, or go to the Cambridge Assessment International Education website.

A curriculum framework correlation document (mapping the Cambridge Lower Secondary Mathematics resources to the learning objectives) and scheme of work are available to download from Cambridge GO (as part of this Teacher's Resource).

> About the assessment

Information concerning the assessment of the Cambridge Lower Secondary Mathematics curriculum framework (0862) is available on the Cambridge Assessment International Education website: www.cambridgeinternational.org/lowersecondary

> Introduction to Thinking and working mathematically

Thinking and working mathematically is an important part of the Cambridge Lower Secondary Mathematics course. The curriculum framework identifies four pairs of linked characteristics: specialising and generalising, conjecturing and convincing, characterising and classifying, and critiquing and improving. There are many opportunities for learners to develop these skills throughout Stage 8. This section provides examples of questions that require learners to demonstrate the characteristics, along with sentence starters to help learners formulate their thoughts.

⬇ You can download a list of the Thinking and working mathematically questions set in this stage and their respective characteristics here.

Specialising
and
Generalising

Conjecturing
and
Convincing

Critiquing
and
Improving

Characterising
and
Classifying

The thinking and working mathematically star
(Cambridge International, 2018)

Specialising and Generalising

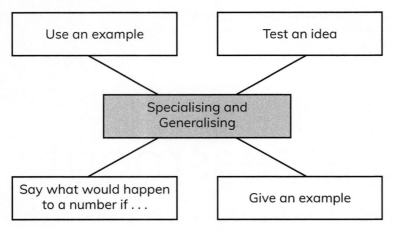

Use an example

Test an idea

Specialising and Generalising

Say what would happen to a number if . . .

Give an example

Specialising

Specialising involves choosing and testing an example to see if it satisfies or does not satisfy specific maths criteria. Learners look at particular examples and check to see if they do or do not satisfy specific criteria.

The Thinking and Working Mathematically star © Cambridge International, 2018

Example:

Look at this expansion. $x(2x + 5) + 3x(2x + 4) = 2x^2 + 5x + 6x^2 + 12x$

a   How would the expansion change if the **+** changed to **−** ?

Here is the expansion again. $x(2x + 5) + 3x(2x + 4) = 2x^2 + 5x + 6x^2 + 12x$

b   How would the expansion change if both of the **+** changed to **−** ?

Learners show they are **specialising** when they change the signs in the expansion and work out the new expansion to see how the expansion changes.

SENTENCE STARTERS

- I could try . . .
- . . . is the only one that . . .
- . . . is the only one that does not . . .

Generalising

Generalising involves recognising a wider pattern by identifying many examples that satisfy the same maths criteria. Learners make connections between numbers, shapes and so on and use these to form rules or patterns.

Example:

c   Write down the missing signs (**+** or **−**) in these expansions

i   ☺(✿ + ❀) + ◯(★ + ◆) = ☺✿ + ☺❀ . . . ◯★ . . . ◯◆

ii   ☺(✿ + ❀) + ◯(★ − ◆) = ☺✿ + ☺❀ . . . ◯★ . . . ◯◆

iii   ☺(✿ + ❀) − ◯(★ + ◆) = ☺✿ + ☺❀ . . . ◯★ . . . ◯◆

iv   ☺(✿ + ❀) − ◯(★ − ◆) = ☺✿ + ☺❀ . . . ◯★ . . . ◯◆

Learners will show they are **generalising** when they notice the effect of **+** and **−** signs in expansions, without needing to use numbers.

SENTENCE STARTERS

- I found the pattern . . . so . . .

Conjecturing and Convincing

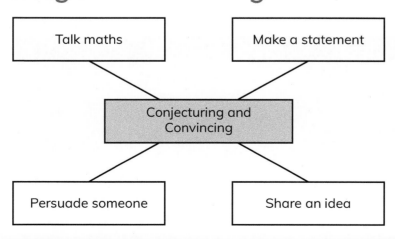

Conjecturing

Conjecturing involves forming questions or ideas about mathematical patterns. Learners say what they notice or why something happens or what they think about something.

Example:

Here are five fraction cards.

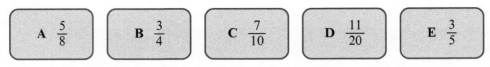

Without doing any calculations, do you think these fractions are terminating or recurring decimals? Explain why.

Learners will show they are **conjecturing** when they look at the denominators of these fractions and ask themselves if they are multiples of 10, 100, 1000, etc. If they are, the fractions can be written as terminating decimals. If not, the fractions are written as recurring decimals.

SENTENCE STARTERS
• I think that . . .
• I wonder if . . .

Convincing

Convincing involves presenting evidence to justify or challenge mathematical ideas or solutions. Learners persuade people (a partner, group, class or an adult) that a conjecture is true.

Example:

Which of these calculation cards is the odd one out?

Explain why.

A $6.3 \div 0.9$	**B** $1.4 \div 0.2$	**C** $4.9 \div 0.7$	**D** $4.8 \div 0.6$	**E** $5.6 \div 0.8$

Learners will show they are **convincing** when they do calculations to show that card D has a different answer from the others.

$A = 7$, $B = 7$, $C = 7$, $D = 8$, $E = 7$

SENTENCE STARTERS
• This is because . . .
• You can see that . . .
• I agree with . . . because . . .
• I disagree with . . . because . . .

Characterising and Classifying

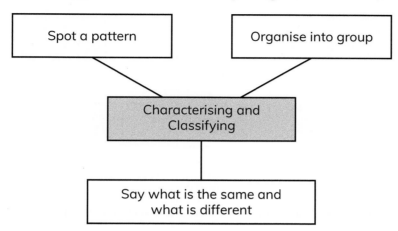

Characterising

Characterising involves identifying and describing the properties of mathematical objects. Learners identify and describe the mathematical properties of a number or object.

Example:

Work with a partner or in a small group to discuss these questions.

a Is a square a rectangle? Is a rectangle a square?

b Is a square a rhombus? Is a rhombus a square?

c Is a parallelogram a rectangle? Is a rectangle a parallelogram?

d Is a parallelogram a rhombus? Is a rhombus a parallelogram?

Discuss your answers with other groups in the class. Learners will show they are **characterising** when they identify and compare the properties of the different shapes and decide if one shape is a special version of another shape.

SENTENCE STARTERS

- This is similar to . . . so . . .
- The properties of . . . include . . .

Classifying

Classifying involves organising mathematical objects into groups according to their properties. Learners organise objects or numbers into groups according their mathematical properties. They may use Venn and Carroll diagrams.

Example:

Sort these cards into groups of **equivalent** expressions.

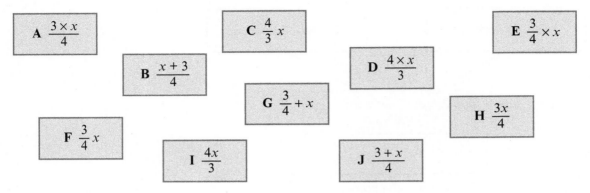

A $\dfrac{3 \times x}{4}$

B $\dfrac{x + 3}{4}$

C $\dfrac{4}{3}x$

D $\dfrac{4 \times x}{3}$

E $\dfrac{3}{4} \times x$

F $\dfrac{3}{4}x$

G $\dfrac{3}{4} + x$

H $\dfrac{3x}{4}$

I $\dfrac{4x}{3}$

J $\dfrac{3 + x}{4}$

Learners will show that they are **classifying** when they sort the cards into groups that have equivalent expressions.

SENTENCE STARTERS

- . . . go together because . . .

- I can organise the . . . into groups according to . . .

Critiquing and Improving

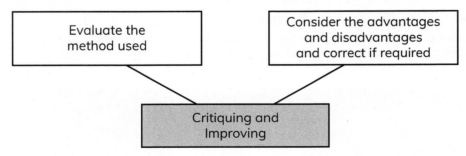

Evaluate the method used

Consider the advantages and disadvantages and correct if required

Critiquing and Improving

Critiquing

Critiquing involves comparing and evaluating mathematical ideas for solutions to identify advantages and disadvantages. Learners compare methods and ideas by identifying their advantages and disadvantages.

Example:

Zara and Arun use different methods to work out the answer to this question.

Work out the diameter of the circle with a circumference of 16.28 cm.
Give your answer correct to 3 significant figures.

This is what they write.

Zara

Step 1: Make d the subject of the formula.

$C = \pi \times d$

$\dfrac{C}{\pi} = d$

$d = \dfrac{C}{\pi}$

Step 2: Substitute in the numbers.

$d = \dfrac{16.28}{\pi}$

$= 5.18208\ldots$

$= 5.18\ cm\ (3\ s.f.)$

Arun

Step 1: Substitute in the numbers.

$C = \pi \times d$

$16.28 = \pi \times d$

Step 2: Solve the equation.

$16.28 = \pi \times d$

$\dfrac{16.28}{\pi} = d$

$5.18208\ldots = d$

$d = 5.18\ cm\ (3\ s.f.)$

a   Look at Zara and Arun's methods.

Do you understand both of these methods?

Do you think you will be able to use both of these methods?

b   Which method do you like the best and why?

This question provides an opportunity for learners to practise **critiquing** when they are shown two different ways to answer the question. They need to be able to follow the working shown and choose the method that they think is the best. It also gives them the chance to explain why they prefer one method over another.

Improving

Improving involves refining mathematical ideas to develop a more effective approach or solution. Learners find a better solution.

Example:

This pattern is made from hexagons.

Pattern 1   Pattern 2   Pattern 3

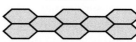

How many hexagons will there be in Pattern 20? Show how you worked out your answer.

Discuss the method you used with other learners. Did you use the same method or a different method? What do you think is the best method to use?

This question provides an opportunity for learners to look at the methods they, and other learners, use to answer a question. They can then describe how they are **improving** their methods to find the best method.

> Approaches to teaching and learning

The following are the teaching approaches underpinning our course content and how we understand and define them.

Active Learning

Active learning is a teaching practice that places student learning at its centre. It focuses on *how* students learn, not just on *what* they learn. We as teachers need to encourage learners to 'think hard', rather than passively receive information. Active learning encourages learners to take responsibility for their learning and supports them in becoming independent and confident learners in school and beyond.

Assessment for Learning

Assessment for Learning (AfL) is a teaching approach that generates feedback that can be used to improve learners' performance. Learners become more involved in the learning process and, from this, gain confidence in what they are expected to learn and to what standard. We as teachers gain insights into a learner's level of understanding of a particular concept or topic, which helps to inform how we support their progression.

Differentiation

Differentiation is usually presented as a teaching approach where teachers think of learners as individuals and learning as a personalised process. Whilst precise definitions can vary, typically the core aim of differentiation is viewed as ensuring that all learners, no matter their ability, interest or context, make progress towards their learning intentions. It is about using different approaches and appreciating the differences in learners to help them make progress. Teachers therefore need to be responsive, and willing and able to adapt their teaching to meet the needs of their learners.

Language awareness

For many learners, English is an additional language. It might be their second or perhaps their third language. Depending on the school context, students might be learning all or just some of their subjects in English.

For all learners, regardless of whether they are learning through their first language or an additional language, language is a vehicle for learning. It is through language that learners access the learning intentions of the lesson and communicate their ideas. It is our responsibility as teachers to ensure that language doesn't present a barrier to learning.

Metacognition

Metacognition describes the processes involved when students plan, monitor, evaluate and make changes to their own learning behaviours. These processes help learners to think about their own learning more explicitly and ensure that they are able to meet a learning goal that they have identified themselves or that we, as teachers, have set.

Skills for Life

How do we prepare learners to succeed in a fast-changing world? To collaborate with people from around the globe? To create innovation as technology increasingly takes over routine work? To use advanced thinking skills in the face of more complex challenges? To show resilience in the face of constant change? At Cambridge we are responding to educators who have asked for a way to understand how all these different approaches to life skills and competencies relate to their teaching. We have grouped these skills into six main Areas of Competency that can be incorporated into teaching, and have examined the different stages of the learning journey, and how these competencies vary across each stage.

These six key areas are:

- Creativity – finding new ways of doing things, and solutions to problems
- Collaboration – the ability to work well with others
- Communication – speaking and presenting confidently and participating effectively in meetings
- Critical thinking – evaluating what is heard or read, and linking ideas constructively
- Learning to learn – developing the skills to learn more effectively
- Social responsibilities – contributing to social groups, and being able to talk to and work with people from other cultures.

Cambridge learner and teacher attributes

This course helps develop the following Cambridge Learner and Teacher attributes.

Cambridge learners	Cambridge teachers
Confident in working with information and ideas – their own and those of others.	**Confident** in teaching their subject and engaging each student in learning.
Responsible for themselves, responsive to and respectful of others.	**Responsible** for themselves, responsive to and respectful of others.
Reflective as learners, developing their ability to learn.	**Reflective** as learners themselves, developing their practice.
Innovative and equipped for new and future challenges.	**Innovative** and equipped for new and future challenges.
Engaged intellectually and socially, ready to make a difference.	**Engaged** intellectually, professionally and socially, ready to make a difference.

Reproduced from Developing the Cambridge learner attributes with permission from Cambridge Assessment International Education.

More information about these approaches to teaching and learning is available to download from Cambridge GO (as part of this Teacher's Resource).

> Setting up for success

Our aim is to support better learning in the classroom with resources that allow for increased student autonomy, whilst supporting teachers to facilitate student learning.

Through an **active learning** approach of enquiry-led tasks, open ended questions and opportunities to externalise thinking in a variety of ways, learners will develop analysis, evaluation and problem solving skills.

Some ideas to consider to encourage an active learning environment:

• Set up seating to make group work easy.

• Create classroom routines to help learners to transition between different types of activity efficiently, e.g. moving from pair-work to listening to the teacher to independent work.

• Source mini-whiteboards, which allow you to get feedback from all learners rapidly.

• Start a portfolio for each learner, keeping key pieces of work to show progress at parent-teacher days.

• Have a display area with learner work and vocab flashcards.

Planning for active learning

We recommend the following approach to planning. A blank Lesson Plan Template is available to download to help with this approach.

1   **Planning learning intentions and success criteria:** These are the most important feature of the lesson. Teachers and students need to know where they are going in order to plan a route to get there!

2   **Plan language support:** Think about strategies to help learners overcome the language demands of the lesson so that language doesn't present a barrier to learning.

3   **Plan starter activities:** Include a 'hook' or starter to engage learners using engaging and imaginative strategies. This should be an activity where all learners are active from the start of the lesson.

4   **Plan main activities:** During the lesson, try to: give clear instructions, with modelling and written support; coordinate logical and orderly transitions between activities; make sure that learning is active and all learners are engaged; create opportunities for discussion around key concepts.

5   **Plan assessment for Learning and differentiation:** Use a wide range of Assessment for Learning techniques and adapt activities to a wide range of abilities. Address misconceptions at appropriate points and give meaningful oral and written feedback which learners can act on.

6   **Plan reflection and plenary:** At the end of each activity, and at the end of each lesson, try to: ask learners to reflect on what they have learnt compared to the beginning of the lesson; extend learning; build on and extend this learning.

7   **Plan homework:** If setting homework, it can be used to consolidate learning from the previous lesson or to prepare for the next lesson.

To help planning using this approach, a blank Lesson plan template is available to download from Cambridge GO (as part of this Teacher's Resource). There are also examples of completed lesson plans.

For more guidance on setting up for success and planning, please explore the Professional Development pages of our website www.cambridge.org/education/PD

⟩ Acknowledgement

The authors and publishers acknowledge the following sources of copyright material and are grateful for the permissions granted. While every effort has been made, it has not always been possible to identify the sources of all the material used, or to trace all copyright holders. If any omissions are brought to our notice, we will be happy to include the appropriate acknowledgements on reprinting.

Thanks to the following for permission to reproduce images:

Cover Photo: ori-artiste/Getty Images

Kitti Boonnitrod/Getty Images

⟩ 1 Integers

Unit plan

Topic	Approximate number of learning hours	Outline of learning content	Resources
Introduction and Getting Started	10–15 minutes		Learner's Book
1.1 Factors, multiples and primes	3	Understand factors, multiples, prime factors, highest common factors and lowest common multiples.	Learner's Book Section 1.1 Workbook Section 1.1 ⬇ Additional teaching ideas Section 1.1
1.2 Multiplying and dividing integers	2	Understand that brackets and operations follow a particular order. Estimate, multiply and divide integers, recognising generalisations.	Learner's Book Section 1.2 Workbook Section 1.2 ⬇ Additional teaching ideas Section 1.2
1.3 Square roots and cube roots	2	Recognise squares of negative and positive numbers, and corresponding square roots. Recognise positive and negative cube numbers, and the corresponding cube roots. Understand the hierarchy of natural numbers, integers and rational numbers.	Learner's Book Section 1.3 Workbook Section 1.3 ⬇ Additional teaching ideas Section 1.3
1.4 Indices	2	Use positive and zero indices, and the index laws for multiplication and division.	Learner's Book Section 1.4 Workbook Section 1.4 ⬇ Additional teaching ideas Section 1.4

Cross-unit resources
⬇ Language worksheet 1.1–1.4
⬇ Diagnostic check
⬇ End of Unit 1 test

BACKGROUND KNOWLEDGE

Before teaching unit 1, you may want to use diagnostic check activity to assess whether the learners are ready to begin Stage 8. This diagnostic check can assist you as the teacher to identify gaps in the learner's understanding which you can use to address before teaching this unit.

CONTINUED

For this unit, learners will need this background knowledge:

- Be able to add and subtract integers (Stage 7).
- Be able to multiply or divide integers, including where one integer is negative (Stage 7).
- Understand highest common factor and lowest common multiple (Stage 7).
- Know the difference between prime numbers and composite numbers (Stage 5).

- Understand the relationship between squares and square roots (Stage 7).
- Understand the relationship between cubes and cube roots (Stage 7).

Each of these areas will be extended during this unit. Throughout this unit, learners will be encouraged to look at number patterns and use them to make rules for themselves, promoting deeper understanding.

TEACHING SKILLS FOCUS

Active learning

It is important learners are given the chance to explore new mathematical situations for themselves so that they can look for patterns and make conjectures. In the section on powers, for example, the rules about multiplying and dividing indices are not given in the introductory material. Instead they are developed through investigations in the subsequent exercise. In this way learners are given the chance to discover and express the rules in their own way. By doing this they are working like mathematicians. They explore a situation and look for a conjecture that they can make and test. At the end of Unit 1, ask yourself:

- Were learners able to recognise and use the number patterns?
- Were the learners able to make and test sensible conjectures from the number patterns?
- Have learners developed a confidence in the conjectures/rules they have deduced?

1.1 Factors, multiples and primes

LEARNING PLAN

Framework codes	Learning objectives	Success criteria
8Ni.03	• Understand factors, multiples, prime factors, highest common factors and lowest common multiples.	• Use a factor tree to write a composite number over 100 as a product of prime numbers, e.g. 135 or 280.

LANGUAGE SUPPORT

Factor tree: a method of finding prime factors

HCF: an abbreviation for highest common factor

Index: the number of times a number is multiplied; $7^3 = 7 \times 7 \times 7 = 343$, so the index is 3

LCM: an abbreviation for lowest common multiple

Prime factor: a factor that is a prime number

Common misconceptions

Misconception	How to identify	How to overcome
Learners sometimes put '1' on one of the branches of a factor tree.	Give them a number and ask 'how can we start?' So 20 could start with 2 and 10 or 4 and 5 but not with 1 and 20.	Emphasise that they should not see 1 on any branch. Ask 'what would happen if we did allow 1?' (You would split 1 as 1 and 1; then split each of those as 1 and 1; it never stops!)
Learners may not factorise as much as possible.	They may stop at 9 and not break it down to 3 and 3.	Learners should be familiar with the prime numbers but take opportunities to remind them and reinforce knowledge.

Starter idea

Prior knowledge (10 minutes)

Resources: 'Getting started' questions in the Learner's Book

Description: Give the learners a few minutes to try the questions. Then go through the answers. Do this by asking different learners to give you their answers. Where possible ask follow-up questions such as 'how did you work that out?' Look for problems or incorrect answers and if necessary ask supplementary questions to make sure of understanding. Knowledge of these topics is essential to the material covered in this unit which takes further the ideas covered in Stage 7.

Main teaching idea

Factor trees (30 minutes)

Learning intention: Investigating the properties of factor trees.

Resources: Learner's Book Exercise 1.1, Question 1

Description: Say that any integer that is not prime can be written as a product of prime numbers. Write some examples such as:

$12 = 2 \times 2 \times 3$; $21 = 3 \times 7$; $40 = 2 \times 2 \times 2 \times 5$

Given a number you can use a **factor tree** to write the number as a product of primes. Use 120 as an example and demonstrate it as shown in the Learner's Book. Build up the diagram step by step as follows:

- start with 12 and 10
- write 12 as 3 and 4
- write 10 as 2 and 5
- 3, 2 and 5 are prime so circle those. You will not go any further with those.

- write 4 as 2 and 2
- 2 is prime so circle those
- all end points are circled, so you stop.

The circled primes have a product of 120.
Write $120 = 2 \times 2 \times 2 \times 3 \times 5$

It is convenient to write them in ascending order like that. Check it is correct. You usually use indices to write it more concisely as $120 = 2^3 \times 3 \times 5$. Learners should be familiar with the use of indices. Now set the learners to do Exercise 1.1, Question 1. This asks them to investigate different number trees for 120. Encourage them to work through this on their own; do not do it as a teacher-led activity. Give them plenty of time, particularly to compare their results with a partner.

When appropriate bring the class back together and discuss what they have found. Possible points that will arise:

- When are two trees considered to be different? Just swapping the order of the numbers on the tree does not make a different tree.
- There are lots of possibilities. Even for the start you could have 2×60 or 3×40 or 4×30 and so on and then subsequent branches can vary too.
- However you draw it, the factor tree should always give the same end points. Each number can be written as a product of primes in just one way if we ignore the order.

Learners can now continue with the exercise.

> **Differentiation ideas:** Some learners might need support in choosing the numbers to start the factor tree. Encourage them to look for two easy numbers. For example, if the number is even then 2 can be one of the numbers. Find the other by halving. More confident learners could be challenged to find how many different trees start with a particular pair.

Plenary idea

What have you learned? (5 minutes)

Resources: None

Description: Ask learners to make summary notes of what they need to remember about this topic. They should choose two numbers, write them as products of primes and show how to find the HCF and LCM. They could use numbers that they have already investigated. Ask one or two learners to describe what they have done.

⟩ **Assessment ideas:** Look particularly at the notes of learners you suspect may not fully understand the process. Assess the accuracy of learners as they explain their notes.

Guidance on selected *Thinking and working mathematically* questions

Specialising and Generalising

Learner's Book Exercise 1.1, Question 11

The questions are arranged in pairs so that learners can look for a common property. In this case the property is that the number of occurrences of each prime factor doubles. Learners need to be able to explain this in their own words. As learners become more familiar with this approach the scaffolding of the preliminary question can be taken away. They should be confident enough to choose their own examples and then move on to generalising.

Homework ideas

Exercise 1.1 in the Workbook gives more questions of a similar type. You could choose specific questions from this exercise or you could set the exercise as two separate homeworks.

An optional extra would be to ask learners to find the largest known prime number. They can easily do this on the internet. In January 2019 it was $2^{82589933} - 1$ which has over 24 million digits.

Assessment ideas

The questions provide opportunities for learners to compare their results with a partner. This can be both peer assessment and self-assessment. They can identify ways to improve their own work and someone else's by making this type of comparison.

1.2 Multiplying and dividing integers

LEARNING PLAN		
Framework codes	**Learning objectives**	**Success criteria**
8Ni.01	• Understand that brackets, indices (squares and square roots) and operations follow a particular order.	• In Question 5, they recognise the need for brackets, to determine the order.
8Ni.02	• Estimate, multiply and divide integers, recognising generalisations.	• If learners are successful in answering Questions 6, 16 and 17, they understand how to use rounding to estimate answers.

LANGUAGE SUPPORT

Conjecture: an opinion, an idea or a suggestion based on what you know

Integer: a whole number that can be positive or negative or zero, with no fractional part

Inverse: the operation that has the opposite effect; the inverse of 'multiply by 5' is 'divide by 5'

Investigate: explore an idea or method

Common misconceptions

Misconception	How to identify	How to overcome
The most likely error is to assume that the answer is negative when two negative integers are multiplied or divided.	It will be clear from learners' answers, either written or oral.	Encourage learners to make their own generalisation of the results so that they can accurately state the sign of the answer when any two integers are multiplied or divided.

Starter idea

Using patterns (10 minutes)

Resources: Learner's Book Worked example 1.2

Description: Write down this sequence. Put the calculations in a column as shown.

$$2-5=-3$$
$$2-4=-2$$
$$2-3=-1$$
$$2-2=\ \ 0$$

Check that learners agree these are correct and then ask for descriptions of any patterns. Look in particular for these suggestions:

- The first number is always 2.
- The number subtracted decreases by one each time you go down the column.
- The answer increases by 1 each time.

Ask learners how you should continue the sequence. You are looking for:

$$2-1=1$$
$$2-0=2$$
$$2--1=3$$
$$2--2=4$$
$$2--3=5$$

and so on.

Ask 'Are these the correct answers?' You could also extend the sequence upward if you wish. $2-6=-4$ and so on. Emphasise that you have not used any rules about subtraction to do these, you have simply used the pattern. This technique is used again in Worked example 1.2. If learners need more practice, work through Worked example 1.2 in the Learner's Book in a similar way.

Main teaching idea

Patterns of multiplication (10 minutes)

Learning intention: To develop their own rules for multiplying integers by recognising a pattern and extending it.

Resources: Learner's Book Exercise 1.2, Question 1

Description: Learners should already have looked at Exercise 1.2, Question 1 of the Learner's Book. Display this pattern which is similar to the ones in Question 1.

$$-8\times4=-32$$
$$-8\times3=-24$$
$$-8\times2=-16$$
$$-8\times1=-8$$

Ask what patterns they can see. Look for these answers:

- The first number is always -8.
- The number you multiply by decreases by 1 each time you go down a row.
- The answer increases by 8 each time you go down a row, although not all learners may see this until the sequence is extended.

Ask learners how the sequence continues. You are looking for:

$$-8\times0=0$$
$$-8\times-1=8$$
$$-8\times-2=16$$
$$-8\times-3=24$$

Ask 'What does this show about the result of multiplying two negative integers?' and 'Does this agree with what you found in Question 1?' Try to get learners to explain any rule in their own words. This will generally involve looking at the signs of the numbers being multiplied to decide the sign of the answer. Resist the temptation to tell learners the 'correct' description. Encourage them to make their own. They have more chance of remembering it if they work it out for themselves.

Learners should now be able to answer multiplication questions involving one or two negative numbers. Give them some new examples to check this.

> **Differentiation ideas:** You may not need as much detail if learners have learnt all they need from Question 1 and can discuss their conclusions.

Plenary idea

Three key facts (10 minutes)

Resources: None

Description: Ask learners to write down three facts that summarise the results in Section 1.2. When everyone has written something ask for examples from as many learners as possible. The examples should cover the ideas of multiplying and dividing positive and negative integers. Ask learners 'Have we missed anything important?' When you have done this ask learners to look again at their three facts and decide if they want to change or replace any of them.

> **Assessment ideas:** As learners offer their suggestions it gives you the chance to make sure that they have understood the ideas of this section and know how to multiply or divide with negative integers. If necessary, you can correct misconceptions and clarify ideas.

Guidance on selected *Thinking and working mathematically* questions

Critiquing and Improving

Learner's Book Exercise 1.2, Question 9

Question 9 asks learners to look at Zara's conjecture and improve it. Zara's statement is partially correct but only when the middle number is not changed. Her statement will be correct if it just talks about exchanging the numbers in the first and third boxes. A more comprehensive conclusion is that there is a maximum of three possible numbers in the top box for a given set of three numbers in the bottom row. The value of the number at the top depends only on which number is placed in the middle of the bottom row.

Homework ideas

Workbook Exercise 1.2 gives more questions of a similar type. You could choose specific questions from the exercise or set the exercise as two homeworks.

Another possible homework idea is to ask learners to complete a multiplication pyramid with integers in the bottom row and the number -36 in the top cell. Can they find different ways to do this? Share learners' answers at the start of the next lesson.

Assessment ideas

The point to assess is that learners can multiply or divide two integers correctly where one or both is negative, where the answer to the division is an integer. There are many opportunities to check learners can do this successfully: in the exercise, the homework and the class activities. Try to identify learners who have not been able to use a general rule (such as dividing a negative by a negative gives a positive answer) and concentrate on them for support.

1.3 Square roots and cube roots

LEARNING PLAN		
Framework codes	**Learning objectives**	**Success criteria**
8Ni.06	• Recognise squares of negative and positive numbers, and corresponding square roots.	• Find both square roots of 64.

CONTINUED

Framework codes	Learning objectives	Success criteria
8Ni.07	• Recognise positive and negative cube numbers, and the corresponding cube roots.	• Find the cube roots of 64 and of −64.
8Ni.04	• Understand the hierarchy of natural numbers, integers and rational numbers.	• Place 3, −4 and $3\frac{1}{4}$ in the correct places in a Venn diagram showing the types of number.

LANGUAGE SUPPORT

Cube root: the number that produces the given number when the number is cubed; the cube root of 125 is 5 because 5^3 is 125

Square root: the square root of a number multiplied by itself gives that number; the square root of 36 is 6 or −6

Learners should already be familiar with the terms square number, square root, cube number and cube root. Natural numbers are what learners have probably called counting numbers in the past, with the addition of 0. Learners need to understand that rational numbers are any numbers that can be written as a fraction, positive or negative, and they include all the integers. It might help to think, for example, of 4 as $\frac{4}{1}$.

Common misconceptions

Misconception	How to identify	How to overcome
Learners may not be aware that every positive square number has two integer square roots.	Ask for the solution of the equation $x^2 = 9$ Learners need to identify 3 and −3 as solutions.	Emphasise that $\sqrt{9} = 3$ is the positive square root of 9 and that $-\sqrt{9} = -3$ is another square root.
Because a negative number can have a cube root, learners can think it also has a square root.	Ask for the square roots of negative numbers such as −9 or −25.	Emphasise the difference between square roots and cube roots in this respect.

Starter idea

Types of number (10 minutes)

Resources: None

Description: Draw a number line. Mark on it the numbers 0, 1, 2, 3, 4, 5, . . . Say that these are called **natural numbers**. They are the counting numbers, the first numbers children learn.

Then mark in −1, −2, −3, −4, . . . Ask for the name of all the numbers marked. These are **integers**. Say that the integers include the natural numbers. All natural numbers are integers.

Ask learners to draw a Venn diagram to show natural numbers and integers. They may need reminding what a Venn diagram is. If some learners cannot remember ask a learner who does know to explain. It is a diagram where sets are represented by overlapping loops.

Learners may draw something like this (N = natural numbers, I = integers):

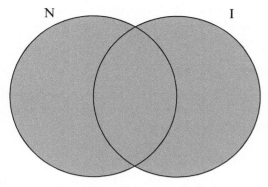

Ask them to choose one number to write in each section. There is no natural number that is not an integer so all the natural numbers will go in the overlap, e.g.

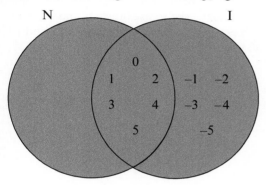

Explain that the diagram should actually look like this.

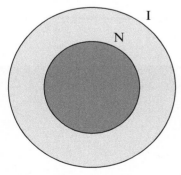

N is a **subset** of I and is entirely inside it. Make sure everyone has a correct copy. Call out some integers (some positive, some negative) and ask each learner to write them in the correct place. Then ask learners to exchange their diagram with a partner to allow peer assessment. Make sure all learners have a correct diagram.

Main teaching idea

Square roots of integers (10 minutes)

Learning intention: To extend the idea of square roots to include negative numbers.

Resources: None

Description: Learners were initially introduced to square roots in the context of natural numbers (0, 1, 2, . . .) Now that they are familiar with integers the concept can be extended to cover them too.

Display this table and ask learners to look at it. You could ask them for the answers as you fill in the second row.

x	−4	−3	−2	−1	0	1	2	3	4
x^2	16	9	4	1	0	1	4	9	16

Now ask for the solution of the equation $x^2 = 9$.

Learners should say $x = 3$ immediately but the table shows that another solution is $x = -3$. The complete solution is that $x = 3$ or -3.

It is unusual for learners to have an equation with more than one solution so it is worth stressing the point that both values are required. Say that $\sqrt{9} = 3$ is the square root of 9 because $3^2 = 9$. In fact it is only one of the two square roots of 9 because $(-3)^2 = -3 \times -3 = 9$, so -3 is also a square root. $\sqrt{9} = 3$ is the positive square root of 9 but $-\sqrt{9} = -3$ is the negative square root of 9.

Ask learners to give the solutions of other similar equations such as $x^2 = 36$ or $x^2 = 100$, making sure that they give both square roots each time. Finally ask for the solutions of the equation $x^2 = -16$. Learners might be tempted to say -4 but in that case point out that $(-4)^2 = -4 \times -4 = 16$ so that is incorrect. They need to realise that the equation has no solution. The square of any positive or negative integer is always positive so a negative integer has no square root.

Mathematical note: strictly speaking we should say that the equation $x^2 = -16$ has no real solution. It does have two complex solutions but that is a long way beyond Stage 8.

> **Differentiation ideas:** If learners find this difficult, spend more time squaring negative numbers, writing out examples in full, such as $(-5)^2 = -5 \times -5 = 25$ until learners become convinced.

Plenary idea

What have we learned? (5 minutes)

Resources: None

Description: Ask learners to describe the differences between square roots and cube roots of integers. The main points they should recall are:

- A positive square number n has two square roots, $\sqrt{n}$ and $-\sqrt{n}$.
- A negative integer does not have a square root.
- Positive cube numbers have a positive cube root and the corresponding negative cube number has a negative cube root.

Ask learners to give numerical examples to illustrate each of these facts.

> **Assessment ideas:** Asking learners for numerical examples gives you a chance to assess the understanding of individual learners.

Guidance on selected *Thinking and working mathematically* questions

Conjecturing and Convincing

Learner's Book Exercise 1.3, Question 10

Question 10 asks learners to decide whether statements are true or false and to give evidence to support their answer. This is a common way in which learners are asked to make conjectures in order to convince someone. In this question, encourage learners to work on just one side of the equals sign at time. They should avoid writing something muddled like $(-3)^2 + (-4)^2 = (-5)^2 = 9 + 16 = 25$.

Homework ideas

Exercise 1.3 in the Workbook has more questions of the same type. You could select particular questions or ask learners to complete them all.

Assessment ideas

When you look at learners' work, make sure that they are being accurate when they write expressions with numbers. Check that they know the difference between -3^2 and $(-3)^2$ or between $\sqrt{-9}$ and $-\sqrt{9}$. They should know when they need to use brackets and when these are unnecessary. You might use questions 9 and 10 in the exercise to check this.

1.4 Indices

LEARNING PLAN		
Framework codes	**Learning objectives**	**Success criteria**
8Ni.05	• Use positive and zero indices, and the index laws for multiplication and division.	• Using the fact that $3^5 = 243$, find 3^7 and 3^4.

LANGUAGE SUPPORT
Generalise: use a set of results to make a general rule **Index:** the number of times a number is multiplied; $7^3 = 7 \times 7 \times 7 = 343$, the index is 3	**Indices:** plural of index **Power:** $2 \times 2 \times 2 = 2^3$ is called '2 cubed' or '2 to the power 3'

Common misconceptions

Misconception	How to identify	How to overcome
Learners read 3^4 as $3 \times 4 = 12$, instead of $3 \times 3 \times 3 \times 3 = 81$.	Make sure learners say '3 to the power 4' and not 'three four' or 'three times 4'.	It helps to reinforce this if you say '3 to the power 4 or $3 \times 3 \times 3 \times 3$', giving both versions.
Learners think that $3^0 = 0$.	Look at or listen to learners' answers.	Stress that it may be surprising but it is not true. Remind them of the patterns in the exercise.

Starter idea

An index of 0 (10 minutes)

Resources: Calculators

Description: Show this table with only the numbers from 2 onwards on the top row.

n	0	1	2	3	4	5
2^n			4	8	16	32
3^n			9	27	81	243
4^n			16	64	256	1024
10^n			100	1000	10000	100000

Start by filling in columns headed 2, 3, 4, 5 one row at a time, asking learners to tell you the numbers to put in. So $2^2 = 4$, $2^3 = 8$, $2^4 = 16$ and $2^5 = 32$ go in first. If learners find this difficult to understand, write out the calculation in full.

Ask learners to describe how the numbers in each row change. They should see that you multiply by 2, 3, 4, 10, . . . when you move one place to the right. Point out that this means that as you move to the *left* you *divide* by 2, 3, 4, 10, . . . Use this fact to fill in the first 2 columns. It looks like this.

n	0	1	2	3	4	5
2^n	1	2	4	8	16	32
3^n	1	3	9	27	81	243
4^n	1	4	16	64	256	1024
10^n	1	10	100	1000	10000	100000

The second column is not surprising and learners are usually happy to accept that $2^1 = 2$ and so on. Learners often insist that 2^0 is 0 and say things like 'there are no 2s and so there is nothing'. The idea of multiplying 2s for a power breaks down here. Stress that

$n^0 = 1$ for *any* positive integer n and it is *never* 0. Use the pattern as justification. There will be more justification as they work through this section.

Main teaching idea

Multiplying powers of an integer (10 minutes)

Learning intention: To discover and test a generalisation. In this case it is the rule for multiplying powers of an integer by adding the indices.

Resources: Learner's Book Exercise 1.2, Question 1

Description: Learners should have completed Exercise 1.4, Question 3 before doing this activity. Write down this multiplication $25 \times 125 = 3125$. Ask what each number is as a power of 5 and then rewrite it as $5^2 \times 5^3 = 5^5$. In Question 3 learners should have found that multiplying powers of 2 or 3 is equivalent to adding the indices and explain that this is another example. Another example is $1296 \times 36 = 46656$. Ask learners to try to write this in terms of powers. The answer is $6^4 \times 6^2 = 6^6$.

Ask learners to write some examples of their own using powers of 7. After a couple of minutes ask for their examples and check them as a class. Now tell learners that $16 \times 16 = 256$ can be written in powers in two different ways. How? You are looking for $2^4 \times 2^4 = 2^8$ and $4^2 \times 4^2 = 4^4$. In both cases the rule about adding indices works. Make sure learners can use the general result about adding indices correctly. Writing an example such as $N^2 \times N^5 = N^7$ may be helpful. Now ask learners to write in powers $27 \times 1 = 27$. You are looking for $3^3 \times 3^0 = 3^3$. This reinforces the definition of 3^0.

> **Differentiation ideas:** For more confident learners, ask if there is a rule for multiplying the *same* power of *different* integers such as $2^3 \times 3^3$. In this case it is $(2 \times 3)^3$ and this is an example of a general result. Beware of confusing less confident learners with this!

Plenary idea

Extending rules (5 minutes)

Resources: None

Description: Ask learners to recap the three rules about indices they have met in this unit. In their own words they should know:

- To multiply powers add the indices
- To divide powers subtract the indices
- To find a power of a power multiply the indices.

Ask learners to make a note to remind themselves of these rules. They could write a general explanation and/or write down some specific examples. Point out that all the examples used powers of positive integers.

Ask do they still work with negative integers? Ask for some numerical examples to check on a calculator. They should find that they still work.

› **Assessment ideas:** This is a chance to review understanding of the rules and give more practice in using them if necessary. Ask each learner to give his or her notes to a partner to check for accuracy and clarity.

Guidance on selected *Thinking and working mathematically* questions

Specialising and generalising

Learner's Book Exercise 1.4, Question 15

For part **a** of Question 15, learners need to do more than say 'yes' or 'they are the same'. The best answer will be to write $(5^2)^3$ as the product of three terms $(5^2 \times 5^2 \times 5^2)$ giving 5^6 and then do something similar

with $(5^3)^2$. For part **b**, learners should consider other specific examples from which they can generalise a rule for solving other questions of this type.

Homework ideas

Exercise 1.4 in the Workbook has more questions of a similar type. You can set all of them or select some questions to concentrate on particular skills.

Assessment ideas

There is less opportunity for peer assessment in this section. Ask learners to explain how they find the answers to questions and what particular rules they are using. The exercise is designed to help the learners to discover rules for themselves rather than being told the rules at the start. Assessment should include checking that learners are able to explain clearly, in their own words, the rules that they use.

> 2 Expressions, formulae and equations

Unit plan

Topic	Approximate number of learning hours	Outline of learning content	Resources
Introduction and Getting Started	10–15 minutes		Learner's Book
2.1 Constructing expressions	1	Understand that letters have different meanings in expressions, formulae, and equations. Understand that order of operations (BIDMAS) rules apply to algebraic terms and expressions. Understand that a situation can be represented either in words or as an algebraic expression.	Learner's Book Section 2.1 Workbook Section 2.1 ⬇ Additional teaching ideas Section 2.1
2.2 Using expressions and formulae	1–1.5	Understand that order of operations (BIDMAS) rules apply to algebraic terms and expressions. Understand that a situation can be represented either in words or as a formula. Understand how to change the subject of a formula by using knowledge of inverse operations.	Learner's Book Section 2.2 Workbook Section 2.2 ⬇ Additional teaching ideas Section 2.2 ⬇ Exit ticket 2.2 ⬇ Resource sheet 2.2A ⬇ Resource sheet 2.2B
2.3 Expanding brackets	1–1.5	Understand how to expand a bracket with a single term.	Learner's Book Section 2.3 Workbook Section 2.3 ⬇ Additional teaching ideas Section 2.3 ⬇ Exit ticket 2.3 ⬇ Resource sheet 2.3

Topic	Approximate number of learning hours	Outline of learning content	Resources
2.4 Factorising	0.5–1	Understand how to factorise by identifying the highest common factor.	Learner's Book Section 2.4 Workbook Section 2.4 ⬇ Additional teaching ideas Section 2.4 ⬇ Resource sheet 2.4
2.5 Constructing and solving equations	1–1.5	Understand that letters have different meanings in expressions, formulae and equations. Understand that a situation can be represented either in words or as an equation and solve the equation.	Learner's Book Section 2.5 Workbook Section 2.5 ⬇ Additional teaching ideas Section 2.5 ⬇ Resource sheet 2.5A ⬇ Resource sheet 2.5B
2.6 Inequalities	0.5–1	Understand that letters can represent open and closed intervals.	Learner's Book Section 2.6 Workbook Section 2.6 ⬇ Additional teaching ideas Section 2.6

Cross-unit resources

⬇ Language worksheet 2.1–2.2

⬇ Language worksheet 2.3–2.6

⬇ Project guidance: Algebra chains resource sheets A and B

⬇ End of Unit 2 test

BACKGROUND KNOWLEDGE

For this unit, learners will need this background knowledge:

- Understand that letters can represent unknown numbers, variables or constants (Stage 7).
- Understand that the order of operations (BIDMAS) rules apply to algebraic terms and expressions involving x, ÷, + and − (Stage 7).
- Be able to manipulate algebraic expressions by collecting like terms and applying the distributive law with a constant (Stage 7).

- Have a knowledge of constructing expressions, inequalities, order of operations (BIDMAS) rules and expanding brackets (Stage 7).

Each of these areas will be extended during this unit. The work in Stage 7 should have reinforced to learners the essential nature of algebra as the key to much of mathematics and its uses in day-to-day life. Throughout this unit, and Stage 8 as a whole, it is important to highlight the role of algebra in mathematics and its applications to life outside the classroom.

2 EXPRESSIONS, FORMULAE AND EQUATIONS

TEACHING SKILLS FOCUS

Active learning

Throughout the six sections of Unit 2, if learners do not understand or they continue to get the same type of question incorrect, you can ask another learner to explain. It is important that you also listen to the explanation given. You need to be able to confirm that the help is of good quality or to ask if another learner could explain the problem in a different way.

Active learning helps to establish good learning patterns and practice. When a learner can explain well, it shows that they really understand what they are doing and know how to improve. Also, learners often feel more confident speaking to other learners, asking more targeted questions, so becoming more active learners themselves. As learners get more used to explaining concepts or asking for specific, targeted help from other learners, these discussions can happen without you being present. The practice learners have had during Stage 7 will mean they are already more confident in this very effective learning skill.

Remind learners that the key to being successfully involved in this type of learning is that there is no judgement. The learner asking for help and the learner giving help are both learning and improving.

At the end of Unit 2, ask yourself:

- Did learners have useful discussions that solved issues one of them was having?
- Did a variety of learners do the explaining or did you rely on just one or two?
- Did the learners who helped others understand the work better themselves because of the help they gave?
- Did learners who received help from others benefit from it? Did they then need help or advice from you?
- Are all learners who require help getting it?
- What other ways could you get learners to explain more to others, e.g. you teach a small group something and then get those learners to teach the whole class?

2.1 Constructing expressions

LEARNING PLAN

Framework codes	Learning objectives	Success criteria
8Ae.01	• Understand that letters have different meanings in expressions, formulae and equations.	• Understanding Question 1. Although these definitions are covered in Year 7 Unit 2, it is useful to revise them.
8Ae.02	• Understand that the laws of arithmetic and order of operations apply to algebraic terms and expressions (four operations, squares and cubes).	• Learners can use order of operations (BIDMAS) rules to find equivalent expressions.
8Ae.04	• Understand that a situation can be represented either in words or as an algebraic expression, and move between the two representations (linear with integer or fractional coefficients).	• If learners are successful at attempting Question 10, they thoroughly understand the requirements of this learning objective.

LANGUAGE SUPPORT

Coefficient: a number in front of a variable in an algebraic expression; the coefficient multiplies the variable

Constant: a number on its own (with no variable); -5, 8 and $10\frac{1}{2}$ are all constants, but so is π as this is also just a number.

Equivalent: equal in value

Expression: a collection of symbols representing numbers and mathematical operations, but not including an equals sign (=)

Linear expression: an expression, with at least one variable, where the highest power of any variable is 1

Solve: calculate the value of any unknown letter(s) in an equation

Term: a single number or variable, or numbers and variables multiplied together

Unknown: a letter (or letters) in an equation, for which the value (or values) is yet to be found

Variable: a symbol, usually a letter, that can represent different values

Common misconceptions

Misconception	How to identify	How to overcome
Not understanding that $\frac{3}{4}x$, $\frac{3}{4} \times x$ and $\frac{3 \times x}{4}$ are all equivalent expressions.	Check answers to Question 7.	Discussions during Questions 4, 6 and 7.
Not using brackets when they are required.	Errors in Question 3.	Discussions during Questions 3 and 12.

Starter idea

Before you start (10–15 minutes)

Resources: Notebooks; 'Getting started' questions in Learner's Book

Description: Check learners' prior understanding. Learners should have little difficulty with the 'Getting started' material if they were confident with Stage 7 Unit 2. It may, however, be useful to have a brief discussion reminding learners that *ab* and *ba* are the same before attempting Question 3. Discuss what learners remember about solving equations and lead them, if necessary, towards discussing inverse operations.

This exercise is a quick reminder of previous work that will help learners to be more effective with this unit. It is not a test. After each question it may be useful to allow self or peer marking, allowing learners to rectify any mistakes after a brief discussion.

Main teaching idea

Think like a mathematician (2–5 minutes)

Learning intention: Understanding equivalent expressions involving fractions.

Resources: Notebooks; Learner's Book Exercise 2.1, Question 7

Description: Learners instinctively think there is a right answer and therefore a wrong answer. Many learners will be looking for the expression that does **not** represent the problem. Learners who find an incorrect answer will require more guidance. They can be helped by other learners, with your help too if there is still a lack of understanding.

> **Differentiation ideas:** For learners who are struggling, suggest they choose a number for *n*, e.g. 12. They can substitute $n = 12$ into the problem given and then into all three of the suggestions to check they get the same answer. This approach will also help many learners with their explanation.

Plenary idea

Explanations (2–5 minutes)

Resources: Notebooks

Description: Ask learners to write an expression for: 'Multiply *n* by 3 and subtract 2' $[3n - 2]$. Ask them to write an explanation of how they worked out the expression. Ask learners to write an explanation of how they would work out an expression for 'Subtract 2 from n then multiply by 3' $[3(n-2)]$.

> **Assessment ideas:** Ask learners to exchange notebooks with a partner. Ask them to read the two explanations and decide if they are clear. Would their explanations help someone to understand how to write an expression for these types of questions? If a learner thinks the explanation is clear, it should be read out to the class. Ask for two or three explanations of each type to be read out. Return notebooks for learners to change their explanations if necessary.

Guidance on selected *Thinking and working mathematically* questions

Characterising and Classifying

Learner's Book Exercise 2.1, Question 8

For this question, learners need to spot patterns in different expressions and put them into groups. More confident learners will do much of this mentally. Many learners, however, will benefit from being asked to write down each expression and to try to simplify it. Explain that only a few expressions can be obviously simplified while others can be written in a slightly different way.

Give an example, if required: $\frac{2}{3}x$, $\frac{2}{3} \times x$, $\frac{2 \times x}{3}$ and $\frac{2x}{3}$

all mean the same thing; that x is multiplied by 2 and divided by 3.

Homework idea

As Section 2.1 will probably take more than one lesson, you can select questions from Workbook Exercise 2.1 at the end of each lesson. Only set questions that can be answered using skills and knowledge gained from that lesson. You can help learners to mark their homework at the start of the next lesson. This means you can address any problems before moving on.

Assessment idea

Every 5 or 10 minutes, ask all learners to answer a question (on a whiteboard, or in the back of their notebooks). Use simple questions such as 'If I had x dollars and spent 5 dollars, write an expression for how much I have left' $[x-5]$; 'Write an expression for: Multiply n by 10 and add 4' $[10n+4]$; 'Write an expression for:
I think of a number n, I divide it by 10 then multiply by 3'
$[\frac{3n}{10}$ or $\frac{n}{10} \times 3$ or $\frac{3}{10}n \dots]$ etc.

Once all learners have answered the question ask them to show you their answer (by raising their whiteboard, or as you walk by). This gives you an opportunity to talk briefly to learners, to identify those who may struggle and to check their working.

2.2 Using expressions and formulae

LEARNING PLAN		
Framework codes	**Learning objectives**	**Success criteria**
8Ae.02	• Understand that the laws of arithmetic and order of operations apply to algebraic terms and expressions (four operations, squares and cubes).	• Success with Question 3 shows understanding when using squares and cubes.
8Ae.04	• Understand that a situation can be represented either in words or as an algebraic expression, and move between the two representations (linear with integer or fractional coefficients).	• Success with Question 7 shows understanding in deriving a formula from a written description of situation.

CONTINUED

Framework codes	Learning objectives	Success criteria
8Ae.05	• Understand that a situation can be represented either in words or as a formula (mixed operations), and manipulate using knowledge of inverse operations to change the subject of a formula.	• Learners can rearrange simple formulae correctly using inverse operations.

LANGUAGE SUPPORT

Changing the subject: rearranging the formula to get a different letter on its own

Derive: construct a formula

Formula: an equation that shows the relationship between two or more quantities

Formulae: plural of formula

Inverse operation: the operation that reverses the effect of another operation

Subject of a formula: the letter than is on its own on one side (usually the left) of the formula

Substitute: replace part of an expression, usually a letter, by another value, usually a number

Common misconceptions

Misconception	How to identify	How to overcome
Confusion when using negative numbers.	Generally, check any incorrect answer where substitution involves negative numbers, specifically Questions 2a, 2f and 4.	Discussion of incorrect answers, possibly ask learners to write and use: $+ + = +$ $+ - = -$ $- + = -$ $- - = +$ if they are still not secure in their knowledge after completing Stage 7 Unit 1 and Stage 8 Unit 1.
Using order of operations (BIDMAS) rules incorrectly when rearranging a formula.	Question 13e, answering 'B'.	Successful learners leading a discussion of why the answer is A and what mistakes have been made when answering B.

Starter idea

Substitution practice (2–5 minutes)

Resources: Mini whiteboards

Description: Put learners into pairs. Write on the board 'Work out the value of $c - de$ when $c = 100$, $d = 2$ and $e = 15$'. Ask learners to show their workings and give the answer. [70] Discuss any errors or misunderstandings.

Allow learners to help other learners if possible. Next, ask learners to write on their boards the answer to $\frac{c}{d} + e$, using the same values. [65] Ask learners what mistakes might have been made when attempting this question, e.g. working out $c + e$ before dividing by d or adding d and e and using that number to divide c by.

Main teaching idea

Rearrange the cards (10–15 minutes)

Learning intention: Ensuring sound knowledge of substitution using positive numbers.

Resources: Resource sheet 2.2A (you can download this resource and answers from Cambridge GO); scissors

Description: (Use this idea after working through the introduction and Worked examples, but before starting Exercise 2.2.)

Ask learners to work individually, in pairs or in small groups. Distribute copies of Resource sheet 2.2A and ask learners to start by cutting their sheets into the rectangular cards. Tell learners that the cards are not in the correct order on the sheet. Learners must match each expression card with a value card and an answer card. Each set of three cards is unique. There is only one way to group the cards. There is no short way of doing this activity; learners will have attempted a great many questions before they have the correct answers. This is an excellent method for sharpening mental arithmetic skills via repeated substitution.

> **Differentiation ideas:** In less confident classes, groups of three or four are recommended.

Plenary idea

Exit ticket (3–5 minutes)

Resources: Exit ticket 2.2 (cut along the dotted lines). You can download this resource from Cambridge GO.

Description: Ask learners to put their name on their ticket, complete it and hand to you.

> **Assessment ideas:** The first two parts of the exit ticket should be well understood by learners, although they may still require practice in expressing their answers in words. Learners need to know how to change the subject of a formula. If they are finding this challenging, you can give them more practice questions to help build their confidence. Learners have not seen this type of question before but some will be able to tackle it.

Learners who cannot answer this question need some support. This can be done by you or you could ask other learners to explain how to rearrange the formula at the

start of the next lesson. You could follow that up with another similar question such as:

Make a the subject of $x = 9a + cd$ or $y = rs + 4a$.

Guidance on selected *Thinking and working mathematically* questions

Critiquing and Improving

Learner's Book Exercise 2.2, Question 17

In this question, learners will compare two different methods and evaluate them. No answer is required for part **a**, although you might decide to allow learners to discuss the advantages and disadvantages of each method. It does not matter which method a learner prefers but they must give a satisfactory reason for their choice. This reason should show that learners understand the difference between the two methods. A learner who prefers Polly's method might give a reason such as: Once n has been made subject of the formula, any values for P and b can be easily substituted. A learner who prefers Theo's method might give a reason such as: I prefer to use numbers when rearranging a formula. Whichever method a learner decides to use, they should use that method for both questions in part **c**.

Homework idea

As Section 2.2 will probably take more than one lesson, you can select questions from Workbook Exercise 2.2 at the end of each lesson. Only set questions that can be answered using skills and knowledge gained from that lesson. You can help learners to mark their homework at the start of the next lesson. This means you can address any problems before moving on.

Assessment idea

Just after completing Question 13, ask learners to write an explanation of how to rearrange the formula $a = 5b - 7$ to make b the subject. You can write this on the board.

Once completed, ask several learners in turn to read out their explanation. You should follow their instructions but deliberately misinterpret any instruction that could be seen as unclear in any way.

2.3 Expanding brackets

LEARNING PLAN

Framework codes	Learning objectives	Success criteria
8Ae.03	• Understand how to manipulate algebraic expressions by applying the distributive law with a single term (squares and cubes).	• Learners can expand a bracket with a single term. Success with Question 7 shows confidence with this learning objective.

LANGUAGE SUPPORT

Brackets: used to enclose items that are to be seen as a single expression

Expand: to multiply all parts of the expression inside the brackets by the term alongside the bracket

Common misconceptions

Misconception	How to identify	How to overcome
As in Section 2.2, confusion when using negative numbers.	Questions 9c and d.	Discussion about incorrect answers. Checking when learners are attempting questions 10 and Activity 2.3.

Starter idea

Stage 7 Brackets (5 minutes)

Resources: Notebooks

Description: Put learners into pairs or small groups. This starter is intended to remind learners how to expand simple brackets. If some learners cannot recall the method, probably other learners will be able to help them.

Write on the board:

a $3(2x+1)$ **b** $4(3y+5)$

c $5(2w+3)$ **d** $6(4z+7v+9)$

Ask learners to copy each question in turn, expand the bracket and check with their partner or group that they all have the same answer. If not, they should only ask you for assistance if they cannot agree who has the correct answer.

Answers: a $6x+3$,   **b** $12y+20$,   **c** $10w+15$, **d** $24z+42v+54$

Main teaching idea

Equivalent expressions (5 minutes)

Learning intention: Practising this important method.

Resources: Notebooks; Learner's Book Exercise 2.3, Question 7

Description: Ask learners to read the question. Then ask them how they intend to answer the question. Discuss various methods, but do not say if one is better than another. Ask learners to answer the question.

While learners are working, copy the cards, in order A to I, vertically on the board:

A $2x(8x^2+6x)=$

B $10x(3x^2+2)=$

C $2x^2(12x+9)=$

D $2x(10+15x^2)=$

E $4x^2(4x+3)=$

F $3x^2(6+8x)=$

G $5(6x^3+4x)=$

H $6x(3x + 4x^2) =$

I $x^2(12 + 16x) =$

After about three minutes stop the class and ask them to look at the board. Ask different learners to expand the terms as you copy down their answers. After each answer check that the other learners agree. Once all expansions are completed, ask learners to self-mark work done so far. Discuss any errors and ask what might have caused them.

Ask learners to complete the question. Once completed, ask learners to compare with partners and self-mark. Ask learners if there are any parts of the question that they would like you to explain again.

Answers: $16x^3 + 12x^2$: A, E, I $30x^3 + 20x$: B, D, G $24x^3 + 18x^2$: C, F, H

> **Differentiation ideas:** Wait until all learners have completed the questions, then peer mark. As extension, ask learners to do the question mentally, only writing down the final answer.

Plenary idea

Brackets (5–10 minutes)

Resources: Notebooks

Description: Tell learners they have done a range of questions on expanding brackets, and ask them to expand the following 10 questions. Write or display on the board:

1 $5(x + 4) =$

2 $3(3 + 2p) =$

3 $10(z - 2) =$

4 $2(3 - 5e) =$

5 $x(y - 9) =$

6 $y(y + 7) =$

7 $p(2 + 3p) =$

8 $e(5e + 2f) =$

9 $4x(x - 2y) =$

10 $w(6w + 2x) - 2y(2y - 9x) =$

Or alternatively, give these questions as an exit ticket. You can download Exit ticket 2.2 from Cambridge GO.

Answers: **1** $5x + 20$ **2** $9 + 6p$ **3** $10z - 20$ **4** $6 - 10e$ **5** $xy - 9x$ **6** $y^2 + 7y$ **7** $2p + 3p^2$ **8** $5e^2 + 2ef$ **9** $4x^2 - 8xy$ **10** $6w^2 + 2wx - 4y^2 + 18xy$

> **Assessment ideas:** If learners have used notebooks, they can check their answers using peer marking. If they have filled in exit tickets, you can review them after the lesson to decide on any revision that learners need.

Guidance on selected *Thinking and working mathematically* questions

Critiquing and Improving

Learner's Book Exercise 2.3, Question 6

Learners will evaluate different methods and give reasons for choosing one. If learners have been struggling with this unit, you could encourage discussion in pairs or small groups for parts **a** and **b** before they write down their answers. Reasons for their choice of method could be very varied. Writing that, e.g. 'Jun's one is easier' is not sufficient. You should expect the learner to be able to explain to you why it is easier than the other two methods. Learners can attempt part **c** individually.

Homework idea

As Section 2.3 will probably take more than one lesson, you can select questions from Workbook Exercise 2.3 at the end of each lesson. Only set questions that can be answered using skills and knowledge gained from that lesson. You can help learners to mark their homework at the start of the next lesson. This means you can address any problems before moving on.

Assessment idea

Allow peer marking throughout this section. Peer marking encourages learners to look at the key parts of each answer. It helps them to spot mistakes in other learners' work and later to avoid making the same mistakes themselves.

2.4 Factorising

Framework codes	Learning objectives	Success criteria
8Ae.03	• Understand how to manipulate algebraic expressions by identifying the highest common factor to factorise.	• Learners can fully factorise expressions containing one letter, two letters and squared letters.

LANGUAGE SUPPORT

Factorisations: expressions that have been factorised

Factorise: write an algebraic expression as a product of factors

Highest common factor (HCF): the largest number, and/or letters, that is a factor of two or more expressions

Common misconceptions

Misconception	How to identify	How to overcome
Learners often find a common factor, but not the *highest* common factor.	Discussion during Question 3, checking answers to Questions 6b and 6d.	Successful learners leading a discussion of why the numbers outside the brackets in 6b and 6d are 4 and 6, not 2 or 3 (4 and 6 are the *highest* common factors).

Starter idea

Worked example (5 minutes)

Resources: Two colours of board marker pen

Description: Read through the Learner's Book Section 2.4, Worked example 2.4. Emphasise the phrase 'the highest common factor', reminding learners that this is the largest number that will divide into both parts of the expression. Many learners will be confident in attempting basic factorisation questions, but some will need further guidance as to the way that factorising 'works'.

On the board copy Question **a**: $2x + 10$

Tell learners that you will rewrite $2x + 10$ using the highest common factor. Think 'out loud': 'What is the highest common factor of $2x$ and 10? Two!', now add to the question, using the two colours of pen:

$2x + 10 = 2 \times x + 2 \times 5$

Tell learners that this can now be factorised. Add to the board:

$2x + 10 = 2 \times x + 2 \times 5 = 2(x + 5)$

This process can be repeated for the rest of the worked examples:

b $8 - 12y = 4 \times 2 - 4 \times 3y = 4(2 - 3y)$

c $4a + 8ab = 4a \times 1 + 4a \times 2b = 4a(1 + 2b)$

d $x^2 - 5x = x \times x - x \times 5 = x(x - 5)$

Learners should understand that the method shown in the worked example and what has been done here are basically the same. Both methods are based upon learners working out the highest common factor.

Exercise 2.4 assumes that learners will use the method shown in Worked example 2.4, but learners should be allowed to use the above method instead.

Main teaching idea

Triangle with squares (5–15 minutes)

Learning intention: Repeated expansion of brackets and factorising, much of it mentally.

Resources: Resource sheet 2.4 (you can download this resource from Cambridge GO); scissors

Description: Learners can do this puzzle after they have completed Exercise 2.4. Give each learner or group a copy of Resource sheet 2.4. Learners should cut out all the individual equilateral triangles. Explain to learners that they should rearrange the small triangles into a large triangle. The question on one side of a small triangle needs to touch the corresponding answer on an adjacent small triangle. If learners require some assistance, you can tell them that the blank sides of small triangles will be on the outside of the finished puzzle.

Answers:

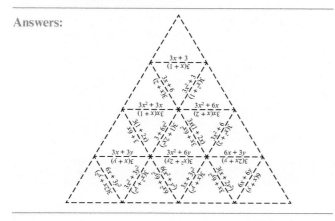

> **Differentiation ideas:** Learners can work individually or in small groups, depending upon ability.

Plenary idea

How to factorise (5 minutes)

Resources: Notebooks

Description: Ask learners to write an explanation of how to factorise $4y - 20$ for someone who has never factorised before.

> **Assessment ideas:** Ask learners to exchange notebooks then to decide if they could factorise $5h + 15$ after reading the explanation in front of them. Ask for learners to put up their hands if they think the explanation is good enough. Ask the writer of two or three of these 'good explanations' to read out their explanation. You should follow their instructions but deliberately misinterpret any instruction that could be seen as unclear in any way.

Guidance on selected *Thinking and working mathematically* questions

Critiquing and Improving

Learner's Book Exercise 2.4, Question 12

Learners are going to find the errors in the working and correct them. They should know by now that the best way to answer this type of question is to do the working themselves and use their working to explain any mistakes made. If learners have shown correct workings, they should notice that when simplifying they did $12 + 8$. Marcus probably did $12 - 8$ instead, meaning he worked out -4×-2 incorrectly, giving an answer of -8 instead of 8. With this many steps to get the answer, it is possible that a learner will get the correct answer $[2(7y + 10)]$ but be unable to recognise the exact mistake Marcus has made, even though they know the answer is incorrect.

Homework idea

As Section 2.4 will probably take more than one lesson, you can select questions from Workbook Exercise 2.4 at the end of each lesson. Only set questions that can be answered using skills and knowledge gained from that lesson. You can help learners to mark their homework at the start of the next lesson. This means you can address any problems before moving on.

Assessment idea

With the teaching focus of active learning, this is another good section for asking learners to peer mark and to give each other feedback. Learners asking *how* something was done or *why* something was done when an error has been made is an excellent way for learners to identify misunderstandings and deepen knowledge.

2.5 Constructing and solving equations

LEARNING PLAN

Framework codes	Learning objectives	Success criteria
8Ae.01	• Understand that letters have different meanings in expressions, formulae and equations.	• Learners remembering the differences between an expression, a formula and an equation in Question 1.
8Ae.06	• Understand that a situation can be represented either in words or as an equation. Move between the two representations and solve the equation (integer or fractional coefficients, unknown on either or both sides).	• Learners can write an equation when presented with a suitable problem, then solve the equation.

LANGUAGE SUPPORT

Construct: use given information to write an equation

Inverse operation: the operation that reverses the effect of another operation

Solve: calculate the value of any unknown letter(s) in an equation

Common misconceptions

Misconception	How to identify	How to overcome
Given 'George thinks of a number. He subtracts 2 then multiplies the result by 3', learners may forget the brackets, writing $n - 2 \times 3$ rather than $3(n - 2)$.	Questions 9c and d.	Check answers and discuss any errors. Emphasise how the word 'then' is used to tell you the order of operations. If something has to be done first, it should be put into brackets, so that order of operations (BIDMAS) rules can be followed correctly.

Starter idea

Solving simple equations (5–10 minutes)

Resources: Notebooks

Description: This is to remind learners of work done in Stage 7 Unit 2. Put learners into pairs or small groups. This is not a test. Encourage learners to help one another and to explain what methods to use, not just give answers. Learners should show all working. Write or display on the board:

1. $x + 7 = 10$
2. $x - 7 = 10$
3. $7 + x = 10$
4. $7x = 21$
5. $20 = x - 5$

6 $20 = 5x$

7 $5x + 10 = 20$

8 $30 = 5x - 10$

As learners answer the questions, read out answers for self-marking. Encourage successful learners to explain methods to those learners who need more assistance.

Answers: **1** $x=3$, **2** $x=17$, **3** $x=3$, **4** $x=3$, **5** $x=25$, **6** $x=4$, **7** $x=2$, **8** $x=8$

Main teaching idea

Think of a number (10–20 minutes)

Learning intention: To be able to represent a situation either in words or as an equation. Move between the two representations and solve the equation.

Resources: Resource sheet 2.5A. You can download this resource from Cambridge GO.

Description: Set this activity after learners have completed Exercise 2.5. Ask learners to work in groups of three to five. Give each group a copy of Resource sheet 2.5A. As they work, allow learners to compare their equations in the same way as they did for Question 9.

Question 1 gives a further opportunity to practise the valuable algebraic skills gained in Exercise 2.5. Note that some questions will produce initial equations with the unknown on both sides.

Answers: **a** 5, **b** 2, **c** 80, **d** 40, **e** 4, **f** 6 (note larger coefficient of n on the right-hand side), **g** 3, **h** 7

Question 2 leads learners to think in a new way, trying to put an equation into words. This will help them more thoroughly understand the mathematical language that they have been using during this Unit.

Question 3 requires learners to solve the equations they have put into words.

Answers: **a** 2, **b** 4, **c** 6, **d** 15, **e** 10, **f** 10, **g** 2

> **Differentiation ideas:** Learners who are struggling should concentrate on Question 1. Working in pairs or small groups is an option here. Questions 4 and 5 should only be attempted by more confident learners who have thoroughly understood this unit. Most learners would find these questions rather challenging.

Plenary idea

I think of a number (5 minutes)

Resources: Mini whiteboards

Description: Ask learners to write each part you say in algebra and then show you their board:

Say 'I think of a number' [ask to see boards, expect to see n, but any letter is correct]

Say 'I multiply it by 4' [ask to see boards, expect to see $4n$, rather than $4 \times n$]

Say 'I now subtract 5' [ask to see boards, expect to see $4n - 5$]

Say 'I multiply the result by 3' [ask to see boards, expect to see $3(4n - 5)$, check brackets are in place]

Say 'The answer is the same as' [ask to see boards, expect to see $3(4n - 5) =$]

Say '6 times my number' [ask to see boards, expect to see $3(4n - 5) = 6n$]

Say 'add 3' [ask to see boards, expect to see $3(4n - 5) = 6n + 3$]

Write '$3(4n - 5) = 6n + 3$' on the board and ask learners what number you were thinking of, i.e. solve the equation to work out the value of n [$n = 3$]

> **Assessment ideas:** At any stage, if an incorrect answer is seen, repeat that sentence and all of those above it. If the answer is not corrected, ask a successful learner to explain their method to the class. The learner with the incorrect answer should then be able to have the same answer as the rest of the class.

Guidance on selected *Thinking and working mathematically* questions

Conjecturing and Convincing

Learner's Book Exercise 2.5, Question 14

Learners will make a conjecture about which combination of cards gives them the largest or smallest value of y, giving their reasons. Any learner who reads the entire question will realise that in order for them to show they are correct they will need to work out answers to all nine possibilities. If they work them all out and then answer parts **a** and **b** they will get correct answers but will have missed out on the most important part of this question: thinking. Instead ask learners *not* to start by working out all possible answers.

Once they have made a conjecture and given their reasons, learners can then check by working out the nine possibilities. For example, they could start by comparing the expressions: $(2y + 14)$ will always give negative values for y because you have to take 14 from both sides so this will be used for the smallest value of y; $8(y - 12)$ will always give big numbers because you will be adding 96 to both sides; $\frac{y}{4} - 18$ will also give large numbers because you are adding 18 and then multiplying by 4. Learners then go on to select the appropriate yellow card.

Answers: Largest value is from $\frac{y}{4} - 18 = 4$, $(y = 88)$
Smallest value is from $2y + 14 = -20$, $(y = -17)$

Homework idea

As Section 2.5 will probably take more than one lesson, you can select questions from Workbook Exercise 2.5 at the end of each lesson. Only set questions that can be answered using skills and knowledge gained from that lesson. You can help learners to mark their homework at the start of the next lesson. This means you can address any problems before moving on.

Assessment idea

Once Question 9 has been completed, give each learner a section from Resource sheet 2.5B. You can download this resource from Cambridge GO. If learners can answer this question, you will know that they understand how to 'move between the two representations and solve the equation' and their answers will show evidence of their success at this learning objective. Any learners with incorrect answers may require some help as the question is very similar to part **d** of Question 9.

Answers: number $= 8$

2.6 Inequalities

LEARNING PLAN		
Framework codes	**Learning objectives**	**Success criteria**
8Ae.07	• Understand that letters can represent open and closed intervals (two terms).	• Learners can explain what inequalities such as $4 < y \leq 7$ mean, listing the possible integer values.

LANGUAGE SUPPORT	
Closed interval: a list of numbers that is not never-ending **Inequality:** a relationship between two expressions that are not equal	**Integer:** a whole number that can be positive or negative or zero, with no fractional part

Common misconceptions

Misconception	How to identify	How to overcome
Treating $<$ and $\leq$ as the same sign.	Errors in Question 1.	Discussions while answering Question 1.
Confusing o and ●.	Errors in questions 3 and 4.	Discussions while answering Questions 3 and 4.

Starter idea

Inequalities (5–10 minutes)

Resources: Mini whiteboards

Description: Do this before reading through the introduction or Worked examples. Remind learners that in Stage 7 Unit 2 they learned about inequalities. Ask learners to write down some examples of what they remember about inequalities on their boards. Allow one to two minutes.

Now ask learners to get into groups of three or four to discuss examples and write a better list of examples between them. Say that you would like one example each for [write on the board] $<$, $\leq$, $>$ and $\geq$.

Once completed ask for one board from each group to be put together where all learners can see the boards.

Ask the class which is the clearest explanation for the inequality $>$. The example should have an inequality, e.g. $x > 5$ *and* also a list of the possible values, e.g. $x = 6, 7, 8, \ldots$ If boards have inaccurate values, discuss possible mistakes. If no board shows a list of values, ask learners to take back their boards and add that to their example for $>$, then look again as a class.

Remind them that we use $\ldots$ to show that the numbers go on for ever and we can't list them all.

Main teaching idea

Inequalities (3 minutes)

Learning intention: To understand better more complex inequalities.

Resources: Notebooks; Learner's Book Exercise 2.6, Question 1; electronic whiteboard

Description: Read Question 1, part **a** with the learners.

Many learners will look at the inequality $6 < x < 11$ and only focus on the fact that the x is between 6 and 11, but not really understand the inequality itself.

Write on the board:

$$6 < x < 11$$
$$6 < x \qquad\qquad x < 11$$

Next, discuss what learners can tell you about each inequality. The aim is to get learners to show/tell you that the $6 < x$ is the same as $x > 6$. For some classes, the following sequence will help learners see the connection:

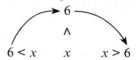

Ask learners to answer part **b**. Check and discuss any incorrect answers.

Ask learners to answer parts **c** and **d**.

Answers:
a x is greater than 6 and less than 11
b x is greater than or equal to 12 and less than or equal to 18
c x is greater than 0 and less than or equal to 20
d x is greater than or equal to −9 and less than −1

> **Differentiation ideas:** Some learners will find it helpful to rewrite $12 \leq x \leq 18$ as $x \geq 12$ and $x \leq 18$ before attempting to answer.

Plenary idea

What is the inequality? (5 minutes)

Resources: Notebooks

Description: Write on the board '6, 7, 8, 9, 10'

Ask learners to write down an inequality whose solution would be this list of integer values.

Once completed, ask learners 'Can you write another inequality that still has the same list of integer values? If yes, write it down.'

Answers: There are four possible solutions: $6 \leq x \leq 10$, $5 < x \leq 10$, $6 \leq x < 11$ and $5 < x < 11$.

> **Assessment ideas:** You can either mark this problem solving question yourself for a formal grading. Alternatively you could allow peer marking followed by a brief discussion about learners' different answers.

Guidance on selected *Thinking and working mathematically* questions

Conjecturing and Convincing

Learner's Book Exercise 2.6, Question 11b

Ask learners to read, answer and self or peer mark Question 11a. When any problems have been dealt with, ask learners to answer part **b** using a mini whiteboard to write their answer. In this part of the question, learners will make a statement based on their observations and then think how to explain it. When learners have answered the question, ask to see their answers. Be aware that some learners may not think clearly and may be tempted to write 'yes, $8 < m < 14$' or 'yes, $8 > m > 14$'. If any learners have written either of these answers write on the board '$m > 14$' and ask for the first three integers that satisfy the inequality. Once given, write '$m = 15, 16, 17, \ldots$'

Next write '$m < 8$' on the board and ask for the first three integers that satisfy the inequality. Once given, write '$m = 7, 6, 5, \ldots$' Ask learners what they notice about the values of m. Hopefully, someone will say that m cannot be both 'only larger than 14' and 'only smaller than 8'.

Homework ideas

As Section 2.6 will probably take more than one lesson, you can select questions from Workbook Exercise 2.6 at the end of each lesson. Only set questions that can be answered using skills and knowledge gained from that lesson. You can help learners to mark their homework at the start of the next lesson. This means you can address any problems before moving on.

You could ask learners to make a list of worked examples containing everything they think they need to remember for the end-of-unit test. The following lesson, it is important to share their lists in class, perhaps spread out over a few desks for everyone to look at. Discuss the different worked examples as a class. Learners should not just have copied out the worked examples from the Learner's Book, but used questions they think will help them with revision at a later date. When the class agree that a point is important, that key point could be copied onto the board. Agree on as many key points as possible. Learners could then improve their individual worked example list if necessary. Learners could store their worked examples list at home as a possible revision tool towards mid-term or end-of-year exams.

Assessment idea

Use Question 8b as a diagnostic question. If any learners struggle with this question, you will need to address their problems before moving on.

PROJECT GUIDANCE: ALGEBRA CHAINS

Why do this problem?

In this problem learners are required to specialise by substituting different values into expressions and noticing how the outputs change. Along the way they will need to work systematically, consider the properties of numbers and think about inverse operations.

Possible approach

Show learners an example of an algebra chain and explain how it works.

Hand out Project 1 Algebra chains resource sheet A with the eight expressions for learners to cut out. (You can download this resource from Cambridge GO. There is also a sheet that includes questions and prompts: Project 1 Algebra chains resource sheet B. You could give this to learners instead or you could use the questions yourself.) Learners can work in pairs. Challenge them to arrange the expressions into four algebra chains that take the inputs 1, 2, 3 and 4 and give the outputs 40, 30, 20 and 10 respectively.

While they are working, walk around the room and listen out for good ideas that help learners to narrow down the possibilities. Bring the class together to share insights such as:

- some expressions will always have an odd/even output
- some expressions will never give an output which is a multiple of 10
- some expressions will give a negative output if the input is too big.

Then give learners time to finish the activity, using these insights to help them. Once each pair has finished they can move on to the follow-up activity.

Key questions

Are there any cards that always give an odd output?

Which cards could give an output of 30?

What would the input need to be?

Possible support

Encourage learners to work together, to experiment and record what they've tried. Reassure them that they may need to try several arrangements before finding a combination that works.

Possible extension

Challenge learners to create and solve algebra chains with three or more cards. They could be invited to create their own expressions that include fractions and decimals or powers and roots.

> 3 Place value and rounding

Unit plan

Topic	Approximate number of learning hours	Outline of learning content	Resources
Introduction and Getting Started	5 minutes		Learner's Book
3.1 Multiplying and dividing by 0.1 and 0.01	1–1.5	Use knowledge of place value to multiply and divide integers and decimals by 0.1 and 0.01.	Learner's Book Section 3.1 Workbook Section 3.1 ⬇ Additional teaching ideas Section 3.1 ⬇ Resource sheet 3.1A ⬇ Resource sheet 3.1B ⬇ Resource sheet 3.1C
3.2 Rounding	0.5–1	Round numbers to a given number of significant figures.	Learner's Book Section 3.2 Workbook Section 3.2 ⬇ Additional teaching ideas Section 3.2 ⬇ Exit ticket 3.2 ⬇ Resource sheet 3.2
Cross-unit resources ⬇ Language worksheet 3.1–3.2 ⬇ End of Unit 3 test			

BACKGROUND KNOWLEDGE

For this unit, learners will need this background knowledge:

- Be able to multiply and divide whole numbers and decimals by 10, 100 and 1000 (Stage 6).
- Be able to round numbers with 2 decimal places to the nearest tenth or whole number (Stage 6).

- Be able to round to a given number of decimal places (Stage 7).

This unit extends to multiplying and dividing by 0.1 and 0.01, and rounding numbers to a given number of significant figures.

TEACHING SKILLS FOCUS

Assessment for learning

A key aspect for assessment for learning is assessing prior knowledge. While the 'Getting started' exercise will help find weaknesses, much of this unit is built on previously learned skills. If any of those skills are weak or missing it is important to revisit that area of the Stage 6 or 7 work. You may need to adapt or stop the planned lesson if the required previous knowledge is missing. If only part of the class lacks a skill, then this is a great opportunity for you to get learners to help teach.

Show the skill required to all learners, set three or four basic questions, put learners in groups with one or two 'learners' with as many 'teachers' as possible. Listen to the groups, make sure that only one 'teacher' is speaking at any time. Regularly check with 'learners' that they understand and that the 'teacher' is giving good feedback to any questions they are asking. Let learners self-mark their answers to the questions.

Now give *slightly* harder questions to all learners, working in pairs - one 'learner' and one 'teacher' per pair if possible. Allow self-marking.

Now give one question for all learners to attempt, without help. Is there evidence of learning? Have the 'teachers' done a good job? Did the 'teachers' understand what they were teaching? Are there any aspects that you need to clarify?

At the end of Unit 3, ask yourself:

- Do you know what the learners know/knew about this topic?
- Have you asked questions to look for evidence of learning, of a depth of understanding of the topic that shows learners understand *how* the maths works, not just that they can get an answer to a question?
- Are learners confident that if they can suggest half-formed ideas about a problem, then they can share it and receive guidance from yourself or another learner?
- Do learners realise that learning from their mistakes is an excellent and invaluable process that is encouraged within the classroom?

3.1 Multiplying and dividing by 0.1 and 0.01

LEARNING PLAN

Framework codes	Learning objectives	Success criteria
8Np.01	• Use knowledge of place value to multiply and divide integers and decimals by 0.1 and 0.01.	• Learners understand that they can work out $3.2 \div 0.1$ by working out 3.2×10.

LANGUAGE SUPPORT

Decimal number: a number in the counting system based on 10; the part before the decimal point is a whole number, the part after the decimal point is a decimal fraction

Equivalent calculations: calculations that use a different method but end up with the same answer

Inverse operation: the operation that reverses the effect of another operation

Common misconceptions

Misconception	How to identify	How to overcome
Learners often find difficulty understanding that 0.1 is the same as $\frac{1}{10}$ and 0.01 is the same as $\frac{1}{100}$.	Introduction 3.1.	Allow learners to use a calculator while working through the introduction proving to themselves that 0.1 is the same as $\frac{1}{10}$, etc. For 0.01, draw a place value table: 	U	.	10ths	100ths	 |---|---|---|---| | 0	.	0	1	 Show that 1/100 is 1 in the 100ths column, and filling in 0s.
Learners often find difficulty understanding and remembering that dividing a number by 0.1 is the same as multiplying that number by 10.	Question 7 and 8.	Check several different divisions (with 0.1 and 0.01) on a calculator, with a variety of whole and decimal numbers. This will help most learners to recognise this fact.

Starter idea

Before you start (5 minutes)

Resources: Notebooks; 'Getting started' questions in Learner's Book

Description: Before learners attempt the questions, discuss what they remember of the rules of rounding to decimal places (looking at the next digit after the required number of decimal places: 0, 1, 2, 3 and 4 round down, 5, 6, 7, 8 and 9, round up). A few basic questions might help recall and discussion, such as Round 4.724/12.159/32.929/32.976 to 1 decimal place or 2 decimal places. It may be worthwhile asking learners 'What is 295 ÷ 10' [29.5] and 'What is 295 ÷ 100' [2.95] to make sure they remember division by 10 and 100.

Main teaching idea

Think like a mathematician (3–5 minutes)

Learning intention: To understand a common method of mental division by a decimal.

Resources: Learner's Book Exercise 3.1, Question 7; calculators

Description: Allow learners to check the answers first using a calculator to help with understanding. Win's method is very clear. Learners should be able to follow what is happening and replicate it. It is more difficult for learners to understand *why* it works.

Remind learners that 0.1 is one tenth, or $\frac{1}{10}$. Ten lots of one tenth is ten tenths or one whole [1], which is why you multiply the 0.1 by 10. If the 0.1 [the denominator] is multiplied by 10, then the numerator must be multiplied by 10.

The reason for this has been explained before, but remind learners that, looking at Win's question 1: $\frac{3.2 \times 10}{0.1 \times 10}$ you see that Win has multiplied by $\frac{10}{10}$, and 10 divided by 10 is 1, so really she has multiplied by 1.

> Differentiation ideas: Some classes or some learners may require you to work through Win's methods before learners get the chance to discuss in pairs or groups and confirm their understanding. To extend, ask for a quicker method of working out Win's Question 2. $[\times \frac{100}{100}]$ Ask why it works. [÷ 0.01 is equivalent to × 100 as $0.01 = \frac{1}{100}$]

Plenary idea

Quick questions (2–3 minutes)

Resources: Mini whiteboards

Description: Ask a variety of multiplication and division questions to be written on the main board, but done mentally by learners. Learners should show their answer on their mini whiteboards. It may be useful to ask learners to make sure their decimal place 'dot' is bigger than usual, making it easier for you to scan answers looking for errors.

Ask questions such as: $99 \div 0.1$ [990], 99×0.1 [9.9], $99 \div 0.01$ [9900], 99×0.01 [0.99]

and $5.5 \div 0.1$ [55], 5.5×0.1 [0.55], $5.5 \div 0.01$ [550], 5.5×0.01 [0.055]

> **Assessment ideas:** Scan learners' answers quickly. If you notice incorrect answers, give the correct answer and either show the method briefly on the board or ask a successful learner to explain how they reached the answer. Give a similar question and make a note of learners who still give incorrect answers. These learners will probably require one-to-one help.

Guidance on selected *Thinking and working mathematically* questions

Conjecturing and Convincing

Learner's Book Exercise 3.1, Question 14

This multi-step problem is best approached via inverse operations rather than by trial and improvement. The question is intended to make learners think clearly about both inverse operations and multiplying and dividing

by 0.1 and 0.01. Learners will say what they notice and share their ideas, making convincing arguments.

If learners struggle to start, ask them to look at the line 'Razi then divides this answer by 0.1 and gets a final answer of 12 500.' Help learners by saying they should start with the final answer, 12 500 and work out 'a number' $\div 0.1 = 12\,500$ [1250]. Once that part has been discussed, the rest should be straightforward.

Homework idea

As Section 3.1 will probably take more than one lesson, you can select questions from Workbook Exercise 3.1 at the end of each lesson. Only set questions that can be answered using skills and knowledge gained from that lesson. You can help learners to mark their homework at the start of the next lesson. This means you can address any problems before moving on.

Assessment idea

With so many 'quick to check' answers, this section is ideal for peer marking. Encourage learners not only to check each other's work, but to try to suggest what mistake has been made, if any. Anyone can say that, e.g. 2.45 is incorrect, but only someone knowledgeable can say *how* the error might have occurred.

3.2 Rounding

LEARNING PLAN

Framework codes	Learning objectives	Success criteria
8Np.02	• Round numbers to a given number of significant figures.	• Learners can round any number (integer or decimal) to any number of significant figures.

LANGUAGE SUPPORT

Decimal places: the digits after the decimal point

Degree of accuracy: the level of accuracy in any rounding

Round: make an approximation of a number, to a given accuracy

Significant figures (s.f.): the first significant figure is the first non-zero digit in a number; for example, 2 is the first significant figure in both 2146 and 0.000024

Common misconceptions

Misconception	How to identify	How to overcome
Not checking that an answer is of the correct order of magnitude when rounding to significant figures, dropping zeros from the end to give, for example, an answer of 5 instead of 500.	Question 1.	When giving answers constantly reinforce the question of 'Is the answer about the same size as the question?'
Confusing rounding to significant figures with rounding to decimal places, especially with numbers less than 1.	Question 4 parts c, d, e and f (especially part d).	Discussion when dealing with incorrect answers. Use Question 5 to check understanding.
Confusion when the significant figure is a 9 and needs to be rounded up.	Question 4 part g and especially 5 part e.	Checking answers and a class discussion during Starter idea 'Decimal place rounding', Questions e, g and h. Also see Worked example 3.2c.
Not counting non-leading zeros as significant figures.	Question 5 part d.	Use Worked example 3.2b to explain to learners. Also discuss Question 5d answer option B, which is the result of this misconception.

Starter idea

Decimal place rounding (5 minutes)

Resources: Electronic whiteboard; Notebooks

Description: Before working through the introduction or Worked examples, display on the board:

Round each of these numbers to the given degree of accuracy.

a   45.982 (2 decimal places)

b   126.99231 (4 d.p.)

c   0.7785 (1 d.p.)

d   0.040056583 (6 d.p.)

e   782.02972 (3 d.p.)

f   3.141592654 (7 d.p.)

g   3.9975 (2 d.p.)

h   99.9961 (1 d.p.)

Answers:

a   45.98,   b   126.9923,   c   0.8,
d   0.040057,   e   782.030,   f   3.1415927,
g   4.00,   h   100.0

Tell learners that this is a question they did last year. Tell them that it is important they remember the rules for decimal place rounding because the rules are almost the same for the next type of rounding. While the last two questions [and perhaps part **e**] are a little more confusing, learners must be able to answer the others with confidence before moving on to Section 3.2.

Main teaching idea

Think like a mathematician (2–5 minutes)

Learning intention: To understand where the first significant figure in a number is, and to understand that the answer and question must be of the same order.

Resources: Notebooks; Learner's Book Exercise 3.2, Question 3

Description: If learners have been successful with questions 1 and 2, understanding that the answers given by Harry are wrong should be straightforward. Some learners, however, might struggle to write down *why* they are wrong. Ask learners to round the numbers themselves, and to compare their answers with those answers given. This will usually help less confident learners understand the reasons behind the mistakes. It is essential to make sure the whole class understands part **a**, in order to help them write useful answers to parts **b** and **c**.

Answers:

a   For example: In **a** he has forgotten the zeros. It should be 45 000. In **b** he has rounded to 2 d.p. not 2 s.f. It should be 0.033.

b   For example: Fill in the gaps between the significant figures and the decimal point with zeros.

c   For example: Fill in the gaps between the decimal point and the significant figures with zeros.

⟩ **Differentiation ideas:** It will usually be enough to work out the correct answers and have a discussion with a partner to identify the misconceptions. If a pair of learners still cannot answer part **a**, hold a brief class discussion so that other learners can explain the errors and why they might have occurred.

Plenary idea

Significant figures (5 minutes)

Resources: Notebooks

Description: Write on the board:
$1 \div 6.2623^2 = 0.025\,499\,535$

Ask learners to round the answer to **a** 1 s.f.; **b** 2 s.f.; **c** 3 s.f.; **d** 4 s.f.; **e** 5 s.f.; **f** 6 s.f. Answer the questions individually.

⟩ **Assessment ideas:** Allow peer comparisons first, then peer or self-marking.

Discuss any incorrect answers, especially those when rounding to 4 and 5 s.f.

Answers:

a 0.03	b 0.025	c 0.0255
d 0.02550	e 0.025500	f 0.0254995

Guidance on selected *Thinking and working mathematically* questions

Critiquing and Improving

Learner's Book Exercise 3.2, Question 11

Learners should attempt this question individually. It asks learners to evaluate what degree of accuracy would be sensible. Allow learners 1–2 minutes to think and write down their answer. Many will just guess.

Put learners into small groups and ask them to share their ideas so that they can improve together. After another 2 or 3 minutes, discuss answers as a class. You may have to lead the class into thinking/discussing that it is sensible to assume that measurements of 0.87 m and 9.6 m have been rounded, probably both to the same degree, i.e. 2 s.f. If these measurements are rounded to 2 s.f. it is unwise to think any further calculations using 0.87 m and 9.6 m could be more accurate than 2 s.f.

Homework ideas

As Section 3.2 will probably take more than one lesson, you can select questions from Workbook Exercise 3.2 at the end of each lesson. Only set questions that can be answered using skills and knowledge gained from that lesson. You can help learners to mark their homework at the start of the next lesson. This means you can address any problems before moving on.

You could ask learners to make a list of worked examples containing everything they think they need to remember for the end-of-unit test. The following lesson, it is important to share their lists in class, perhaps spread out over a few desks for everyone to look at. Discuss the different worked examples as a class. Learners should not just have copied out the worked examples from the Learner's Book, but used questions they think will help them with revision at a later date. When the class agree that a point is important, that key point could be copied onto the board. Agree on as many key points as possible. Learners could then improve their individual worked example list if necessary. Learners could store their worked examples list at home as a possible revision tool towards mid-term or end-of-year exams.

Assessment idea

Use Learner's Book Exercise 3.2, Question 6 as a hinge point question, i.e. to check whether learners are ready to move on. If learners struggle to write or to answer other learner's questions you may need to return to rounding to decimal places to remind them of the rules of rounding. Always try to get other learners to explain how and why to a confused learner, only helping if the explanations are not clear enough.

❯ 4 Decimals

Unit plan

Topic	Approximate number of learning hours	Outline of learning content	Resources
Introduction and Getting Started	5–10 minutes		Learner's Book
4.1 Ordering decimals	0.5–1	Understand the relative size of quantities to order and compare decimals (positive and negative) using the symbols =, ≠, >, <, ≤ and ≥.	Learner's Book Section 4.1 Workbook Section 4.1 ⬇ Additional teaching ideas Section 4.1 ⬇ Resource sheet 4.1
4.2 Multiplying decimals	1	Estimate and multiply decimals by integers and decimals.	Learner's Book Section 4.2 Workbook Section 4.2 ⬇ Additional teaching ideas Section 4.2 ⬇ Resource sheet 4.2
4.3 Dividing by decimals	1–1.5	Estimate and divide decimals by numbers with one decimal place.	Learner's Book Section 4.3 Workbook Section 4.3 ⬇ Additional teaching ideas Section 4.3 ⬇ Resource sheet 4.3A ⬇ Resource sheet 4.3B
4.4 Making decimal calculations easier	0.5–1	Use knowledge of the laws of arithmetic and order of operations (including brackets) to simplify calculations containing decimals.	Learner's Book Section 4.4 Workbook Section 4.4 ⬇ Additional teaching ideas Section 4.4

Cross-unit resources
⬇ Language worksheet 4.1–4.4
⬇ Project guidance: Diamond decimals resource sheet
⬇ End of Unit 4 test

BACKGROUND KNOWLEDGE

For this unit, learners will need this background knowledge:

- Understand the relative size of quantities and how to order and compare decimals and fractions using the symbols =, ≠, > and < (Stage 7).

- Be able to multiply and divide decimals by whole numbers and estimate an answer (Stage 7).

- Be able to divide numbers with one or two decimal places by whole numbers (Stage 6).

- Use knowledge of common factors, laws of arithmetic and order of operations (BIDMAS) to simplify calculations containing decimals or fractions (Stage 7).

Learners will deepen their knowledge and extend their use of ordering, multiplying and dividing decimals. Learners will also extend their skills of simplifying calculations using factors and order of operations.

TEACHING SKILLS FOCUS

Metacognition

A complex area of learning that can be simplified to 'thinking about thinking'. Throughout this unit ask learners, whenever possible, to say out loud what they are thinking. Usually ask at the start or a short way through answering a problem. If a question has already been answered, ask what they were thinking while they were attempting a problem and if they would now do the problem a different way. If done regularly, this questioning leads to a process that can be used throughout their schooling: 'think about a problem, plan what to do, do the plan, look back and decide if you could have done anything better'. This process teaches learners to understand how to solve problems effectively, not just get the answer to a particular question.

At the end of Unit 4, ask yourself:

- Are learners able to explain what they are thinking? If the answer is 'No, not really', was

that just because they are not used to giving explanations and so need much more practice?

- Are learners getting better at explaining their reasoning?

- Are learners getting better at explaining what mistakes have been made and what to do next in a problem?

- Are learners more confident explaining when in pairs or small groups rather than as a whole class?

- With the more complicated problems, can learners tell you what they will do to improve, i.e. make a plan?

Remember, if you are the first teacher to use this very powerful learning tool, your learners may find it difficult to explain what they are thinking. They need more practice.

4.1 Ordering decimals

LEARNING PLAN

Framework codes	Learning objectives	Success criteria
8Nf.06	• Understand the relative size of quantities to order and compare decimals (positive and negative) using the symbols =, ≠, >, <, ≤ and ≥.	• Learners can order a pair or list of numbers. These numbers may be positive or negative decimals or measurements with different units.

LANGUAGE SUPPORT

Compare: to look at and see what is the same or different

Decimal measurements: measurements of length, capacity and mass that are written as a decimal number

Decimal number: a number in the counting system based on 10; the part before the decimal point is a whole number, the part after the decimal point is a decimal fraction

Decimal part: the part of the decimal number to the right of the decimal point

Hundredths: the second digit after the decimal point in a decimal number

Order: to arrange from the smallest to the largest or largest to smallest

Tenths: the first digit after the decimal point in a decimal number

Term-to-term rule: a rule to find a term of a sequence, given the previous term

Whole-number part: the part of the decimal number to the left of the decimal point

Common misconceptions

Misconception	How to identify	How to overcome
Learners may think, for example, that 13.2 is smaller than 13.11 because there are fewer digits in 13.2 than in 13.11, or because 2 is smaller than 11.	Discussion during Worked example 4.1, checking answers for Questions 1d, 2d and 2e.	Discuss relevant parts of the Worked example again, or remind learners that they can add zeros for empty columns to any numbers to make each have the same number of decimal places.

Starter idea

Before you start (5–10 minutes)

Learning intention: Check learners' prior understanding.

Resources: Notebooks; Learner's Book 'Getting started' questions

Description: Learners should have little difficulty with the 'Getting started' material. Carefully check and discuss any incorrect answers using Question 3. Some classes might need a little help with the inequality signs. Write '<' on the board and ask if anyone can remember what the sign means. Hopefully most learners will remember but, if necessary, add to the '<' sign '<ess than' as a reminder.

The 'Getting started' section is not a test. This is a quick method of making sure all learners have the basic skills in order to start the section. This is an ideal place for metacognition (thinking about thinking). Ask learners what they were thinking when they answered a particular question, especially the first three. This discussion can be on a one-to-one basis with yourself, or with a group or whole class.

Main teaching idea

Think like a mathematician, Question 3 (3–5 minutes)

Learning intention: To understand a potentially new method of ordering decimals.

Resources: Notebooks; Learner's Book Exercise 4.1

Description: This shows a very commonly used, and easily understood, alternative method of ordering decimals. The basic idea is to have each number to contain the same number of decimal places. This is done by looking for the number with the most digits after the decimal place. Then add zeros to any other decimal number so all numbers in the list end up with the same number of decimal places.

> **Differentiation ideas:** If a learner struggles with the concept, write the numbers from the list in a column:

2 6 . 5

2 6 . 4 1

2 6 . 0 9

2 6 . 0 0 1

2 6 . 9 2

And then add the zeros, reminding learners that as the numbers are still in the same columns as before, they are the same size.

2 6 . 5 0 0

2 6 . 4 1 0

2 6 . 0 9 0

2 6 . 0 0 1

2 6 . 9 2 0

Now you can compare the decimal numbers by simply comparing the last three digits.

Plenary idea

How to order decimals (3–5 minutes)

Resources: Notebooks

Description: Write on the board '11.3, 11.205, 11.27'

Ask learners to write out a list of instructions for someone else to follow that will help them rewrite the numbers in order, starting with the smallest. Assume the other person understands what a decimal is, but has never put them in order before.

> **Assessment ideas:** Exchange notebooks with a partner. Each learner now follows the instructions on how to order the three decimals [11.205, 11.27, 11.3]. If the instructions are not clear enough to get to the correct answer they can be discussed in pairs or with the whole class. Discuss briefly two or three very clear instructions with the class.

Guidance on selected *Thinking and working mathematically* questions

Conjecturing and Convincing

Learner's Book Exercise 4.1, Question 11

In this question, learners will say what they notice and explain it. In part **a**, Learners will often just look for the smallest or largest number and not consider the units. Any learners that do not choose 25 km should be encouraged to take more time to think clearly about the question. Part **b** is effectively an extension of part **a**. Learners must find the smallest [0.2 km] and largest [1.64 km] and check the statement is true. Part **c** requires basic logic. Learners should realise that half of Shen's distances are only divisible by 25 m [250 m, 1.25 km, 1.75 km, 750 m and 0.75 km]. Most of Mia's distances are only divisible by 20 m [240 m, 1.64 km, 820 m, 640 m, 1.42 km, 960 m and 0.88 km].

Homework idea

As Section 4.1 will probably take more than one lesson, you can select questions from Workbook Exercise 4.1 at the end of each lesson. Only set questions that can be answered using skills and knowledge gained from that lesson. You can help learners to mark their homework at the start of the next lesson. This means you can address any problems before moving on.

Assessment idea

At various times during Section 4.1, ask individual learners short, easy to answer questions that check knowledge. Ask questions without warning, and only ask three or four learners questions. Later in the lesson, ask three or four others, etc. Questions such as: 'Which is larger: 3.44 or 3.399?', 'Which is smaller: 3.44 or 3.399?', 'Which is larger: −3.44 or −3.399?' 'Which is smaller: −3.44 or −3.399?', 'Say a number that is larger/smaller than 5.25/−5.25', 'Say a number that is equal to 4.3', 'Which is larger: 4.3 kg or 999 g?', etc.

4.2 Multiplying decimals

LEARNING PLAN		
Framework codes	**Learning objectives**	**Success criteria**
8Nf.07	• Estimate and multiply decimals by integers and decimals.	• Learners can use written and mental methods to multiply decimals by integers or decimal numbers.

LANGUAGE SUPPORT

Estimation: approximation of an answer, based on a calculation with rounded numbers

Mentally/mental method: work out in your head

Place value: the value of the digit in a number based on its position in relation to the decimal point

Written method: work out on paper

Common misconceptions

Misconception	How to identify	How to overcome
Learners can forget to insert the decimal point after they have completed the multiplication.	Worked examples.	Discussion during Worked examples, reminding learners that rounding numbers to one s.f. can give a good estimate of the final answer, which they can use to check their work. Repeated practice throughout this section.
Learners can give answers to questions such as 0.2×0.3 (Q4) incorrectly (in this case, for example, as 0.6), when they have worked out the 2×3 correctly but have not understood the place value issues.	Question 4.	Discussion during Question 4.

Starter idea

Five fives (5 minutes)

Resources: Notebooks

Description: You will be writing a series of multiplications, starting with 5×5, on the board, and ending up with:

5×500	=	2500
5×50	=	250
5×5	=	25
5×0.5	=	2.5
5×0.05	=	0.25
5×0.005	=	0.025
5×0.0005	=	0.0025

Start by writing '$5 \times 5 =$'. Ask for the answer. Write '25'.

Write '$5 \times 50 =$' above it. Ask for the answer. Write '250'.

Write '$5 \times 0.5 =$' below. Ask for the answer. Write '2.5'.

Point to the '$5 \times 50 = 250$' line. Ask learners 'What happens when I make the 50 ten times bigger, and write 500 instead?' [Answer is 10 times bigger too, so is 2500]

Write '$5 \times 500 = 2500$' above.

Point to the '$5 \times 0.5 = 2.5$' line. Ask learners 'What happens when I make the 0.5 ten times smaller, and write 0.05 instead?' [Answer is 10 times smaller too, so is 0.25]

Show learners that the number of decimal places in the question is the same as the number of decimal places in the answer.

Write '$5 \times 0.005 =$' and '$5 \times 0.0005 =$' at the bottom of the list and ask learners to copy and complete the list.

Main teaching idea

Think like a mathematician, Question 4 (5 minutes)

Learning intention: To understand place value when multiplying two decimals.

Resources: Notebooks; Learner's Book

Description: Allow each pair or group to discuss and write their explanation.

Discuss several groups' explanations as a class, writing on the board any particularly clear methods. After you have a few good examples on the board, discuss what makes them a clear explanation. Allow learners to alter their explanations if appropriate.

> **Differentiation ideas:** For some learners it may be necessary to point out these patterns:

The first line, $2 \times 3 = 6$, has no decimals in either the question or the answer.

The second line, $0.2 \times 3 = 0.6$, has one decimal place in the question [point to the 2] and one decimal place in the answer [point to the 6].

The third line has two decimal places in the question [point to the 2 and the 3] and two decimal places in the answer [point to the 06].

Then ask how many decimal places the learner can see in the fourth line [3], and so how many decimal places should there be in the answer [3]. This is usually enough for a learner to understand the link between the number of decimal places in both the question and the answer.

Plenary idea

Simple decimal multiplication online (2–10 minutes)

Resources: Electronic whiteboard; mini whiteboards or notebooks

Description: Type 'transum.org, decimal times' into a search engine. When directed to the page, learners will complete the level 1 material. This material changes every time it is clicked on, so no two sessions are the same. This is a free resource and learners can access this too. They may wish to practise at home so make sure they write down the web address of this resource. There are many other similar resources available.

Ask learners to draw a 3×4 grid on their board:

Display the level 1 material on the board then tell learners they have 2 minutes 30 seconds to write in their grid as many answers as possible. After 2 mins 30 secs, stop the class. Ask learners to swap boards with a partner. Ask for answers and put them into the answer boxes in the level 1 questions. Click the 'Check' button to make sure all answers are correct. Each learner can give a score out of 12 and hand back the board to their partner. Ask how many got 12 out of 12. Ask the others why they didn't get 12 out of 12. Was it lack of speed recalling the multiplications or was it getting the decimal point in the wrong place?

> **Assessment ideas:** All learners will peer mark. If many learners have fewer than 9 correct answers it may be useful to go back and do this plenary again. This website will automatically show a similar, but different, set of questions.

Guidance on selected *Thinking and working mathematically* questions

Conjecturing and Convincing

Learner's Book Exercise 4.2, Question 11

In this question, learners will look at the working and decide whether it is correct, giving their reasons. Ideally when estimating, it is usual to round to 1 s.f. to make the question as simple as possible.

For most learners, part **a** will be rounded to 0.5×3 giving an estimate of 1.5. This will show learners that the answer is probably incorrect. For more confident learners show that as the 2.8 will be rounded *up* to 3, it might make sense to round the 0.45 *down* to 0.4 giving an estimate of 1.2 [showing that Syra has correctly used rounding to get the digits 126, but has misplaced the decimal point]. 1.26 would be a better estimate to the question.

Learners should have no difficulty with part **b** as $8 \times 0.009 = 0.072$. Part **c** can be done using 0.07×0.04 [0.0028]. If learners used 0.4×3 in part **a**, check they haven't used 0.06×0.04 for this question.

Homework idea

As Section 4.2 will probably take more than one lesson, you can select questions from Workbook Exercise 4.2 at the end of each lesson. Only set questions that can be answered using skills and knowledge gained from that lesson. You can help learners to mark their homework at the start of the next lesson. This means you can address any problems before moving on.

Assessment ideas

Resource sheet 4.2 can be given as an extension to Section 4.2 or as an assessment. Although Resource sheet 4.2 can be done individually, it can also be used for pair work, encouraging collaboration and peer checking. Each individual or pair needs a copy of Resource sheet 4.2. All 15 questions involve multiplication of decimals. Encourage learners to read the questions, which are put into realistic contexts.

They should not just blindly multiply two numbers together! As learners read the questions, they will identify a variety of ways in which an examiner can ask them to multiply decimals. They should quickly realise that multiplication is a skill that they must develop.

Please note that none of the answers has been rounded. If learners have rounded to the same number of s.f. as the question, congratulate them for their thinking. Remind them that they should always show full answers before any rounding, and also that these questions did not ask for the answers to be given to an appropriate degree of accuracy.

Answers: 1 0.96 kg, **2** 2.4 kg, **3** 10.5 cm, **4** 0.1 kg, **5** 25.2 tonnes, **6** 10.5 inches, **7** 4.05 m, **8** 0.0924 kg, **9** 0.87 kg, **10** 0.1912 kg, **11** 0.0144 kg, **12** 1.65 kg, **13** 6.43 troy ounces, **14** 3.12 kg, **15** 0.4095 grams

4.3 Dividing by decimals

LEARNING PLAN

Framework codes	Learning objectives	Success criteria
8Nf.08	• Estimate and divide decimals by numbers with one decimal place.	• Learners can divide any number by a decimal number, with one decimal place, correctly placing the decimal point.

LANGUAGE SUPPORT

Equivalent calculation: calculations that use a different method but end up with the same answer

Reverse calculation: a method of checking your answer by working backwards through the calculation using inverse operations

Short division: a method of division where remainders are simply placed in front of the following digit

Common misconceptions

Misconception	How to identify	How to overcome
Confusing simplifying decimal division (e.g. multiplying both by 10) with simplifying decimal multiplication (e.g multiplying one number by 10, but dividing the other number by 10).	Question 3.	Discussion while answering Question 3.

Starter idea

Halves into one (5 minutes)

Resources: Notebooks

Description: Ask learners, 'How many halves go into one?' [2]

Write on the board '$1 \div 0.5 = 2$'. Say that another way of writing this is [write on board] '$\frac{1}{0.5} = 2$'.

Write on the board $\frac{1}{0.5} \times 1 = 2$. Ask if learners agree.

Next ask 'What is 10 divided by 10?' [1] Tell learners that if 10 divided by 10 is 1 then [write on board] $\frac{1}{0.5} \times \frac{10}{10} = 2$.

Say that if this were a normal fraction question, you would now just multiply the top two numbers and the bottom two numbers – so you will . . . [rub out the last '2' written and write on the board $\frac{1}{0.5} \times \frac{10}{10} = \frac{10}{5}$.

Now ask learners 'what is 10 divided by 5?' [2], so $1 \div 0.5 = \frac{1}{0.5} = \frac{1}{0.5} \times \frac{10}{10} = \frac{10}{5} = 2$. Ask learners to copy this to their notebooks.

Write on the board '$1 \div 0.2 = \frac{1}{0.2} =$' and ask learners to copy and complete the question. [5]

Main teaching idea

Dividing decimals online (5–10 minutes)

Learning intention: To speed up decimal division skills.

Resources: Electronic whiteboard; mini whiteboards or notebooks

Description: Type 'transum.org, decimal times' into a search engine. When directed to the page, learners will complete the level 5 material. This material changes every time it is clicked on, so no two sessions are the same. This is a free resource and learners can access this too. They may wish to practise at home so make sure they write down the web address of this resource. There are many other similar resources available.

The first six questions are of the type used in Section 4.3. Display the six questions on the board. Ask learners to answer the first three individually.

Once completed, ask for answers and discuss any differences in opinions. Put the three answers into the answer boxes on the site and click the 'Check' button.

Assuming all three are correct, ask learners to answer the last three. Repeat discussion, and check. If required, click 'Level 4' and re-click 'Level 5' and ask learners to answer the first six of these new questions. Discuss and check as before.

> **Differentiation ideas:** To extend, more confident learners could be allowed to answer the last six on the level 5 material. Make sure they understand that $\div 0.0x$ means they multiply by 100 rather than $\times 10$ for a $0.x$ number.

Plenary idea

Is it correct? (5–10 minutes)

Resources: Mini whiteboards or notebooks

Description: Write on the board:

1 $23.4 \div 0.3 = 78$
2 $123 \div 0.4 = 307.5$
3 $-228 \div 1.2 = -190$
4 $149.52 \div 0.6 = 249.2$

For each question, learners should write down how they would estimate the answer to check if it is probably correct.

Answers:
Possible answers:
1 $24 \div 0.3 = 240 \div 3 = 80$,
2 $120 \div 0.4 = 1200 \div 4 = 300$,
3 $-240 \div 1.2 = -2400 \div 12 = -200$ or $-200 \div 1 = -200$,
4 $150 \div 0.6 = 1500 \div 6 = 250$.

> **Assessment ideas:** Once learners have completed the questions, put them into pairs or small groups. Ask them to look at each other's estimations. If there are different answers, they should decide which is the best option. Tell learners that all four questions are correct. Discuss briefly as a class the best ways to estimate these questions. You could also discuss estimations that are useful but more complicated to do.

Guidance on selected *Thinking and working mathematically* questions

Conjecturing and Convincing

Learner's Book Exercise 4.3, Question 2

As with the majority of questions of this type, the best method is to work out the answer to each question carefully. Then learners need to decide which is the 'odd one out' (the one that is not like the others) and explain why.

Homework idea

As Section 4.3 will probably take more than one lesson, you can select questions from Workbook Exercise 4.3 at the end of each lesson. Only set questions that can be answered using skills and knowledge gained from that lesson. You can help learners to mark their homework at the start of the next lesson. This means you can address any problems before moving on.

Assessment ideas

Resource sheet 4.3B can be given as an extension to Section 4.3 or as an assessment. You can download this resource from Cambridge GO. Although Resource sheet 4.3B can be done individually, it can also be used for small group work, encouraging collaboration and peer checking. Each individual or group needs a copy of Resource sheet 4.3B. Tell learners they should answer each of the 10 problems in two different ways, one for a friend and the other for a scientist. The friend would prefer a rounded answer that is fairly easy to understand. The scientist would prefer a more accurate answer, which could still be rounded but not as much as for the friend.

The task is to answer the questions, but also to decide how accurate their answers need to be when giving them to the different people. They must think about what each person wants to be told. The answer they are to be given should be appropriate to the problem. First, learners should work out the actual answer themselves before the group work starts. Second, learners check each other's accurate answers. You may decide to allow learners to use a calculator at this point. Then they can move on to discuss how accurate they would want the answers to be themselves and how accurate a scientist might want them to be. The accurate answers are given here.

Answers: 1 $1.\dot{3}$ m, **2** $0.\dot{2}8571\dot{4}$ litres, **3** $333.\dot{3}$ m,
4 $1486.\dot{6}$ m, **5** $5785.71428\dot{5}$ m, **6** $0.08\dot{3}$ kg,
7 $54.71\dot{6}$ g, **8** $0.079\dot{2}\dot{7}$ kg, **9** $\$3.70\dot{6}$, **10** $1.1\dot{2}$ kg

---

4.4 Making decimal calculations easier

LEARNING PLAN		
Framework codes	**Learning objectives**	**Success criteria**
8Nf.04	• Use knowledge of the laws of arithmetic and order of operations (including brackets) to simplify calculations containing decimals.	• Learners can use order of operations rules (BIDMAS) and a variety of other skills to simplify calculations involving decimal numbers.

LANGUAGE SUPPORT
Factor: a whole number that divides exactly into another whole number

Common misconceptions

Misconception	How to identify	How to overcome
Not choosing the most effective method to simplify a calculation.	Most questions after Question 3.	Repeated class discussions about choice of simplification. Learners explaining what they were thinking when they started the simplification process.

Starter idea

6 times tables (5–10 minutes)

Resources: Notebooks

Description: Ask learners to make a grid showing the six times table up to 6×10.

1	2	3	4	5	6	7	8	9	10
6	12	18	24	30	36	42	48	54	60

Tell learners that you will say a question about the six times table. You expect them to write down the question and work out the answer. Tell learners it would be best to show working.

Ask 'What is one and a half times six?' [9] After 15 to 20 seconds, ask for the answer, and then ask how the learner worked out the answer. Discuss whether others used a different method.

Ask 'What is two and a half times six?' [15] After 15 to 20 seconds, ask for the answer, and then ask how the learner worked out the answer. Discuss whether others used a different method.

Ask 'What is five and a half times six?' [33] After 15 to 20 seconds, ask for the answer, and then ask how the learner worked out the answer. Discuss whether others used a different method.

Ask 'What is 25 times six?' [150] After 20 to 30 seconds, ask for the answer, and then ask how the learner worked out the answer. Discuss whether others used a different method.

Ask 'What is 26 times six?' [156] After 20 to 30 seconds, ask for the answer, and then ask how the learner worked out the answer. Discuss whether others used a different method. [Expect learners to say the answer is 6 more than the last answer.]

Ask 'What is 75 times six?' [450] After 20 to 30 seconds, ask for the answer, and then ask how the learner worked out the answer. Discuss whether others used a different method.

Ask 'What is 74 times six?' [444] After 20 to 30 seconds, ask for the answer, and then ask how the learner worked out the answer. Discuss whether others used a different method. [Expect learners to say the answer is 6 less than the last answer.]

Main teaching idea

Think like a mathematician, Question 5 (5 minutes)

Learning intention: For learners to invent their own method of simplification.

Resources: Notebooks; Learner's Book Exercise 4.4

Description: Let pairs or groups discuss part **a** and write down an answer. Discuss different answers with the class. The class should make a decision as to what is the best method, i.e. $52 \times (10 - 0.1)$ [$= 52 \times 10 - 52 \times 0.1 = 520 - 5.2 = 514.8$].

Once they have discussed part **a**, learners should be able to understand that, as $0.99 = 1 - 0.01$, the method should be $52 \times (1 - 0.01)$ [$= 52 \times 1 - 52 \times 0.01 = 52 - 0.52 = 51.48$].

Once both parts **a** and **b** have been discussed, learners can attempt part **c** either in their pairs/groups or individually.

> **Differentiation ideas:** For learners who struggle to start part **a**, remind them that for $\times 0.9$, as 0.9 is close to 1, they did $\times (1 - 0.1)$. So, as $\times 9.9$ is close to $\times 10$, ask what should they do? [$\times (10 - 0.1)$].

Plenary idea

Explaining (5 minutes)

Resources: Notebooks or mini whiteboards

Description: Write on the board '$(0.6 + 0.5) \times 0.3$'. Put learners into pairs: learner 1 and learner 2.

Without looking at the working of learner 2, learner 1 tells learner 2 how to answer the question $(0.6 + 0.5) \times 0.3$. Once completed, both learners look at the working and answer to check its accuracy [$= 1.1$ (order of operations says brackets first) $\times 0.3 = 0.33$].

Ask the 'learner 2' of the pair if their 'learner 1' told them about order of operations or just told them to answer the $0.6 + 0.5$ first. Ask who received a clear instruction on how to multiply 1.1 by 0.3. Ask to hear a few clear instructions. Ask, 'What makes it clear?' Ask, 'What type of instructions would not be clear?'

Write on the board '32×0.9'. Without looking at the working of learner 1, learner 2 tells learner 1 how to answer the question 32×0.9. Once completed, both learners look at the working and answer to check its accuracy. [$32 \times (1 - 0.1) = 32 - 3.2 = 28.8$]

Ask who received a clear instruction on why to multiply 32 by $(1 - 0.1)$. Ask to hear a few clear instructions on any aspect of the help. Ask, 'What makes it clear?' Ask, 'What type of instructions would not be clear?'

> **Assessment ideas:** Peer assessment and class discussion for both questions. To continue to develop explanation and instructing skills, ask questions such as 32×9.9, 34×0.35, 440×0.12, etc.

Guidance on selected *Thinking and working mathematically* questions

Conjecturing and Convincing

Learner's Book Exercise 4.4, Question 14

In this question, learners will look at the working in order to explain the answer. Most learners will substitute 0.4 then 0.3 into the calculation to work out the answer. Some learners will try to rearrange the calculation to make the missing number the subject. This is good practice for more confident learners. If learners use the substitution method, you should also encourage them to attempt the rearranging method.

Homework ideas

As Section 4.4 will probably take more than one lesson, you can select questions from Workbook Exercise 4.4 at the end of each lesson. Only set questions that can be answered using skills and knowledge gained from that lesson. You can help learners to mark their homework at the start of the next lesson. This means you can address any problems before moving on.

You could ask learners to make a mind map containing everything they think they need to remember for the end-of-unit test. The following lesson, it is important to share the mind maps in class [e.g. spread out over a few desks for everyone to look at]. Discuss the different mind maps as a class. When the class agree that a point is important, that key point could be copied onto the board (by you or a learner). Agree on as many key points as possible. Learners could then improve or update their individual mind map if necessary. Learners could store their mind map at home as a possible revision tool towards mid-term or end-of-year exams.

Assessment idea

Ask learners to write three questions that, when answered, would show three different methods of making decimal calculations easier. They should write the answers to the questions on a separate piece of paper. Ask them to exchange questions with a partner and answer the partner's three questions. Exchange back and check the answers. Learners can discuss any errors and whether they used three different methods of making decimal calculations easier.

PROJECT GUIDANCE: DIAMOND DECIMALS

Why do this problem?

In this problem, learners can practise adding, subtracting and dividing decimals in a context that invites them to conjecture and generalise.

Possible approach

Show learners the first Decimal Diamond.

Invite them to think for a moment about how the numbers in the squares were calculated. Make sure everyone appreciates that the value in each square is the average of the values in the two adjacent circles.

Next, introduce an example of a Decimal Diamond where w, x, y and z form a sequence with a constant gap g between the terms.

Invite learners to choose a few different values for w and g and work out the rest of the values in their decimal diamonds. Once they have done a few examples, they should be ready to notice that the values in the five squares also form a sequence, and that the gap between the terms is half the original gap g.

Then set the inverse problem: given a sequence for the squares, can they work out the values that go in the circles?

Key questions

What is the relationship between the values in the squares and the values in the adjacent circles?

How does the sequence in the squares relate to the sequence in the circles?

How can you use this to predict all the values if you only know the values of w and g?

Possible support

Learners could start by exploring examples where all of the numbers are whole numbers or multiples of 0.5.

Possible extension

Challenge learners to complete Decimal Diamonds when they are only given two of the entries. They may need to work algebraically to do this.

› 5 Angles and constructions

Unit plan

Topic	Approximate number of learning hours	Outline of learning content	Resources
5.1 Parallel lines	2	Recognise and describe the properties of angles on parallel and intersecting lines, using geometric vocabulary such as alternate, corresponding and vertically opposite.	Learner's Book Section 5.1 Workbook Section 5.1 ⤓ Additional teaching ideas Section 5.1
5.2 The exterior angle of a triangle	2	Derive and use the fact that the exterior angle of a triangle is equal to the sum of the two interior opposite angles.	Learner's Book Section 5.2 Workbook Section 5.2 ⤓ Additional teaching ideas Section 5.2
5.3 Constructions	3	Construct triangles, midpoint and perpendicular bisector of a line segment, and the bisector of an angle.	Learner's Book Section 5.3 Workbook Section 5.3 ⤓ Additional teaching ideas Section 5.3

Cross-unit resources
⤓ Language worksheet 5.1–5.3
⤓ End of Unit 5 test

BACKGROUND KNOWLEDGE

For this unit, learners will need this background knowledge:

- Know that the sum of the angles around a point is 360° (Stage 7).
- Use the fact that the sum of the angles of a triangle is 180° (Stage 6).
- Use the fact that the sum of the angles of a quadrilateral is 360° (Stage 7).

- Recognise the properties of angles on parallel lines and transversals (Stage 7).
- Draw parallel and perpendicular lines (Stage 7).

Learners will deepen and extend this knowledge, using the correct geometric language to make convincing arguments. They will also learn and practise further constructions.

TEACHING SKILLS FOCUS

Assessment for learning

An important part of assessment for learning is peer assessment and self-assessment. There are opportunities for both in this unit. Learners write explanations in several steps with a reason at each stage. It is inefficient for the learner to have to wait for the teacher to read the explanation and comment on it. It is better for a partner to read it, give feedback, and allow the learner to take more responsibility for his or her own learning.

The learner will also learn to make accurate drawings using protractor, ruler and compasses. In many cases learners are asked to make a further measurement on their drawing. If this is incorrect they know that they have made an error.

They can look at each stage of the drawing, identify any mistakes and correct them. They have the opportunity for self-assessment and taking responsibility for their own learning. This is at the heart of assessment for learning.

At the end of Unit 5, ask yourself:

- Do you know what the learners know/knew about this topic?
- Have learners developed better skills in their explanations through sharing ideas with their peers?
- Do learners realise that learning from their mistakes and those of their peers is an excellent and invaluable process that is encouraged within the classroom?

5.1 Parallel lines

LEARNING PLAN

Framework codes	Learning objectives	Success criteria
8Gg.11	• Recognise and describe the properties of angles on parallel and intersecting lines, using geometric vocabulary such as alternate, corresponding and vertically opposite.	• The learner can identify equal angles in a diagram with parallel lines and can give reasons using the correct mathematical terms.

LANGUAGE SUPPORT

Alternate angles: two equal angles between two parallel lines on opposite sides of the transversal

Corresponding angles: two equal angles formed by parallel lines and a transversal

Transversal: a line that crosses two or more parallel lines

Vertically opposite angles: two equal angles formed where two straight lines cross

Common misconceptions

Misconception	How to identify	How to overcome
Learners sometimes think that equal angles like those in the diagram below are alternate angles. 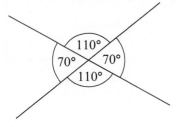	Ask learners to identify all pairs of alternate angles when you have two parallel lines and a transversal. There are only 2 pairs.	Imagine alternate angles as those inside a letter Z as shown in the Learner's Book. This will reinforce the fact than they are between the two parallel lines.

Starter idea

Review of prior knowledge (20 minutes)

Resources: Learner's Book 'Getting started' questions

Description: Give learners 10 minutes to complete the questions. These cover the bullet points in the Background knowledge section. As learners finish they can start to compare their answers with a partner. When they have all finished, go through each question, checking the answers, and ask what knowledge is being checked in each one. There is an opportunity here to identify any gaps in learners' knowledge.

Main teaching idea

Geometrical terms (10 minutes)

Learning intention: To use correct words to justify conclusions.

Resources: Diagrams drawn on the board

Description: First draw two intersecting straight lines.

Label one acute angle 70°, and ask learners for the sizes of the other angles, giving reasons for their answers.

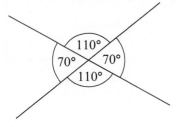

They should know that angles on a straight line add up to 180° and use this to find all four angles. Generalise the result showing that $a + b = 180°$ and there are two pairs of equal angles:

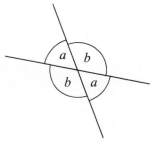

Explain that the equal angles are called *vertically opposite angles*. It is a general result that **vertically opposite angles are equal**.

Now draw two parallel lines and a transversal. Label one angle 65° and ask learners to fill in the rest.

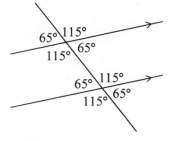

They should be able to identify all eight angles, which should be familiar from Stage 7. Ask learners to indicate the vertically opposite angles.

Explain that angles in the same position on each parallel line are *corresponding angles*. Add arcs to one pair of corresponding angles on your diagram. Ask learners to indicate any more pairs. They should be able to identify four pairs, and discover they are equal. This gives the general result that **corresponding angles are equal**.

Next mark a pair of alternate angles, and ask learners to find another pair.

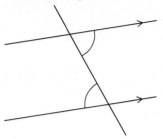

Emphasise that alternate angles are on different sides of the transversal (hence the term 'alternate'), and they are *between* the parallel lines. They should notice that they are also equal, giving the general result that **alternate angles are equal**.

Draw another pair of parallel lines and a transversal in a different orientation. Say that there are 4 pairs of corresponding angles and 2 pairs of alternate angles. Ask learners to identify them. Repeat the process, if necessary, until learners are confident with the three general rules.

Corresponding angles are sometimes called F angles and alternate angles are called Z angles. Ask learners why they think this is. Say this is a useful way to remember them but they should always use the correct words.

> **Differentiation ideas:** If learners find this difficult, ask them to draw their own diagrams to show the different types of angles.

Plenary idea

Parallel and non-parallel lines (10 minutes)

Resources: None

Description: Show this diagram:

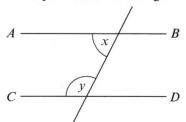

Say 'If *AB* and *CD* are parallel, what can you say about *x* and *y*?' Ask further questions to ensure that learners know that $x + y = 180°$ and also that they can give an explanation using correct geometric terms. This can be done in different ways. Now ask learners what they can say if $x + y$ is *not* equal to 180°. Let them discuss this in pairs before you take suggestions. They may simply say the lines are not parallel, which is true, but you are looking for an answer in two parts:

If $x + y < 180°$ the two lines will meet on the *left* to form a triangle.

If $x + y > 180°$ the two lines will meet on the *right* to form a triangle.

> **Assessment ideas:** By asking learners to give different explanations you can check their understanding of particular geometric terms.

Guidance on selected *Thinking and working mathematically* questions

Conjecturing and Convincing

Learner's Book Exercise 5.1, Question 9

Learners are asked to look at an incorrect explanation and correct it. Learners should see that all the statements about angles are correct. However the reasons given are not. Emphasise the point that the reasons as well as the statements themselves need to be correct for an argument to be correct. Their correct argument will not change the statements about the angles, only the reasons.

Homework ideas

Further questions of a similar type are in Exercise 5.1 in the Workbook. You could set a selection of questions or the whole exercise.

Assessment ideas

The aim of this section is to use geometrical terms correctly. Make sure that learners are doing this in written answers. In class discussion or in conversations with individuals use the correct terms yourself and insist that they do the same.

5.2 The exterior angle of a triangle

LEARNING PLAN

Framework codes	Learning objectives	Success criteria
8Gg.10	• Derive and use the fact that the exterior angle of a triangle is equal to the sum of the two interior opposite angles.	• Learners can give a clear explanation for any angle of any triangle.

LANGUAGE SUPPORT

Exterior angle of a triangle: the angle formed by extending one of the sides of a triangle

Common misconceptions

Misconception	How to identify	How to overcome
Learners may think that an exterior angle is formed when both the sides of a triangle are extended at one point like this:	Ask learners to draw a triangle and indicate an exterior angle.	Emphasise that an exterior angle of a triangle is *next to* an interior angle, *not* opposite it.

Starter idea

The angles of a triangle (5 minutes)

Resources: None

Description: Say that one angle of a triangle is 60°.

Ask 'Could it be an equilateral triangle?' Ask for an explanation of the answer. This uses the fact that every angle of an equilateral triangle is 60°.

Ask 'Could it be a right-angled triangle?' Ask for an explanation of the answer. In this case the angles must be 90°, 60° and 30°.

Ask 'Could it be an isosceles triangle?' Then ask for an explanation of the answer. If two angles are the same then the only possibility is that all three angles are 60°. It is a special sort of isosceles triangle. Often learners are reluctant to admit that an equilateral triangle is a special

sort of isosceles triangle, just as a square is a special sort of rectangle, so this is a useful point to discuss. This activity reinforces the fact that the sum of the angles of a triangle is 180°.

Main teaching idea

Exterior angles of a triangle (10 minutes)

Learning intention: See a proof that the exterior angle of a triangle is equal to the sum of the two interior opposite angles.

Resources: Diagrams following

Description: Ask learners to draw a triangle and extend one side. Their diagram could look like this but there will be variations.

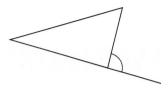

Say that the angle formed (marked in the diagram) is called an *exterior angle* of the triangle. The 3 angles inside the triangle are *interior* angles. Ask them to add a line parallel to the opposite side like this:

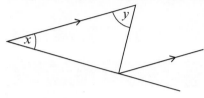

Ask how we can use angle properties of parallel lines to show that the exterior angle is equal to the sum of x and y. This diagram shows why.

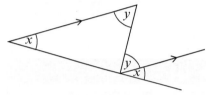

The angles labelled x are equal corresponding angles.

The angles labelled y are equal alternate angles.

Learners should label their own angles in a similar way.

This shows that the exterior angle of a triangle is equal to the sum of the two interior opposite angles ($= x + y$).

⟩ **Differentiation ideas:** If learners find the proof difficult, ask them to draw a different triangle and try to write a similar explanation. Ask more confident learners to show that the exterior angle on one of the other vertices is equal to the sum of its two interior opposite angles.

Plenary idea

The sum of the external angles (10 minutes)

Resources: Blackboard or whiteboard

Description: Show learners this diagram of a triangle.

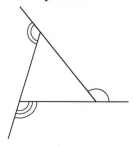

Three external angles are marked with arcs. Now add a parallel line.

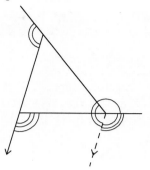

How does this show that the sum of the external angles is 360°?

Discussion should bring out these points:

- there are two pairs of corresponding angles
- the three angles at a point make a full turn so add up to 360°.

⟩ **Assessment ideas:** This is another opportunity to check that learners can recognise corresponding angles.

Guidance on selected *Thinking and working mathematically* questions

Conjecturing and Convincing

Learner's Book Exercise 5.2, Question 4

This question gives more opportunities to form ideas and make convincing arguments. This is one of the main themes of this unit. In Stage 7, learners learned to calculate angles. In Stage 8, there is an emphasis on giving reasons for each stage of an argument. It is important for learners to be familiar with correct geometric terminology and to use it correctly.

Homework ideas

Exercise 5.2 has further questions. It can be used for one or two homeworks or you could set selected questions.

Assessment ideas

Some of the questions involve setting out an argument and giving reasons for each step. Peer assessment is useful to give learners feedback quickly. The learner can check that the reasoning is clear and accurate.

5.3 Constructions

LEARNING PLAN

Framework codes	Learning objectives	Success criteria
8Gg.12	• Construct triangles, midpoint and perpendicular bisector of a line segment, and the bisector of an angle.	• Learners can accurately carry out the constructions listed. Measure another side or angle to assess accuracy.

LANGUAGE SUPPORT

Arc: part of a circle

Bisector: a line that divides a line segment or an angle into two equal parts

Hypotenuse: the side of a right-angled triangle opposite the right angle

Common misconceptions

Misconception	How to identify	How to overcome
Learners sometimes try to do constructions by measuring only with a ruler and without using a pair of compasses.	Look for construction lines on any diagram.	Emphasise the importance of leaving construction lines, such as arcs. Do not give credit if these are not shown.

Starter idea

Drawing triangles (10 minutes)

Resources: Learner's Book for Section 5.3

Description: Draw a sketch of this triangle on the board, and ask learners to draw it accurately.

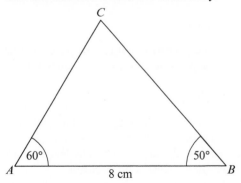

Learners have experience of drawing quadrilaterals and they should be able to draw this without being told what to do. If they need help, the Learner's Book shows the steps required in the introduction to Section 5.3. To check the accuracy, they should give their drawing to a partner. The partner should measure angles *A* and *B* and the length of *AB*. Now repeat the exercise with this triangle.

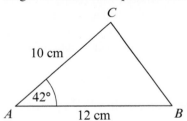

Once again, the learners should not need guidance but this is available in the introduction to the Learner's Book Section 5.3 if necessary. Point out that in the first case you knew two angles and the side between them. This is sometimes called ASA (angle/side/angle). In the second case you knew two sides and the angle between them. This is sometimes called SAS (side/angle/side).

In both cases you have three pieces of information that are enough to draw the triangle accurately.

Main teaching idea

Drawing a triangle when the sides are known (15 minutes)

Learning intention: How to use compasses to draw a triangle.

Resources: Compasses, ruler for each learner

Description: Tell the learners that they are going to draw a triangle with sides 4 cm, 4.5 cm and 5 cm. Go through the steps shown in the introduction to Section 5.3 with each learner drawing a triangle. When complete, give to a partner to measure the length and check accuracy. Now ask learners to draw the same triangle but to start with a different side. Use a partner to check as before.

> **Differentiation ideas:** Some learners may need more practice. If necessary give them another triangle to draw.

Plenary idea

Bisectors by folding (10 minutes)

Resources: Plain paper; scissors

Description: Ask learners to draw a large triangle on a piece of plain paper then to cut it out. By folding the paper, they can find the bisector of one of the angles of the triangle. In the same way ask them to find the bisector of each of the other two angles. Say, 'You now have three folds on your triangle. What do you notice about them?' Learners should find that they meet at a single point. If this is not the case, they should check the accuracy of their folding.

Now ask them to draw a second triangle and cut it out. This time they should fold it to find the perpendicular bisector of each side. Do the perpendicular bisectors all meet at one point? If the learners think they do, ask them to try it with a triangle with an obtuse angle. In

this case the intersection of the three bisectors is outside the triangle so the folds will not intersect.

> **Assessment ideas:** This activity will show if the learners understand the properties of a perpendicular bisector of a line segment and the bisector of an angle.

Guidance on selected *Thinking and working mathematically* questions

Conjecturing and Convincing

Learner's Book Exercise 5.3, Question 12

Both the conjectures are correct. By drawing their own triangles, and looking at triangles drawn by others, learners can see that the result seems to be correct. They can look at examples where it is apparently not the case and check by measuring that the construction has been done accurately. Of course this is not a proof but learners can gather enough evidence between them to show that the result is reasonable. A possible extension is to look at special cases such as equilateral triangles, isosceles triangles and right-angled triangles.

Homework ideas

Exercise 5.3 in the Workbook has further questions on this topic. It can be used for one homework or two, or you could set selected questions. You could also ask learners to make notes of the points that they need to remember from this unit.

Assessment ideas

Many of the questions allow for self-assessment. Where learners are asked to measure a length or an angle they can check the answer. If they are incorrect they can look back at their construction and check it. They can either correct the errors or do the question again.

> 6 Collecting data

Unit plan

Topic	Approximate number of learning hours	Outline of learning content	Resources
6.1 Data collection	2	Choose and justify appropriate methods to collect data and choose a sample.	Learner's Book Section 6.1 Workbook Section 6.1 ⬇ Additional teaching ideas Section 6.1
6.2 Sampling	2	Know different sampling methods and their advantages and disadvantages.	Learner's Book Section 6.2 Workbook Section 6.2 ⬇ Additional teaching ideas Section 6.2

Cross-unit resources
⬇ Language worksheet 6.1–6.2
⬇ End of Unit 6 test

BACKGROUND KNOWLEDGE

For this unit, learners will need this background knowledge:

- Plan and conduct an investigation (Stage 6).
- Consider the type of data to collect: categorical, discrete or continuous (Stage 7).
- Select a sampling method (Stage 7).
- Understand the effect of sample size on data collection and analysis (Stage 7).

TEACHING SKILLS FOCUS

Active learning

In this section there is an emphasis on being an active learner, especially focusing on critiquing and improving. Learners are asked to consider what data to collect and how to take an appropriate sample. They should evaluate for themselves different approaches, stating advantages and disadvantages and making informed choices. Learners can be encouraged to do this orally during class discussion and also in writing in response to questions in exercises. Try to avoid telling them which method is better but give them a chance to decide for themselves.

At the end of Unit 6, ask yourself:

- Did I give learners opportunities to make their own decisions or did I just tell them the answer?

6.1 Data collection

LEARNING PLAN

Framework codes	Learning objectives	Success criteria
8Ss.01	• Select, trial and justify data collection and sampling methods to investigate predictions for a set of related statistical questions, considering what data to collect (categorical, discrete and continuous data).	• Given a set of questions, learners can decide what data to collect and how to collect it, including the selection of a sample.

LANGUAGE SUPPORT

Categorical data: data that is descriptive, rather than numerical

Continuous data: data that can take any value within a given range

Discrete data: data that can only take exact values

Common misconceptions

Misconception	How to identify	How to overcome
Learners sometimes rush to collect the data before they have thought about exactly what data they need.	Ask learners how they decided what data to collect.	Ask learners always to justify their choice of data before they start to collect it.

Starter idea

Getting started (10 minutes)

Resources: Learner's Book 'Getting Started' questions

Description: Give learners a few minutes to answer the 'Getting Started' questions.

Go through the answers. Take as many possible answers as possible to Question 1 to make sure learners remember the different types of data. In Question 2 learners should be aware of different ways of choosing a sample. Question 4 should remind learners about questionnaires and interviews.

Main teaching idea

A worked example (15 minutes)

Learning intention: Learners start to justify their choice of data to collect.

Resources: Learner's Book Worked example 6.1

Description: Read out the task and make sure it is clear. Then go through each section of the question in turn, discussing in detail each part.

For part **a**, ask the class what factors can affect a learner's reply. They should think of gender and age but there may be other factors. It is important to collect all the data necessary to answer the questions.

For part **b**, the sample should reflect the answer to part **a**. The sample should include boys and girls. The sample should include older and younger learners. If there are unequal numbers of boys and girls this should be reflected in the sample chosen.

For part **c** discuss ways of collecting the data. This could be using a questionnaire or interviewing learners individually or by talking to a group of learners together. Ask learners if they can think of advantages or disadvantages. They have learnt about collecting data before so these are not new ideas to them.

> **Differentiation ideas:** In this unit, learners will be asked to justify their choices of data collection and sampling methods. You may want to pay particular attention to how they do this in writing by providing some model sentences.

Plenary idea

Sport in school (5 minutes)

Resources: None

Description: Tell learners you have been asked to find the opinions of learners about sport in your school. Give learners a couple of minutes to discuss in pairs each of these questions:

- What questions could you ask?
- What data do you need to collect?
- How could you choose a sample?
- How would you gather the data?

Set the questions one at a time with a couple of minutes for discussion in pairs after each one. The point to emphasise is that these are the things to think about whenever you have a set of statistical questions to investigate.

> **Assessment ideas:** As learners discuss this in pairs it will help to clarify their understanding. You could ask particular learners to feed back their ideas if you want to check.

Guidance on selected *Thinking and working mathematically* questions

Critiquing and Improving

Learner's Book Activity 6.1

This activity asks learners to trial a data collection method and then look for ways to improve it. The purpose is to make sure their chosen method works effectively and gives the data required in a way that makes it easy to process. The focus here is not on the project itself but on the method used to collect data and making that as efficient as possible. This process of refinement is an important skill that learners sometimes neglect because they want to get on with the task as quickly as possible.

Homework ideas

Exercise 6.1 in the Workbook has further questions of a similar type. You could set them all or a selection.

You may have used the Additional teaching idea 'A real example' on opinion polls (you can download this resource from Cambridge GO). If so, you may wish to ask learners to find a report of a similar survey as an extra homework.

Assessment ideas

Learners have collected data before. The new feature in this section is considering beforehand the data required to answer a series of questions. They have to decide on the data they need before they start any data collection. They should be able to justify their choice of data. When questioning learners you can ask what data they plan to collect. Then follow this up with further questions about why they have chosen that particular data.

6.2 Sampling

LEARNING PLAN

Framework codes	Learning objectives	Success criteria
8Ss.02	• Understand the advantages and disadvantages of different sampling methods.	• Learners can choose a sampling method and justify their choice.

LANGUAGE SUPPORT

Population: all the possible people from whom you choose a sample

Common misconceptions

Misconception	How to identify	How to overcome
Learners do not realise that a sample needs a justification.	Ask why a particular sample was chosen.	Ask learners to describe more than one sampling method and decide which is better.

Starter idea

Choosing a sample (10 minutes)

Resources: None

Description: Say that you want to choose a sample of five people from the class. Ask learners in pairs to discuss different ways of doing this. Then ask for a suggestion from each pair. There are no right answers but you are looking for as many different ways as possible of choosing five people. Make sure it includes putting all the names in a hat and taking out five names. Which methods would give a representative sample?

Main teaching idea

Ways of choosing a sample (10 minutes)

Learning intention: Learners consider the merits of different sampling methods.

Resources: None

Description: Say that there are advantages and disadvantages to different sampling methods. Say that we want a sample of 50 that is *representative*, i.e. one that is a *fair* representation of the whole population. Suppose you want a sample of all the people at a football match. What factors do you need to think about to make it representative? Make sure the suggestions include age and gender.

Now say that one way to take a sample is to choose names out of a hat. Could you do that in this case? No. What methods could you use? Ask learners to discuss this in pairs. Then ask for suggestions. For each suggestion ask for advantages and disadvantages. For example, asking 50 people as they enter the ground is easy and quick but might not be representative. It would be better to take batches at different times. You might decide to make sure you have a particular number of men and women or particular numbers of older and younger people.

The important point is that any method will have advantages and disadvantages and learners need to be able to describe these.

> **Differentiation ideas:** Learners may need more support and examples to be clear what we mean by a representative sample. For more confident learners you could ask if they want equal numbers of men and women. Discuss the idea of choosing numbers in the sample in proportion to the numbers in the crowd. So if a quarter of the crowd are men, choose a quarter of the sample to be men.

Plenary idea

Progress check (5 minutes)

Resources: Learner's Book Unit 6 'Check your progress'

Description: Ask learners to look at the questions, if they have not already done so. Ask them, in pairs, to look at each other's answers. Then ask for individual answers, looking at the data they will collect and how they will do it. There will be variations in what they ask the girls and boys to do. Do they just get one throw, or five throws, or some other number? There will also be variations in how the sample is chosen. Learners should be able to justify their choice. There is not one right answer here so the justifications are important.

> **Assessment ideas:** Self-assessment and peer assessment are involved in the paired activity at the start. By asking for justifications you can check that learners understand what is required for a justification.

Guidance on selected *Thinking and working mathematically* questions

Critiquing and Improving

Learner's Book Exercise 6.2, Question 3

The important point here is that learners consider the advantages and disadvantages of one method of choosing a sample. Then they use this knowledge to make a choice of their own. It is important that they justify their choice. They can identify both advantages and disadvantages for their method.

Homework ideas

Workbook Exercise 6.2 has more examples. You could set all of them or a selection.

Assessment ideas

Once again the emphasis is on giving reasons for choices. Learners should be able to describe different ways to choose a sample and be able to list advantages and disadvantages for each. They must show that they can make their own choices and give reasons for them. The reason will involve looking at alternatives and deciding which is best in any particular case. Look for this reasoning in any questioning you do.

⟩7 Fractions

Unit plan

Topic	Approximate number of learning hours	Outline of learning content	Resources
Introduction and Getting Started	10 minutes		Learner's Book
7.1 Fractions and recurring decimals	1–1.5	Recognise fractions that are equivalent to recurring decimals.	Learner's Book Section 7.1 Workbook Section 7.1 ⬇ Additional teaching ideas Section 7.1 ⬇ Resource sheet 7.1
7.2 Ordering fractions	1–1.5	Understand how to order and compare decimals and fractions.	Learner's Book Section 7.2 Workbook Section 7.2 ⬇ Additional teaching ideas Section 7.2 ⬇ Resource sheet 7.2
7.3 Subtracting mixed numbers	1	Subtract mixed numbers, writing the answer as a mixed number in its simplest form, and estimate the answer.	Learner's Book Section 7.3 Workbook Section 7.3 ⬇ Additional teaching ideas Section 7.3 ⬇ Exit ticket 7.3
7.4 Multiplying an integer by a mixed number	0.5–1	Multiply an integer by a mixed number and estimate the answer.	Learner's Book Section 7.4 Workbook Section 7.4 ⬇ Additional teaching ideas Section 7.4 ⬇ Resource sheet 7.4
7.5 Dividing an integer by a fraction	1	Multiply an integer by a proper fraction and estimate the answer.	Learner's Book Section 7.5 Workbook Section 7.5 ⬇ Additional teaching ideas Section 7.5
7.6 Making fraction calculations easier	1–1.5	Use the laws of arithmetic and order of operations to simplify calculations containing fractions.	Learner's Book Section 7.6 Workbook Section 7.6 ⬇ Additional teaching ideas Section 7.6
Cross-unit resources ⬇ Language worksheet 7.1–7.3 ⬇ Language worksheet 7.4–7.6 ⬇ Resource sheet 7.6 Key words ⬇ End of Unit 7 test			

BACKGROUND KNOWLEDGE

For this unit, learners will need this background knowledge:

- Recognise that fractions, terminating decimals and percentages have equivalent values (Stage 7).
- Understand the relative size of quantities to order and compare decimals and fractions using the symbols =, ≠, > and < (Stage 7).
- Estimate and add mixed numbers and write the answer as a mixed number in its simplest form (Stage 7).
- Estimate and multiply two proper fractions (Stage 7).
- Use knowledge of common factors, laws of arithmetic and order of operations to simplify calculations containing fractions (Stage 7).

Much of this unit extends work completed in Stage 7.

TEACHING SKILLS FOCUS

Language awareness

To help you to highlight and concentrate on language awareness, it is a good idea to be aware of the key words learners will meet during this unit. Make sure you are clear in your understanding of the key words before the lesson. Use the Glossary if necessary.

Give all learners a copy of Resource sheet 7.6 Key words. (You can download this resource from Cambridge GO.) Read out each word in turn. Afterwards, ask learners 'Do you know what any of these key words mean?' Discuss any ideas learners have. Emphasise that by the end of the unit learners will know the meaning of all of these key words. Refer to the worksheet as you work through the unit. Encourage learners to fill in the meaning of a word in the list when they meet each one in the unit, including an example too.

During each section, refer to the key words as often as possible and encourage learners to use the key words during any classroom discussions. When the opportunity arises, e.g. when one learner has used a key word, ask another learner what the key word means. If you do this throughout the unit, you could give learners another copy of Resource sheet 7.6 Key words as a class test at the end of Section 7.6.

When you reach the end of Section 7.6, ask yourself:

- Do the learners understand and feel confident in using the key words? If the answer is yes, then this work has been successful. If the answer is no, then think how you can change the way you approached discussing and using the key words.

7.1 Fractions and recurring decimals

LEARNING PLAN

Framework codes	Learning objectives	Success criteria
8Nf.01	• Recognise fractions that are equivalent to recurring decimals.	• Learners can identify fractions, using pencil and paper or calculator methods, that are equivalent to recurring decimals.

Equivalent decimal: a decimal number that has the same value as a fraction

Improper fraction: a fraction in which the numerator is larger than the denominator

Mixed number: a number which is the sum of a whole number and a proper fraction

Recurring decimal: in a recurring decimal, a digit or group of digits is repeated forever

Terminating decimal: a decimal number that does not go on forever

Unit fraction: a fraction that has a numerator of 1

Common misconceptions

Misconception	How to identify	How to overcome
Learners may not recognise when decimals are recurring if there are more than four or five digits in the recurring group, as in sevenths and thirteenths.	Questions 1f and 8.	Discussion during Questions 1f and 8 (especially part c where some calculators may not show enough decimal places for learners to realise that it is a recurring decimal).
Learners may think that a number displayed on a calculator, for example, as 6.666666667 is terminating because of the 7.	Question 5.	Discussion during Question 5a.

Starter idea

Getting started (10 minutes)

Learning intention: Check learners' prior understanding.

Resources: Notebooks; Learner's Book Unit 7 'Getting started' questions

Description: If required, remind learners:

- why $\frac{6}{5}$ is equivalent to $1\frac{1}{5}$

- to compare $\frac{2}{3}$ and $\frac{3}{5}$ you need to work out the lowest common multiple for the denominators. (Also see the Starter idea for Section 7.1 on Cambridge GO for an extended piece of work relating to finding LCM of denominators). LCM of 3 and 5 is 15,

$$\overset{\times 5}{\frown}\qquad\overset{\times 3}{\frown}$$
$$\text{so } \frac{2}{3} = \frac{10}{15} \text{ and } \frac{3}{5} = \frac{9}{15}$$
$$\underset{\times 5}{\smile}\qquad\underset{\times 3}{\smile}$$

- to add or subtract fractions, the denominators must be the same
- to multiply fractions, multiply the numerators and multiply the denominators, e.g. $\frac{2}{3}\times\frac{3}{5}=\frac{6}{15}$, but remember to try to cancel down. In this fraction

both parts of the fraction are divisible by 3,

$$\overset{\div 3}{\frown}$$
$$\text{so } \frac{6}{15} = \frac{2}{5}$$
$$\underset{\div 3}{\smile}$$

- to divide a fraction by a fraction, turn the second fraction upside-down (invert the fraction) and then

$$\overset{\div 2}{\frown}$$
$$\text{multiply, e.g. } \frac{2}{5} \div \frac{4}{7} = \frac{2}{5} \times \frac{7}{4} = \frac{14}{20} = \frac{7}{10}$$
$$\underset{\div 2}{\smile}$$

Main teaching idea

Think like a mathematician, Question 5 (2–5 minutes)

Learning intention: To understand that a calculator may show a rounded number as an answer.

Resources: Notebooks; Learner's Book Exercise 7.1, Question 5; calculators

Description: Different learners in your class probably own different types of scientific calculators.

The conversion from fraction to decimal and back again is most commonly the $\boxed{\text{S⇔D}}$ button. There are, however, two other common types. Some calculators, especially graphical calculators, have a 'MATHS' button which gives a drop-down menu. The first item in the list is usually the 'FRACTION' option. For other calculators, pressing the a$\frac{b}{c}$ button converts fractions to decimals and back again. Check that all learners are able to use their calculators correctly.

Answers:

a Learners' answers. For example: it has rounded the last 8 on the screen to a 9.

b $\frac{8}{9}$ 0.888888889 $\frac{1}{9}$ 0.111111111

   $\frac{11}{15}$ 0.733333333 $\frac{7}{18}$ 0.388888889

c Learners' answers. For example: changes the fraction to a decimal.
Learners' answers. For example: changes the decimal back to a fraction.

d i $\frac{7}{15} = 0.4\dot{6}$ ii $\frac{8}{11} = 0.\dot{7}\dot{2}$

> **Differentiation ideas:** To assist those who do not understand, ask learners to work out $\frac{8}{9}$ by division.

After 4 or 5 decimal places ask learners to stop and ask what will happen [0.888 . . .] Ask learners to round to 3 decimal places [0.889]. Point out that the calculator in the question has been programmed to round numbers when they are longer than the display. Some of their calculators will do the same.

Plenary idea

Ran# (10 minutes)

Resources: Mini whiteboards or notebooks; calculators

Description: You will need to generate random decimal numbers to 3 d.p. Use the Ran# button on a calculator or an online random decimal number generator, such as Random.org.

Generate a 3-digit random decimal number [0. _ _ _] and write it on the board.

Learners use fractions with denominators between 2 and 99 to match or get as close as possible to the random decimal. Learners must write each fraction and its decimal equivalent (to 3 d.p.)

Allow a set time. Depending on the random decimal number, allow 1 to 4 minutes for the first random number, then between 1 and 2 minutes for any

subsequent random numbers, before asking to see learners' results.

> **Assessment ideas:** Often there will be no fraction that gives the exact decimal. Learners should be encouraged to discuss their method of improving each attempt.

Guidance on selected *Thinking and working mathematically* questions

Conjecturing and Convincing

Learner's Book Exercise 7.1, Question 3

Ideally, learners will look back at their table from Question 2a. They can use the answers from the unit fractions to determine whether the five fractions in Question 3 are terminating or recurring. Learners will need to think differently about $\frac{11}{20}$. There are many options for learners to understand and explain that $\frac{11}{20}$ is a terminating decimal. Learners could easily find the equivalent percentage mentally, e.g. use the fact that all the factors of $\frac{1}{20}$ ($\frac{1}{2}, \frac{1}{4}, \frac{1}{5}$ and $\frac{1}{10}$) are terminating decimals; that $\frac{5.5}{10}$ would be a terminating decimal; or that $11 \div 2$ is not recurring, etc.

Discussing part **a** gives useful feedback to you (and the rest of the class) about the different mental strategies learners are using. This question encourages them to convert fractions to decimals in order to justify their decisions.

Homework ideas

As Section 7.1 will probably take more than one lesson, you can select questions from Workbook Exercise 7.1 at the end of each lesson. Only set questions that can be answered using skills and knowledge gained from that lesson. You can help learners to mark their homework at the start of the next lesson. This means you can address any problems before moving on.

Assessment ideas

Use Question 6 as a hinge point question to help you check whether learners are ready to move on.

It is essential at this point that learners can use a calculator and understand their calculator display. Once Question 6 has been completed, ask learners to round their answers to a suitable degree of accuracy, if they think they need to. Hold a brief class discussion about any differences between their first answer and their second (rounded) answer.

7.2 Ordering fractions

LEARNING PLAN

Framework codes	Learning objectives	Success criteria
8Nf.06	• Understand the relative size of quantities to order and compare decimals and fractions (positive and negative) using the symbols =, ≠, >, <, ⩽ and ⩾.	• Learners can work with positive and negative proper and improper fractions as well as mixed numbers to decide on the largest number, using decimals where necessary.

LANGUAGE SUPPORT

Advantages: the good points
Disadvantages: the bad points

Improve: make better/easier

Common misconceptions

Misconception	How to identify	How to overcome
Not changing improper fractions to mixed numbers before comparing, resulting in large numerators.	Questions 1 to 4.	Discussions about the reasoning for the methods used during Questions 1 and 2.

Starter idea

Unit fractions (5–10 minutes)

Resources: Resource sheet 7.2 (you can download this resource from Cambridge GO)

Description: A useful activity for practising finding common denominators and developing use of logic with adding unit fractions. Tell learners that, in Ancient Egypt, fractions were *only* written in the form of unit fractions. If necessary, remind learners a unit fraction is one in which the numerator is 1, for example, $\frac{1}{2}, \frac{1}{3}, \frac{1}{4}$.

Each learner, pair or small group will need a copy of Resource sheet 7.2, although to save printing a copy can be projected to the board. Ask: 'Which of the fractions on the sheet can be found by adding two unit fractions?' Learners may use the same unit fraction twice, but no more than twice for any fraction. Learners should find as many answers as possible in a given time, for example, 10 minutes. If learners struggle to start, discuss as a class how to make $\frac{2}{3}$ $[\frac{1}{3} + \frac{1}{3}]$ and $\frac{3}{4}$ $[\frac{1}{2} + \frac{1}{4}]$.

Fractions that cannot be expressed in terms of just two unit fractions are $\frac{4}{5}, \frac{3}{7}, \frac{5}{7}, \frac{6}{7}, \frac{7}{8}, \frac{7}{9}, \frac{8}{9}$ and $\frac{9}{10}$.

Answers: Some questions have several possible answers. The ones below are the most obvious.

$\frac{2}{3} = \frac{1}{3} + \frac{1}{3}$	$\frac{3}{8} = \frac{1}{4} + \frac{1}{8}$
$\frac{3}{4} = \frac{1}{2} + \frac{1}{4}$	$\frac{5}{8} = \frac{1}{2} + \frac{1}{8}$
$\frac{2}{5} = \frac{1}{5} + \frac{1}{5}$	$\frac{7}{8} = \frac{1}{2} + \frac{1}{4} + \frac{1}{8}$
$\frac{3}{5} = \frac{1}{2} + \frac{1}{10}$	$\frac{2}{9} = \frac{1}{9} + \frac{1}{9}$
$\frac{4}{5} = \frac{1}{2} + \frac{1}{5} + \frac{1}{10}$	$\frac{2}{5} = \frac{1}{5} + \frac{1}{5}$
$\frac{5}{6} = \frac{1}{2} + \frac{1}{3}$	$\frac{5}{9} = \frac{1}{2} + \frac{1}{18}$

$\dfrac{2}{7} = \dfrac{1}{7} + \dfrac{1}{7}$	$\dfrac{7}{9} = \dfrac{1}{2} + \dfrac{1}{4} + \dfrac{1}{36}$
$\dfrac{3}{7} = \dfrac{1}{7} + \dfrac{1}{7} + \dfrac{1}{7}$	$\dfrac{8}{9} = \dfrac{1}{2} + \dfrac{1}{3} + \dfrac{1}{18}$
$\dfrac{4}{7} = \dfrac{1}{2} + \dfrac{1}{14}$	$\dfrac{3}{10} = \dfrac{1}{5} + \dfrac{1}{10}$
$\dfrac{5}{7} = \dfrac{1}{2} + \dfrac{1}{7} + \dfrac{1}{14}$	$\dfrac{7}{10} = \dfrac{1}{2} + \dfrac{1}{5}$
$\dfrac{6}{7} = \dfrac{1}{2} + \dfrac{1}{3} + \dfrac{1}{42}$	$\dfrac{9}{10} = \dfrac{1}{2} + \dfrac{1}{3} + \dfrac{1}{15}$

If you have time, you could extend this activity for more confident learners by asking them to explain why fractions such as $\dfrac{4}{5}$ cannot be found using just two unit fractions. Let them investigate finding these fractions by adding three unit fractions. Your learners may also be interested to research the ancient Egyptians and their fraction system.

Main teaching idea

Think like a mathematician, Question 7 (3–5 minutes)

Learning intention: To investigate ways to determine the relative size of fractions with negative signs.

Resources: Notebooks; Learner's Book Exercise 7.2

Description: Question 7 asks learners to discuss and decide upon the best method to answer the question, not actually to do it. However, some learners may prefer to do the question first, then discuss the method afterwards. There is a wide range of possible methods learners might suggest, such as: ignoring the negative signs, then ordering, then putting in reverse order with the negative signs; converting the two improper fractions to mixed numbers then comparing fractions; converting to common denominator and comparing, etc.

Answers:

$-3\dfrac{1}{4}, -\dfrac{13}{6}, -\dfrac{17}{8}, -\dfrac{7}{13}$ and learners' answers.

> **Differentiation ideas:** If learners struggle to start answering the question, ask them to look at the numbers. Can they decide, without calculation, which is the largest number, i.e. the number closest to zero $[-\dfrac{7}{13}]$?

If a learner suggests $-3\dfrac{1}{4}$, they will need immediate advice and practice with ordering negative integers before continuing with this question. Suggest that it may help to make all of the fractions look the same, i.e. all mixed numbers or all improper fractions.

Plenary idea

Mini test (3–10 minutes)

Resources: Notebooks

Description: This mini test is for learners to do individually to ensure they have understood the basics of this section. Write or display on the board:

1 Write these pairs of fractions so they have the same denominator:

   a $\dfrac{7}{3}$ and $2\dfrac{7}{15}$ b $\dfrac{13}{4}$ and $4\dfrac{2}{5}$

2 Work out which is larger, $-2\dfrac{2}{3}$ or $-\dfrac{25}{9}$. Show your working.

3 Write $\dfrac{13}{6}$ as a decimal.

Answers:

1a $2\dfrac{5}{15}$ and $2\dfrac{7}{15}$ or $\dfrac{35}{15}$ and $\dfrac{37}{15}$,

1b $3\dfrac{5}{20}$ and $4\dfrac{8}{20}$ or $\dfrac{65}{20}$ and $\dfrac{88}{20}$

2 $-2\dfrac{2}{3}$ as $-\dfrac{24}{9} > -\dfrac{25}{9}$

3 $2.1\dot{6}$

> **Assessment ideas:** This test can be peer marked followed by a discussion on any incorrect answers and muddled methods, ready for the end-of-unit test. Alternatively, collect in learners' answers and mark them yourself for any individually targeted help that may be required.

Guidance on selected *Thinking and working mathematically* questions

Critiquing and Improving

Learner's Book Exercise 7.2, Question 3

In this question, learners will be considering the advantages and disadvantages of two different methods. Then they will think how to improve on the methods.

If any learners are confused by Steps 1 and 2 at the start, they will need your help before continuing.

Zara's method is a valid one. However, many learners are initially confused by this method. If the class has difficulty understanding the process, remind them that with 2, 7 and 10, 10 is the largest number. With -2, -7 and -10, -2 is the largest number. So $2 < 10$, but $-2 > -10$.

Sofia's method is easier for learners to visualise but is more time-consuming.

Homework ideas

As Section 7.2 will probably take more than one lesson, you can select questions from Workbook Exercise 7.2 at the end of each lesson. Only set questions that can be answered using skills and knowledge gained from that lesson. You can help learners to mark their homework at the start of the next lesson. This means you can address any problems before moving on.

Assessment ideas

Use Question 4a as a hinge point question to check learners' understanding before you move on. It is essential that learners can deal with negative fractions when comparing them.

The question of which is larger, $-\frac{7}{4}$ or $-1\frac{13}{16}$, means learners should be comparing $-1\frac{12}{16}$ and $-1\frac{13}{16}$.

Regardless of method, learners must be able to order the two fractions.

A possible method includes: drawing a number line, thinking which fraction is closer to zero, working out whether $1\frac{12}{16}$ or $1\frac{13}{16}$ is larger and reversing that decision to take into account the negative signs. If learners still struggle with this, compare some negative integers first. Then compare some negative decimals before moving back to negative fractions.

7.3 Subtracting mixed numbers

LEARNING PLAN

Framework codes	Learning objectives	Success criteria
8Nf.02	• Estimate and subtract mixed numbers, and write the answer as a mixed number in its simplest form.	• Learners can subtract one mixed number from another with different denominators using a variety of methods.

LANGUAGE SUPPORT

Improper fraction: a fraction in which the numerator is larger than the denominator

Mixed number: a number which is the sum of a whole number and a proper fraction

Common misconceptions

Misconception	How to identify	How to overcome
Learners might still just multiply the denominators to get a common multiple, but this can result in large numbers and significant cancelling.	Questions 2b and 2c. Check Question 4 answers.	Checking answers and discussing better methods.

Starter idea

Adding mixed numbers (5–10 minutes)

Resources: Notebooks

Description: This skill was developed in Stage 7 Unit 7. Practising this skill will help most learners to cope better with the subtraction of mixed numbers in this section.

Ask learners to answer the following addition questions. Each question is slightly harder than the one before. Working in pairs or even small groups will speed up the recall of the methods used in Stage 7. After each question is written down, learners attempt to work out the answer, all working to be shown. Give the answer for self-marking and briefly discuss the method/methods used before writing down the next question.

1 $2\frac{4}{9}+1\frac{4}{9}$ **2** $3\frac{7}{10}+4\frac{9}{10}$ **3** $2\frac{1}{2}+1\frac{1}{4}$

4 $1\frac{5}{12}+3\frac{3}{4}$ **5** $5\frac{3}{8}+7\frac{5}{6}$

Answers: **1** $3\frac{8}{9}$, **2** $8\frac{3}{5}$, **3** $3\frac{3}{4}$, **4** $5\frac{1}{6}$, **5** $13\frac{5}{24}$

Main teaching idea

Question 6 (2–10 minutes)

Learning intention: To think about an alternative method for subtracting mixed numbers.

Resources: Notebooks; Learner's Book; electronic whiteboard

Description: Allow learners to answer the question. Once completed, allow self-marking.

Tell learners of one particular method for answering this, and many similar, questions:

First, add a $\frac{1}{4}$ to $1\frac{3}{4}$ making 2. Then add the $\frac{3}{8}$.

Now write on the board: $\frac{1}{4}+\frac{3}{8}=\frac{2}{8}+\frac{3}{8}=\frac{5}{8}$.

Many learners have been taught this method of 'counting on' during integer and decimal subtraction in primary school. Some learners think this is especially helpful when trying to do a subtraction without full working (mentally or with minimal jottings).

If you have time, ask learners to look at the questions in Question 4 again. Prior to asking for the answers for Question 4, ask learners to explain to each other, using Marcus' method from Question 5, an estimate for each

of the answers. They already have the answers, so this will help them practise a method which they may find very useful.

Answer: $\frac{5}{8}$ m

> **Differentiation ideas:** Work through the first two questions in Question 4 with the class, allowing paired working for the last two questions.

Plenary idea

Exit ticket (2–5 minutes)

Resources: Exit ticket 7.3 (you can download this resource from Cambridge GO)

Description: Give each learner an exit ticket cut out from the sheet. Ask learners to write their name on the ticket. Learners should complete the exit ticket before handing it in to you at the end of the lesson.

> **Assessment ideas:** When you read through the learners' comments this will help you to determine the effectiveness of the lesson. If you have regularly used exit tickets, learners will be familiar with saying what would help them achieve at a higher level. These can be returned unmarked for self or peer marking and discussion or marked by you as a more formal record of individual success. $[4\frac{5}{12}, 3\frac{7}{12}]$

Guidance on selected *Thinking and working mathematically* questions

Conjecturing and Convincing

Learner's Book Exercise 7.3, Question 12

This is a type of question learners have seen quite regularly. They are asked to find a mistake in a written solution and explain it, then to work out the correct answer. Learners may, therefore, think it is easier to start by working out the answer carefully. Then they could explain the mistake by comparing their solution to the printed one. This is usually a good idea. Learners might see one mistake but possibly miss another one. In this case, however, the obvious mistake of $6-9=3$ is the only mistake.

Homework ideas

As Section 7.3 will probably take more than one lesson, you can select questions from Workbook Exercise 7.3 at the end of each lesson. Only set questions that can be answered using skills and knowledge gained from that lesson. You can help learners to mark their homework at the start of the next lesson. This means you can address any problems before moving on.

Assessment ideas

Encourage peer marking as there are several possible methods for many of the questions in Exercise 7.3.

Emphasise that, while marking, learners should concentrate on making sure that workings are clear and logical, not just that the answer is correct. Remind learners constantly that getting *one particular* question wrong is not very important, unless they get all those questions like it wrong. To check this, they must show clear, logical working. Then they can see if they are making the same mistake over and over again.

7.4 Multiplying an integer by a mixed number

LEARNING PLAN

Framework codes	Learning objectives	Success criteria
8Nf.03	• Estimate and multiply an integer by a mixed number.	• Learners can multiply an integer by a mixed number using a variety of methods and understand if their answer is approximately correct by estimation.

LANGUAGE SUPPORT

Mean: an average of a set of numbers, found by adding all the numbers and dividing the total by how many numbers there are in the set

Partitioning: a method of multiplying two numbers where the units, tens, hundreds, etc. in one of

the numbers are multiplied separately by the other number

Simplified: to have written an answer in its simplest form

Common misconceptions

Misconception	How to identify	How to overcome
Problems can occur when attempting to solve mentally, e.g. $2\frac{1}{2} \times 3$. Learners do $2 \times 3 = 6$ then just add the $\frac{1}{2}$ giving $6\frac{1}{2}$.	Check Question 2 answer.	Practice, showing written working.

Starter idea

Finding fractions of a quantity (10 minutes)

Resources: Resource sheet 7.4 (you can download this resource from Cambridge GO); scissors

Description: Arrange the class into groups of two to five learners. Give each group a set of cards cut from Resource sheet 7.4. Learners must put together the cards in their correct groups of three: fraction, amount and answer.

Answers: $\frac{1}{3} \times 18 = 6$, $\frac{1}{4} \times 20 = 5$, $\frac{2}{3} \times 12 = 8$, $\frac{3}{4} \times 28 = 21$,

$\frac{2}{5} \times 25 = 10$, $\frac{3}{8} \times 24 = 9$, $\frac{5}{7} \times 49 = 35$, $\frac{1}{9} \times 63 = 7$, $\frac{5}{12} \times 36 = 15$,

$\frac{2}{15} \times 30 = 4$.

If learners are having trouble knowing what to do, suggest they start with the '$\frac{1}{3}\times$' and '$\frac{2}{3}\times$' cards. Then they can make a pile of all the number cards that are divisible by 3. If necessary, tell them to work out $\frac{1}{3}$ and $\frac{2}{3}$ of each of these numbers and see if their answers are among the answer cards. If necessary, tell them to do the same with the '$\frac{1}{4}\times$' and '$\frac{3}{4}\times$' cards, and so on.

Main teaching idea

Fraction cards (10–15 minutes)

Learning intention: Practise skills learned in lesson.

Resources: Notebooks; mini whiteboards or a scrap of paper for workings; calculators

Description: To be used any time after completing Question 7.

This is a game for two to six learners. Each group will need a piece of paper large enough to be cut into 16 equally sized 'cards'. Learners write the integers 6, 7, 8, 9, 10, 11, 12 on seven of the cards, one integer per card. The other nine cards to be distributed to the group as evenly as possible. Learners take turns to write a fraction on a card followed by a '$\times$' sign, using only the digits 2 to 9, for example, $\frac{2}{5}\times, \frac{7}{9}\times, \frac{4}{8}\times, \ldots$

Put the fraction cards together, shuffle them and put them face down in a pile on the desk.

Put the integer cards together, shuffle them and put them face down in a pile on the desk.

Learners take turns to take two integer cards and one fraction card, putting them together to make a question,

for example, $\boxed{3}\quad\boxed{\frac{2}{5}\times}\quad\boxed{8}$

The whole group multiplies the mixed number formed by the first integer together with the fraction, by the second integer on the revealed cards. The first player to give the correct answer wins a point. Once answered and checked (using a calculator to speed up the game), the cards are returned to the bottom of their original pack. Play the game seven times. The player with the most points wins.

> **Differentiation ideas:** More confident learners should be put into groups of five or six learners of similar ability.

Plenary idea

Show your workings (5 minutes)

Resources: Notebooks

Description: Ask learners to write down two methods to work out [write on board] $3\frac{2}{3}\times5$

> **Assessment ideas:** The answer is $18\frac{1}{3}$. It is, however, the workings that are more important. Allow peer marking. Ask for a show of hands from learners who think the answer they have is correct. Ask one of those with a raised hand to write the workings on the board. Once written, ask for any way to improve the workings shown.

Next ask for someone with the correct answer, but different workings, to volunteer to write those workings on the board. Again, discuss the workings looking for ways to make them easier and clearer.

Guidance on selected *Thinking and working mathematically* questions

Conjecturing and Convincing

Learner's Book Exercise 7.4, Question 6

The area of the rectangle is $7\frac{1}{5}$ m^2. Learners then have to decide on the cost. There are three methods that learners will usually employ:

- $8\,\text{m}^2\times\$42=\$336$, then say that Martha has the wrong answer. This answer is only partially correct. The cost is correct, but learners should show that they understand Martha's error.

- $7\frac{1}{5}\,\text{m}^2\times\$42=\$302\frac{2}{5}$ [or $302.40] and, as above, say that Martha has the wrong answer. This time the answer is also incorrect as they have not read the information: 'She can only buy a whole number of square metres.'

- $7\,\text{m}^2\times\$42=\$294$, then say that Martha is correct. Here, the learner rounds down to 7 rather than up to 8. This is a surprisingly common mistake. Some learners automatically reason that $7\frac{1}{5}$ is closer to 7 than 8 but do not realise that, in this case, $\frac{1}{5}$ m^2 of the garden will not be paved.

Homework ideas

As Section 7.4 will probably take more than one lesson, you can select questions from Workbook Exercise 7.4 at the end of each lesson. Only set questions that can be answered using skills and knowledge gained from that lesson. You can help learners to mark their homework at the start of the next lesson. This means you can address any problems before moving on.

Assessment ideas

At various times during exercise 7.4, ask a small group (3, 4 or 5) of similar ability learners a short, easy to answer question that checks their knowledge. Set the question as a race. Learners can work out the answer mentally or with workings, but speed is the key. Ask questions without warning, and to only one small group of learners. Later in the lesson, ask another small group, etc.

Examples of questions are: Work out $2\frac{1}{2}\times12$, $2\frac{1}{3}\times12$, $2\frac{1}{4}\times12$, $2\frac{3}{4}\times12$, $2\frac{5}{6}\times12$, $2\frac{1}{5}\times12$, $2\frac{2}{5}\times12$, etc.

7.5 Dividing an integer by a fraction

LEARNING PLAN

Framework codes	Learning objectives	Success criteria
8Nf.03	• Estimate and divide an integer by a proper fraction.	• Learners can divide an integer by a proper fraction using a variety of methods.

LANGUAGE SUPPORT

Reciprocal: the multiplier of a number that gives 1 as the result. For example, the reciprocal of 2 is $\frac{1}{2}$ because $\frac{1}{2}\times2=1$

Upside down: when you turn a fraction upside down you swap over the numerator and the denominator. For example, $\frac{2}{3}$ turned upside down is $\frac{3}{2}$

Common misconceptions

Misconception	How to identify	How to overcome
Learners may forget to invert the second fraction before multiplying.	Questions 8c, d, e and 9.	Repetition of the correct methods throughout the section.

Starter idea

Dividing by fractions (3–5 minutes)

Resources: Notebooks

Description: Use this Starter idea before working through the introduction or worked examples for Section 7.5. Ask the following questions, each time asking learners to copy the answer from the board to their notebooks.

Ask 'How many halves make a whole?' [2]. After the answer is given, write on the board: '$1\div\frac{1}{2}=2$'

Ask 'How many halves can go into two?' [4]. After the answer is given, write on the board: '$2 \div \frac{1}{2} = 4$'.

Ask 'What is 3 divided by a half?' [6]. After the answer is given, write on the board: '$3 \div \frac{1}{2} = 6$'.

Ask 'How many thirds make a whole?' [3]. After the answer is given, write on the board '$1 \div \frac{1}{3} = 3$'.

Ask 'How many thirds can go into two?' [6]. After the answer is given, write on the board: '$2 \div \frac{1}{3} = 6$'.

Ask 'What is 3 divided by a third?' [9]. After the answer is given, write on the board '$3 \div \frac{1}{3} = 9$'.

Learners now have six fraction divisions written in their notebooks. Ask if anyone notices a link between the questions and the answers.

- If there are no suggestions, move on to the introduction and worked examples.
- If there are suggestions, guide them to discuss that the whole number multiplied by the denominator gives the answer in these questions.

Main teaching idea

Sharing pizza (5–10 minutes)

Learning intention: Divide an integer by a proper fraction, using knowledge of dividing an integer by a unit fraction.

Resources: Mini whiteboards; Notebooks; Learner's Book Exercise 7.5

Description: Set this activity either after Question 6 or Question 7. You could use this activity after the Starter activity 'Pizza! (you can download this resource from Cambridge GO).

Go through the main points from 'Pizza!' again: say, 'Angelo has 10 pizzas. He wants to give each member of his very large family *two* slices of pizza.' Ask 'How many people get two slices if he cuts the pizzas into thirds?' [15]

See learners' boards and discuss any correct answers, asking what methods they used. Write on the board '$10 \div \frac{2}{3} = 15$'. At this point, someone may say that if

they gave two of the three slices away, there would be a slice left over [$\frac{1}{3}$ of a pizza]. In this case, explain that slicing two pizzas would give two slices left over, enough for another person [two lots of $\frac{1}{3}$ of a pizza, making $\frac{2}{3}$ of a pizza].

If learners are struggling with the concept, ask how many people would get a slice if they had just $\frac{1}{3}$ of a pizza each, i.e. one slice. [30] Remind learners that as they are having double the number of slices each, Angelo can only give pizza to half as many people.

Ask 'How many people get two slices if he cuts the pizzas into fifths?' [25] See learners' boards and discuss any correct answers asking what methods were used.

Write on the board '$10 \div \frac{2}{5} = 25$'.

Ask 'How many people get two slices if he cuts the pizzas into ninths?' [45] See learners' boards and discuss any correct answers asking what methods were used.

Write on the board '$10 \div \frac{2}{9} = 45$'.

Say 'Angelo decides he wants to give five slices of pizza to each member of his very large family.'

Ask 'How many people get five slices if he cuts the pizzas into sixths?' [12] See learners' boards and discuss any correct answers, asking what methods were used.

> **Differentiation ideas:** Learners may prefer to draw one, some or all 10 'pizzas' and mark on thirds and/or fifths. Ninths have been used to force learners into thinking mathematically rather than drawing the fractions and counting. Those learners who have used drawing as a method for the thirds and fifths may need guidance when dealing with ninths. Ask other learners to explain to them.

Plenary idea

Winner stays up (5 minutes)

Resources: Whiteboard or blackboard

Description: Play this game at any stage of Exercise 7.5. The winner is the fastest at saying the answer to a division by a fraction question. Write on the board:

$$2 \div \frac{1}{3} \qquad\qquad 4 \div \frac{1}{4}$$

$$3 \div \frac{1}{5} \qquad\qquad 20 \div \frac{1}{2}$$

$$7 \div \frac{1}{6} \qquad\qquad 30 \div \frac{1}{3}$$

$$5 \div \frac{1}{10} \qquad\qquad 6 \div \frac{1}{6}$$

$$9 \div \frac{1}{3} \qquad\qquad 2 \div \frac{1}{8}$$

Answers: clockwise from $4 \div \frac{1}{4}$: 16, 40, 90, 36, 16, 27, 50, 42, 15, 6

Ask all learners to stand. Put learners into pairs. One pair plays at a time. Point to one pair of learners, then one of the division questions [e.g. $7 \div \frac{1}{6}$]. The first learner of the pair to say the answer [42] is the winner and remains standing. The other learner sits down. Then point to another pair and a different question. Repeat until each pair have had a turn.

Next put 'winners' into pairs (they do not need to move next to each other) and repeat. Then put the 'winners' from that round into pairs and repeat until you have one final winner.

> **Assessment ideas:** Playing the game several times will speed it up but be aware that some learners will start to remember the answers rather than work them out.

You could ask all learners at the end of the game to write down the 10 answers, exchange notebooks and peer mark.

Guidance on selected *Thinking and working mathematically* questions

Conjecturing and Convincing

Learner's Book Exercise 7.5, Question 11

By now, many learners will understand the process of division by a proper fraction and will work through this question rapidly. Other learners, however, may need further guidance. This question is very good for peer to peer support. Learners who are finding it difficult should be guided by those learners who understand. Paired, group or class discussions are very useful for allowing successful learners to spot patterns and explain reasons to other learners. Allow all learners to attempt part **a** of the question before asking them to explain their methods and reasoning to others. You can do the same with parts **b**, **c**, **d** and **e**.

Homework ideas

As Section 7.5 will probably take more than one lesson, you can select questions from Workbook Exercise 7.5 at the end of each lesson. Only set questions that can be answered using skills and knowledge gained from that lesson. You can help learners to mark their homework at the start of the next lesson. This means you can address any problems before moving on.

Assessment ideas

At various times during Exercise 7.5, ask individual learners short, easy to answer questions that check knowledge. Ask questions without warning, and only ask three or four learners each time. Later in the lesson, ask three or four others, etc. Suitable questions are:

$2 \div \frac{1}{3}$, $4 \div \frac{1}{4}$, $3 \div \frac{1}{5}$, $20 \div \frac{1}{2}$, $5 \div \frac{1}{10}$, $6 \div \frac{1}{6}$, etc. After learners have looked at Exercise 7.5, Question 8, give non-unit fractions as divisors. Make sure answers are integers, such as: $2 \div \frac{2}{3}$, $6 \div \frac{2}{3}$, $6 \div \frac{3}{4}$, $6 \div \frac{2}{5}$, $7 \div \frac{7}{10}$, $9 \div \frac{3}{4}$, etc.

7.6 Making fraction calculations easier

LEARNING PLAN

Framework codes	Learning objectives	Success criteria
8Nf.04	• Use knowledge of the laws of arithmetic and order of operations (including brackets) to simplify calculations containing fractions.	• Learners can identify a suitable method to simplify a calculation containing fractions.

LANGUAGE SUPPORT

BIDMAS: the order of operations of a calculation; Brackets, Indices, Division, Multiplication, Addition, Subtraction

Strategies: methods

Common misconceptions

Misconception	How to identify	How to overcome
When dividing by a fraction, learners may divide by the denominator and multiply by the numerator, especially when trying to work mentally.	Question 7, especially if attempted mentally.	Discussion when incorrect answers are given (e.g. Question 7 c $4\frac{1}{2}$, d $2\frac{2}{5}$). Repeated practice, especially with simpler fractions, is essential. Ask learners to tell you what they are doing/thinking as they work through a mental problem.

Starter idea

What is the denominator? (3–5 minutes)

Resources: Mini whiteboards or notebooks

Description: This starter idea helps to revise finding the lowest common denominator when adding or subtracting fractions. You are going to write some fraction questions on the board. Tell learners not to answer the fraction questions, but to write down just the denominator they would use to work out the addition or subtraction. Many classes will benefit if you take each question in turn, writing it, waiting for learners to answer it and discussing it.

$$\frac{2}{3}+\frac{1}{6}, \ \frac{2}{5}-\frac{9}{10}, \ \frac{1}{2}+\frac{7}{8}, \ \frac{11}{15}-\frac{1}{5}, \ \frac{1}{2}+\frac{2}{3}, \ \frac{2}{5}-\frac{1}{4}, \ \frac{5}{6}-\frac{3}{8}$$

Answers: 6, 10, 8, 15, 6, 20, 24

Main teaching idea

Learner's Book Exercise 7.6, Question 7 (5–10 minutes)

Learning intention: To think about an alternative mental method for dividing an integer by a fraction.

Resources: Notebooks; Learner's Book

Description: Ask learners to copy and complete parts **a** and **b**. Discuss answers and allow self-marking. Ask learners to answer the remaining four parts. Discuss answers and allow self-marking.

Tell learners that you will show a slightly different method to Question 7. Write on the board:

a $4\div\frac{2}{3}=4\div 2\times 3=\square$ **b** $8\div\frac{4}{5}=8\div 4\times 5=\square$

Ask learners to think why this method might be easier than the method shown in the question [dividing first means you have smaller numbers to multiply]. Ask them to use this method to work out the other answers to Question 7. Do they prefer this new method? Ask them when this method might not be so useful [when the division does not give an integer answer]. For any of the questions c to f, ask individual learners to explain each step of the workings to you (or possibly a partner) before they attempt it. The final answer is not required, but learners should be clear in their understanding of each step leading to the answer.

Answers: a 6, b 10, c 18, d 15, e 12, f 12

> **Differentiation ideas:** Work through the two questions on the screen and parts **c** and **d** in Question 7 with the class. Allow paired working for the last two parts of the question.

Plenary idea

Learner's Book Exercise 7.6, Question 12d (5–10 minutes)

Resources: Notebooks; Learner's Book

Description: Either ask learners to look back at Question 12d or write on the board: $\frac{11}{12} - \left(\frac{1}{2} + \frac{1}{3} \right)$

Tell learners they are going to write down the steps to help someone else to work out the question. This person *has not used brackets or fractions with different denominators* before. Their guidance must include clear instructions on what to do and the reasons for that.

> **Assessment ideas:** Exchange notebooks and ask each learner to follow *exactly* the instructions given. Once completed, discuss which were clear instructions and which instructions would allow them to work out a different question, such as $\frac{3}{20} + \left(\frac{1}{5} + \frac{1}{4} \right)$.

Encourage learners to think about how clear their instructions are. This is important because they follow their own instructions in tests and exams!

Guidance on selected *Thinking and working mathematically* questions

Conjecturing and Convincing

Learner's Book Exercise 7.6, Question 13

This question uses several of the methods taught in this unit. Learners will spot a pattern in a sequence of answers and find the term-to term rule, learned in Stage 7.

When learners have found the answers [$1\frac{1}{2}$, 3, $4\frac{1}{2}$ and 6], they must put the answers in order. Most of them will

start with the smallest and work out that the rule is '$+1\frac{1}{2}$'. At this point many will struggle, not realising that if the answers were put in order with the largest first, they will make a different sequence. This time the term-to-term rule is $-1\frac{1}{2}$.

Some learners may try to use two of the answers to make one sequence and the other two to make another sequence. Even with this error, they are still practising the skill of finding term-to-term rules.

Homework ideas

As Section 7.6 will probably take more than one lesson, you can select questions from Workbook Exercise 7.6 at the end of each lesson. Only set questions that can be answered using skills and knowledge gained from that lesson. You can help learners to mark their homework at the start of the next lesson. This means you can address any problems before moving on.

You could ask learners to make a poster containing everything they think they need to remember from the unit. The following lesson, it is important to share the posters in class, perhaps spread out over a few desks for everyone to look at. Discuss the different posters as a class. When the class agree that a point is important, that key point could be copied onto the board (by you or a learner). Agree on as many key points as possible. Learners could then improve their individual poster if necessary. Learners could store their poster at home as a possible revision tool towards mid-term or end-of-year exams.

Assessment ideas

Give one copy of Resource sheet 7.6 Key words to each learner (you can download this resource from Cambridge GO). Learners should write in an example or an explanation (a basic definition) for each key word they have seen in Unit 7. This should highlight any key words that need reinforcing. The understanding of these words is important for learners to succeed in exams.

Once completed, you could give them the answers. Alternatively, you could put learners into pairs or small groups to look at the key words box in each section and also the Glossary. Discuss with learners which of their explanations or examples show understanding and which need to be clearer.

If learners have been filling in a copy of Resource sheet 7.6 Keywords since the start of Unit 7, this assessment should be easier for them.

> 8 Shapes and symmetry

Unit plan

Topic	Approximate number of learning hours	Outline of learning content	Resources
Introduction and Getting Started	10–15 minutes		Learner's Book
8.1 Quadrilaterals and polygons	1–1.5	Identify and describe the hierarchy of quadrilaterals. Understand that the number of sides of a regular polygon is equal to the number of lines of symmetry and the order of rotation.	Learner's Book Section 8.1 Workbook Section 8.1 ⬇ Additional teaching ideas Section 8.1
8.2 The circumference of a circle	1–1.5	Know that π is $\dfrac{\text{circumference}}{\text{diameter}}$. Know and use $C = \pi d$.	Learner's Book Section 8.2 Workbook Section 8.2 ⬇ Additional teaching ideas Section 8.2 ⬇ Resource sheet 8.2
8.3 3D shapes	1–1.5	Understand and use Euler's formula: $F + V = E + 2$ Represent front, side and top view of 3D shapes to scale.	Learner's Book Section 8.3 Workbook Section 8.3 ⬇ Additional teaching ideas Section 8.3

Cross-unit resources
⬇ Language worksheet 8.1–8.3
⬇ Project Guidance Quadrilateral tiling resource sheet
⬇ End of Unit 8 test
⬇ Mid-point test

BACKGROUND KNOWLEDGE

For this unit, learners will need this background knowledge:

- Identify, describe and sketch regular polygons, including reference to sides, angles and symmetrical properties (Stage 7).
- Identify reflective symmetry and order of rotational symmetry of 2D shapes and patterns (Stage 7).
- Know the parts of a circle: centre, radius, diameter, circumference, chord, tangent (Stage 7).

- Identify and describe the combination of properties that determine a specific 3D shape (Stage 7).
- Visualise and represent front, side and top view of 3D shapes (Stage 7).

The focus of this unit is understanding many of the properties of 2D and 3D shapes. Learners will extend their knowledge of symmetry of 2D shapes and 2D representations of 3D shapes.

TEACHING SKILLS FOCUS

Active learning

Throughout the three sections of Unit 8, if learners do not understand or they continue to get the same type of question incorrect, ask another learner to help them. It is important that you also listen to the explanation given by another learner. You need to be able to confirm that the help is of good quality.

Active learning helps to establish good learning patterns and practice. When a learner can explain well, it shows that they really understand what they are doing and know how to improve. Also, learners often feel more confident speaking to other learners. By asking more targeted questions, they become more active learners themselves. As learners get more used to explaining concepts or asking for specific, targeted help from other

learners, these discussions can happen without you being present. Remind learners that the key to being successfully involved in this type of learning is that there is no judgement. The learner asking for help and the learner giving help are both learning and improving.

At the end of Unit 8, ask yourself:

- Did learners have useful discussions that solved issues one of them was having?
- Were learners actively learning from each other?
- In what other ways could you get learners to explain more to others, e.g. you teach a small group something and then get those learners to teach it to the whole class.

8.1 Quadrilaterals and polygons

LEARNING PLAN

Framework codes	Learning objectives	Success criteria
8Gg.01	• Identify and describe the hierarchy of quadrilaterals.	• Learners can use the hierarchy of quadrilaterals flow chart.
8Gg.09	• Understand that the number of sides of a regular polygon is equal to the number of lines of symmetry and the order of rotation.	• Learners can give the symmetry properties of any regular polygon.

LANGUAGE SUPPORT

Hierarchy: a system in which things are arranged in order of their importance

Lines of symmetry: a line of symmetry divides a shape into two parts, where each part is the mirror image of the other

Quadrilateral: a flat shape with four straight sides

Regular polygon: a 2D shape with three or more straight sides. All the sides are equal in length

Rotational symmetry: a shape has rotational symmetry if, in one full turn, it fits exactly onto its original position at least twice

Common misconceptions

Misconception	How to identify	How to overcome
Not remembering the meaning of the prefixes to polygon names.	Question 1.	Regularly say the name of a polygon putting emphasis on the prefix, and learners tell you how many sides it has.
Not remembering the names of different quadrilaterals.	Question 2 onwards.	Regularly say the name of a quadrilateral and learners describe it to you, giving some properties of that quadrilateral.

Starter idea

Getting started (10–15 minutes)

Resources: Notebooks; 'Getting started' questions in Learner's Book

Description: Learners should have little difficulty with most of the 'Getting started' material. However, before learners attempt these questions discuss what they remember about the names of various parts of a circle. Some learners may have forgotten what a vertex is (plural is vertices). A brief discussion on faces, edges and vertices of cubes and cuboids might be useful.

Learners might be confused that algebra is included in a unit on 'Shapes and symmetry'. Their algebra skills will be required when working out the circumference of circles. Algebra is also needed when studying the connection between the number of faces, edges and vertices of various 3D shapes.

Main teaching idea

What quadrilateral am I describing? (5–10 minutes)

Learning intention: To be able to recall quadrilateral facts.

Resources: Notebooks

Description: Tell learners you will read out one line of description at a time. You will allow them enough time to draw all possible quadrilaterals that the descriptions could relate to or to write down the answer in words.

	What quadrilateral am I describing?	Answers
1	This quadrilateral has two pairs of parallel sides	square, rectangle, parallelogram, rhombus
2	All angles in this quadrilateral are 90°	square, rectangle
3	All sides in this quadrilateral are equal in length	square, rhombus
4	This quadrilateral has order four rotational symmetry	square
5	This quadrilateral has no lines of symmetry	trapezium, parallelogram
6	This quadrilateral has order two rotational symmetry	rectangle, rhombus parallelogram
7	Opposite sides in this quadrilateral are equal in length	square, rectangle, parallelogram, rhombus

Continued

	What quadrilateral am I describing?	Answers
8	This quadrilateral has two pairs of sides of equal length	square, rectangle, parallelogram, rhombus, kite
9	This quadrilateral has one line of symmetry	kite, isosceles trapezium

> **Differentiation ideas:** Some learners may need to have the Learner's Book open so they can see the seven quadrilaterals together in the introduction.

Plenary idea

Lines of symmetry (3–5 minutes)

Resources: Mini whiteboards

Description: Ask learners to write the numbers 1 to 8 down the left-hand side of their whiteboard.

Tell them that you will say the name of a regular polygon, learners will write down how many lines of symmetry that shape has.

Say the names, giving about 10 seconds for learners to think and write down a number.

1 Octagon, 2 Decagon, 3 Square, 4 Hexagon, 5 Equilateral triangle, 6 Pentagon, 7 Heptagon, 8 Nonagon.

> **Assessment ideas:** Self-mark, or ask learners to exchange boards and peer mark.

Answers:

1	8,	2	10,	3	4,	4	6,	5	3,
6	5,	7	7,	8	9				

You should expect all learners to get 6 to 8 answers correct. If anyone gets fewer answers correct you can ask them to revise the names of polygons and their number of sides as extra homework. Then you can

re-test them later. If you prefer, instead of asking for the lines of symmetry, you could ask for the order of rotational symmetry.

Guidance on selected *Thinking and working mathematically* questions

Characterising and Classifying

Learner's Book Exercise 8.1, Question 10

Most learners will not have seen many flow charts. This one will help them to think about the properties of quadrilaterals so that they can classify them. Make sure learners understand that in each rhombus is a question with a 'yes' or 'no' answer. Learners must know the characteristics of each shape to use the flow chart effectively. Encourage learners to use their memory rather than looking back at information in the book. This will help them to realise whether or not their knowledge is sufficient.

Homework idea

As Section 8.1 will probably take more than one lesson, you can select questions from Workbook Exercise 8.1 at the end of each lesson. Only set questions that can be answered using skills and knowledge gained from that lesson. You can help learners to mark their homework at the start of the next lesson. This means you can address any problems before moving on.

Assessment idea

At various times during Exercise 8.1, ask individual learners to tell you how many sides a particular polygon has, e.g. you say 'How many sides has an octagon?' They should reply '8'. Alternatively, ask for the names of polygons with a certain number of sides, e.g. 'What is the name of the polygon with 10 sides' and they should reply 'decagon'.

8.2 The circumference of a circle

LEARNING PLAN

Framework codes	Learning objectives	Success criteria
8Gg.02	• Understand π as the ratio between a circumference and a diameter. • Know and use the formula for the circumference of a circle.	• Learners understand why the value of π is approximately 3.14. • Learners can work out the circumference of a circle given either the radius or diameter.

LANGUAGE SUPPORT

Accurate: exact

Approximate value: a number rounded to a suitable degree of accuracy

Circumference: the perimeter of a circle

Diameter: a straight line between two points on the circumference of a circle (or surface of a sphere) that passes through the centre of the circle (or sphere)

Pi (π): the ratio of the circumference of a circle to the diameter of the circle

Radius: a straight line from the circumference of a circle (or surface of a sphere) to the centre of a circle (or sphere)

Semicircle: half a circle

Common misconceptions

Misconception	How to identify	How to overcome
Some learners are confused about what π is and how they use it. Stress that it is a constant number relating the circumference to the diameter of a circle.	All questions.	Repeatedly ask learners what π is [the number that you get when you divide the circumference of a circle by its diameter]. Common values of π used are 3.14, 3.142 or $\frac{22}{7}$, or the button on the calculator, depending on the degree of accuracy needed.

Starter idea

Pi (10–15 minutes)

Resources: Rulers; string; felt pens; notebooks; calculators (and perhaps Resource sheet 8.2; you can download this resource from Cambridge GO)

Description: The aim is for learners to calculate the value of pi for themselves and use it to derive the formula for circumference. Make sure that there is a variety of cylindrical objects available, such as straight-sided cans and bottles. It is easier for learners to do this activity in pairs. One learner can hold the object and the other one can measure it.

Ask learners to find the diameter of a cylindrical object. Some learners may find it easier to place two books

or two rulers, one either side of the object. If they line them up so they are parallel, they can measure the perpendicular distance between them. Next, ask them to use a piece of string to measure the circumference of the same object. Some learners may find it helpful to wrap the string around the object they are measuring and mark, with felt pen, where the string overlaps. Then they can measure the distance between the marks on the string.

Now they divide the measurement of the circumference by the diameter of the circle. Learners repeat this, with circles of various sizes. Encourage them to record their results in a table. Learners should realise that the value (circumference divided by the diameter) is always about the same. Once learners have established that the answer is always 'a bit more than 3', explain that although mathematicians have calculated this value, called pi, very accurately, in this unit they will use a rounded value of 3.14 or 3.142 (to 2 or 3 decimal places).

Show learners the symbol for pi, π, and explain that this stands for the value of the circumference divided by the diameter for all circles. Write on the board $\frac{C}{d} = \pi$. Then you can either ask learners to make C the subject of the formula or show them that they can rearrange this to get $C = \pi d$.

You could use Resource sheet 8.2 to support this activity or for homework. Learners will use coins and roll them along a straight line.

Main teaching idea

Question 10 (5 minutes)

Learning intention: To practise two common assessment questions.

Resources: Notebooks; Learner's book

Description: Draw a sketch of the semicircle from Question 10 on the board. Add some extra information:

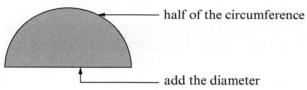

half of the circumference

add the diameter

This will help to remind learners of the parts they need to work out to give the perimeter of the semicircle and, hopefully, the quadrant.

It is a common error, when working out the perimeter of semicircles or quadrants, to include the curved distance but not the straight lines.

Answers:

$$\text{Semicircle: } P = \frac{\pi \times 15}{2} + 15 = 38.56\,\text{m}$$

$$\text{Quarter-circle: } P = \frac{\pi \times 10}{2} + 2 \times 10 = 35.71\,\text{m}$$

Zara is correct as 38.56 m > 35.71 m

> **Differentiation ideas:** If it is needed, make a sketch of the quadrant from Question 10 on the board:

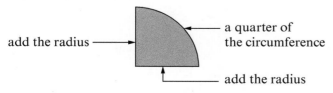

add the radius

a quarter of the circumference

add the radius

Plenary idea

Diameter and radius (5 minutes)

Resources: Mini whiteboards; calculators

Description: Ask learners to work out the circumference of two circles, using π as 3.14. One circle has a diameter of 10 cm and the other has a radius of 10 cm.

Answers:
31.4 and 62.8 cm, so when the diameter is doubled [10 cm and 20 cm] the circumference is doubled too.

> **Assessment ideas:** After checking learners' answers, discuss the different methods learners used to work out the answer. Ask learners to imagine they had to work out the difference in the circumference of two different circles. This time one circle has a radius of 6 cm and the other one a diameter of 6 cm. What method would they use?

Guidance on selected *Thinking and working mathematically* questions

Critiquing and Improving

Learner's Book Exercise 8.2, Question 6

In this question, learners will be comparing two written methods then deciding which they prefer and why. If you think that your learners might struggle with this question, put them into small groups. This should promote discussion about how each method works. Part **b** is often best set as a class discussion. After discussing the different methods, learners will be more able to decide on the one most suited to them.

Point out to learners that, when they rearrange a formula containing π, they should write π and not 3.14.

Homework idea

As Section 8.2 will probably take more than one lesson, you can select questions from Workbook Exercise 8.2 at the end of each lesson. You can help learners to mark their homework at the start of the next lesson. This means you can address any problems before moving on.

Assessment idea

Repeatedly ask learners what pi is. Expect learners to reply that it is a number, approximately 3.14, that you get when you divide the circumference by the diameter.

Repeatedly ask learners what the formula for the circumference of a circle is. Expect learners to reply that it is $C = \pi d$ or $C = \pi \times$ diameter. Insist they start the formula properly, i.e. $C =$ or circumference $=$.

8.3 3D shapes

LEARNING PLAN

Framework codes	Learning objectives	Success criteria
8Gg.05	• Understand and use Euler's formula to connect number of vertices, faces and edges of 3D shapes.	• Learners identify a formula that connects the number of faces (F), vertices (V) and edges (E) of 3D shapes with flat faces.
8Gg.07	• Represent front, side and top view of 3D shapes to scale.	• Learners can identify and draw front, side and top view of 3D shapes to scale.

LANGUAGE SUPPORT

Front view, front elevation: a 2D drawing of a solid shape seen from the front

Side view, side elevation: a 2D drawing of a solid shape seen from the side

Top view, plan view: a 2D drawing of a solid shape seen from above

Common misconceptions

Misconception	How to identify	How to overcome
Trying to give a 3D view when asked for front, side or top view.	Question 2 onwards.	Checking diagrams drawn for Question 2.
Ignoring measurements, assuming each short length of a diagram is 1 cm.	Question 4.	Checking that diagrams do not assume the shape is made from four $1\,cm^3$ blocks.

Starter idea

Front, side and top view of 3D shapes (3–5 minutes)

Resources: Mini whiteboards

Description: To be used before starting Section 8.3.

Draw or display a cuboid on the board:

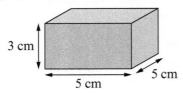

Ask learners to sketch the front, side and top view of the cuboid. Ask learners to peer mark:

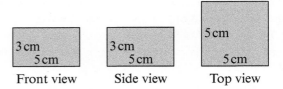

Front view   Side view   Top view

Point out that the front and side views are the same height in the cuboid, so they should also be in their sketch. Make it clear also that the diagrams are 2D (they look flat), and they must **not** attempt to make any of the diagrams look 3D.

Next, draw/display a cylinder on the board:

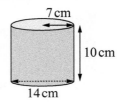

Ask learners to sketch the front, side and top view of the cylinder. Ask learners to peer mark:

Front/side view   Top view

10 cm
14 cm

14 cm

Point out that the front and side views are the same, which is why they have been grouped like this. Also the width of the rectangle and the diameter of the circle are the same, so should look the same in their sketch.

Main teaching idea

Think like a mathematician, Question 1 (10–15 minutes)

Learning intention: To introduce Euler and his formula.

Resources: Notebooks; Learner's Book Exercise 8.3

Description: Ask learners to copy and complete the table in part **a**. Either give them the answers or allow pairs or groups to look at each other's tables to compare their answers. Explain to learners that 300 years ago Euler, a Swiss mathematician, worked out the connection between faces, edges and vertices in certain 3D shapes.

Part **b** of the question asks the learner to look at this connection. Once learners realise that the number of faces + the number of vertices is two more than the number of edges, parts **c** and **d** should be straight forward.

In part **e**, learners may require some guidance. For example, you could suggest 3D shapes with curved edges, such as sphere, hemisphere, cylinder, hemi-cylinder, ovoid prism, cone. You could also suggest that learners try to use the formula for E, F and V for some of the 3D shapes with curved edges.

Answers:

a

3D Shape	Number of faces	Number of vertices	Number of edges
Cube	6	8	12
Cuboid	6	8	12
Tetrahedron	4	4	6
Square-based pyramid	5	5	8
Triangular prism	5	6	9
Trapezoidal prism	6	8	12

b number of faces + number of vertices is two more than the number of edges **or** any rearrangement of this, e.g. number of faces + number of vertices − number of edges = 2

c $E = F + V - 2$ **or** any rearrangement of this, e.g. $F + V = E + 2$

d Learners' discussions

e The formula only works for shapes with flat faces. Learners' explanations. Example: a cylinder has 1 curved surface, 2 flat faces, 0 vertices and 2 edges. If you use the formula $F + V = E + 2$ then $F + V = 3 + 0 = 3$ and $E + 2 = 2 + 2 = 4$, and $3 \neq 4$

⟩ **Differentiation ideas:** If learners cannot find a connection, suggest that they add the number of faces to the number of vertices and look again.

Plenary idea

Front, side and top view (10 minutes)

Resources: Centimetre-squared paper

Description: Have ready multiples of two or three different shapes made from interlocking cubes, e.g.

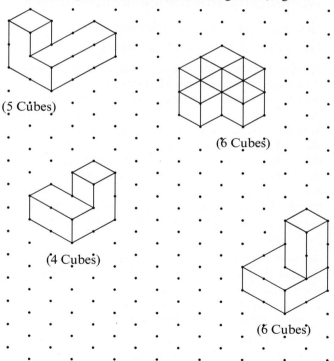

(5 Cubes)

(6 Cubes)

(4 Cubes)

(6 Cubes)

Put learners into pairs or groups and give each learner a piece of centimetre-squared paper. Give a shape to each pair or group and ask learners to sketch the front, side and top view of the shape to a scale of 2 : 1 (without a ruler). Assuming each interlocking cube has a side length of 2 cm, each block will be a single square. Ask pairs or groups with the same shape to compare diagrams and self-mark, asking you for guidance only if necessary.

Exchange shapes between pairs or groups so that each learner is looking at a different shape. Ask learners to sketch the front, side and top view of the shape to a scale of 2 : 1 (without a ruler). Assuming again that each interlocking cube has a side length of 2 cm, each block will be a single square. Again, ask pairs or groups with the same shape to compare diagrams and self-mark, asking you for guidance only if necessary.

> **Assessment ideas:** No formal assessment is needed here, but listen to the larger groups when they are comparing diagrams. If there is lots of discussion it probably means that there is some disagreement, which could mean there is some form of misunderstanding. Asking about that discussion might be useful for informal assessment of certain learners.

Guidance on selected *Thinking and working mathematically* questions

Conjecturing and Convincing

Learner's Book Exercise 8.3, Question 8

In this question, learners will consider 3D shapes and their different views. They will think about what is possible and how to explain it. Interlocking cubes can be very useful for learners who find it difficult to visualise 3D shapes from a drawing (see Plenary idea 'Front, side and top view'). Give learners loose interlocking cubes for them to make the shape in this question. Alternatively, you could produce the shapes ready to give to learners. Most interlocking cubes have a side length of 2 cm. Learners will have to imagine that one cube has a side length of 1 cm rather than its actual 2 cm. This is rarely a problem.

Suggest to learners that they put the shape flat on the desk, as shown in the question, rather than hold it in their hand. Rotating the shape and standing over it to look directly downwards will help all learners decide which shape represents which view.

In part **b** learners should realise that having the same plan view is easy. They can just increase or decrease

the height of the 'tower' part of the shape. Are they able to see that they can also add other 'towers' on the same base?

In part **c**, they should realise that, if all three views are the same as for the shape shown, it can only be that shape. Adding *any* blocks would change *at least one* of the views. There may be learners who think there are other shapes possible. This can lead to useful discussions where learners disagree and try to convince others of their argument. If the disagreement is not resolved using words, give out blocks to be made into the 'impossible' shape.

Homework idea

As Section 8.3 will probably take more than one lesson, you can select questions from Workbook Exercise 8.3 at the end of each lesson. You can help learners to mark their homework at the start of the next lesson. This means you can address any problems before moving on.

You could ask learners to make a list of worked examples containing everything they think they need to remember for the end-of-unit test. The following lesson, it is important to share the lists in class perhaps spread out over a few desks for everyone to look at. Discuss the different worked examples as a class. Learners should not just have copied out the worked examples from the Learner's Book, but used questions they think will help them with revision at a later date. When the class agree that a point is important, that key point could be copied onto the board. Agree on as many key points as possible. Learners could then improve their individual worked example list if necessary. Learners could store their worked examples list at home as a possible revision tool towards mid-term or end-of-year exams.

Assessment idea

Use Learner's Book Exercise 8.3, Question 5 as a class 'test'. It is not necessary to tell learners that this is a test. Just tell them that you wish to mark the question. Give learners centimetre-squared paper for their drawing. If learners can draw the house, they obviously understand how to 'represent front, side and top view of 3D shapes to scale'. Their drawing will show evidence of their success at this learning objective.

PROJECT GUIDANCE: QUADRILATERAL TILING

Why do this problem?

This problem provides an engaging context in which learners can apply their knowledge of the angle properties of quadrilaterals in order to produce convincing arguments and generalisations.

Possible approach

Learners may need squared paper or dotty paper.

Start by sharing an image of tessellating rectangles and invite learners to comment on what they notice. Draw attention to the fact that the angles around each point are all right angles and so we know that they add up to 360°.

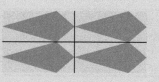

Next, invite learners to draw a kite and to surround their kite with a rectangle. Then ask them to draw a few copies of their rectangles in a tessellation pattern. Rotated kites should emerge.

Take some time to discuss the transformation needed to get from one kite to another, and how they know that the darker and lighter kites are the same.

Then invite learners to explore parallelograms, and after that, trapezia. Can they justify that all parallelograms and all trapezia will tessellate?

Finally, invite learners to explore tessellations of irregular quadrilaterals on dotty grids. An image such as this one could be used to prompt a discussion about how to replicate the quadrilateral, and to draw attention to the angles that meet around each point.

Key questions

What do the angles in a quadrilateral add up to?

What do you know about angles in a parallelogram?

What happens if I rotate a quadrilateral 180° around the midpoint of one of its sides?

Possible support

Learners could use dotty paper throughout, rather than just for the final part.

Possible extension

Challenge learners to prove that all quadrilaterals, including concave ones, will tessellate.

❯ 9 Sequences and functions

Unit plan

Topic	Approximate number of learning hours	Outline of learning content	Resources
Introduction and Getting Started	10–15 minutes		Learner's Book
9.1 Generating sequences	1–1.5	Extend knowledge of term-to-term rules and generate more complex numerical sequences.	Learner's Book Section 9.1 Workbook Section 9.1 ⬇ Additional teaching ideas Section 9.1
9.2 Finding rules for sequences	0.5–1	Use knowledge of term-to-term rules and generate sequences from spatial patterns.	Learner's Book Section 9.2 Workbook Section 9.2 ⬇ Additional teaching ideas Section 9.2
9.3 Using the nth term	1–1.5	Extend knowledge of nth term rules.	Learner's Book Section 9.3 Workbook Section 9.3 ⬇ Additional teaching ideas Section 9.3
9.4 Representing simple functions	0.5–1	Extend knowledge of function machines.	Learner's Book Section 9.4 Workbook Section 9.4 ⬇ Additional teaching ideas Section 9.4 ⬇ Resource sheet 9.4 ⬇ Exit ticket 9.4

Cross-unit resources
⬇ Language worksheet 9.1–9.4
⬇ End of Unit 9 test

BACKGROUND KNOWLEDGE

For this unit, learners will need this background knowledge:

- Understand term-to-term rules using integers (Stage 7).
- Generate sequences from numerical and special patterns (Stage 7).

- Understand and describe simple nth term rules (Stage 7).
- Understand that a function is a relationship where each input has a single output, generate outputs from a given function and identify inputs from a given output by considering inverse operations (Stage 7).

CONTINUED

The focus of this unit is to understand and use more complex sequences than those covered in Stage 7. With these more complex sequences, learners' knowledge of term-to-term rules will be extended. Learners will also describe the general (nth) term.

Learners' knowledge of function machines is extended to include operations that lead to fractional answers.

TEACHING SKILLS FOCUS

Metacognition

A complex area of learning that can be simplified to 'thinking about thinking'. Throughout this unit ask learners, whenever possible, to say out loud what they are thinking. Usually ask at the start or a short way through answering a problem. If a question has already been answered, ask what they were thinking while they were attempting a problem and if they would now do the problem a different way. If done regularly, this questioning leads to a process that can be used throughout their schooling: 'think about a problem, plan what to do, do the plan, look back and decide if you could have done anything better'.

This process teaches learners to understand how to solve problems effectively, not just get the answer to a particular question.

At the end of Unit 9, ask yourself:

- Are learners getting better at explaining their reasoning?
- Are learners more confident explaining when in pairs or small groups rather than as a whole class?

Remember that the more your learners practise this powerful learning tool, the more effective learners they will become.

9.1 Generating sequences

LEARNING PLAN

Framework codes	Learning objectives	Success criteria
8As.01	• Understand term-to-term rules and generate numerical sequences (including fractions).	• Learners can generate increasing and decreasing sequences involving integers, decimals and fractions.

LANGUAGE SUPPORT

Generate: to make or to form

Common misconceptions

Misconception	How to identify	How to overcome
With term-to-term rules such as 'subtract 3 then multiply by 2' learners may use BIDMAS rules: multiplying first, subtracting second.	Questions 6b and 7a.	Ask successful learners to explain their reasoning and method in working out both answers. If there are still problems, read out the question, emphasising the word 'then', and discuss how that gives you the order in which to do the operations.

Starter idea

Before you start (10–15 minutes)

Learning intention: To check learners' prior understanding.

Resources: Notebooks; Learner's Book 'Getting started' questions

Description: Learners should have little difficulty with questions 1, 2, 3 and 5 of the 'Getting started' material. Before they attempt Question 4, discuss what they remember about the nth term. Ask 'What are the first three terms of a sequence with an nth term of $3n$?' [3, 6, 9] Ask 'What are the first three terms of a sequence with an nth term of $n + 4$?' [5, 6, 7] Some learners will require reminding. Encourage other learners to give any explanations or help as necessary. Make sure that explanations include phrases such as 'For the first term $n = 1$, for the second term $n = 2$' and '$3n$ is basically the three times table'.

Main teaching idea

Online sequences (5 minutes)

Learning intention: To practise working out and using the term-to-term rule.

Resources: Electronic whiteboard or suite of computers/tablets; calculators may be useful

Description: Type 'Transum.org, Arithmetic Sequences' into a search engine. When directed to the page, learners will complete the level 1 material. This material changes every time it is clicked on, so no two sessions are the same. This is a free resource and learners can access this too. They may wish to practise at home so make sure they write down the web address of this resource. There are many other similar resources available. Remember that the questions get harder further down the page, so you should think about which learner to ask which question. If you use an electronic whiteboard all learners see the same questions. If you use a suite of computers/tablets, learners see different questions.

Ask learners in turn for an answer (or get them into pairs or small groups first and ask each pair or group in turn). You type the answer. Ask the rest of the class if they agree. If learners disagree, they should be asked to explain why, not just say the correct answer. Check using the check button below the questions. Then either get learners to try again (if incorrect) or congratulate them and continue.

Alternatively, ask each learner in turn to type in their answer and then click the 'check' button. They can then get help from the class if required. Other learners can explain any mistakes, but not give the answer. If each learner has individual access to the site you may wish to limit the time taken on the activity. This will lead to differentiation by outcome, but hopefully all learners will be successful and practise a valuable skill.

> **Differentiation ideas:** If learners have individual access to the site, some may find difficulty with the second half of the sequences. If these learners have been successful with the earlier sequences then it is the mental arithmetic slowing them down. A calculator is usually sufficient to deal with this.

Plenary idea

Generating increasing sequences (3–5 minutes)

Resources: Mini whiteboards

Description: Answering the following questions successfully will show that your learners satisfy the learning objective 'Understand term-to-term rules and generate numerical sequences (including fractions)' for increasing sequences. Write or display on the board:

1   Write down the term-to-term rule and the next two terms of these sequences:

   a $3, 5\frac{1}{4}, 7\frac{1}{2}, 10\frac{3}{4}, \ldots$ **b** $12.4, 13.7, 15, 16.3, \ldots$

2   Write down the first three terms of these sequences:

   a The first term is 9, the term-to-term rule is to multiply by 2 then subtract 8.

   b The first term is 3, the term-to-term rule is to multiply by 2 then subtract $2\frac{1}{2}$.

3   The 10th term of a sequence is 50. The term-to-term rule is add $2\frac{1}{2}$. What is the 20th term of the sequence?

⟩ **Assessment ideas:** These questions can be informally marked by self marking or peer marking. Alternatively, you could mark them formally as proof of understanding part of the learning objective. You could use this information, together with information gained from the end-of-unit test, to help plan for future revision.

Answers:

1   **a** $+2\frac{1}{4}$; $13, 15\frac{1}{4}$ **b** $+1.3$; $17.6, 18.9$

2   **a** $9, 10, 12$ **b** $3, 3\frac{1}{2}, 4\frac{1}{2}$

3   75

Guidance on selected *Thinking and working mathematically* questions

Conjecturing and Convincing

Learner's Book Exercise 9.1, Question 12

In this question, learners will say what they notice and explain why the method is wrong. Their explanations as to why it is wrong will differ. Discuss these differences, trying to get learners to decide which

they find to be the clearest explanation. Tell learners that their explanations should not include the correct method, but only need to convince someone why Tania's method is not correct.

Most learners will understand, or at least remember, that doubling the 10th term to find the 20th term will not work (unless the nth term is in the form an, e.g. $2n$, $3n$).

Working out the actual answer will depend on their level of understanding. Some learners will start by repeatedly adding $4\frac{3}{5}$, hoping to spot a pattern in the numbers. This is effective, but difficult and very time consuming. Those with a clear understanding may immediately multiply $4\frac{3}{5}$ by 10 [46] and add the result to $50\frac{2}{5}$ $\left[96\frac{2}{5}\right]$.

Homework idea

As Section 9.1 will probably take more than one lesson, you can select questions from Workbook Exercise 9.1 at the end of each lesson. Only set questions that can be answered using skills and knowledge gained from that lesson. You can help learners to mark their homework at the start of the next lesson. This means you can address any problems before moving on.

Assessment idea

Use Learner's Book Exercise 9.1, Question 4 as an extended hinge point question. It will help you to check whether learners are ready to move on.

Understanding and correctly answering Question 4 with these sequences means that learners are on track to fulfil the success criteria 'Learners can generate increasing and decreasing sequences involving integers, decimals and fractions'. Any lack of understanding here must be dealt with. A class discussion, with learners explaining the methods/reasoning used to answer each part, will deal with almost all problems other learners encounter.

9.2 Finding rules for sequences

LEARNING PLAN

Framework codes	Learning objectives	Success criteria
8As.01	• Understand term-to-term rules and generate sequences from spatial patterns.	• Learners can recognise a simple spatial pattern and use their own term-to-term rule to help draw the next pattern in the sequence.

LANGUAGE SUPPORT

Position number: the position of a term in a sequence of numbers

Position-to-term rule: a rule that allows any term in a sequence to be calculated, given its position number

Sequence of patterns: patterns made from shapes; the number of shapes in each pattern forms a sequence of numbers

Common misconceptions

Misconception	How to identify	How to overcome
Learners may confuse the term-to-term rule with the position-to-term rule.	Question 2.	Checking answers, class discussion regarding any incorrect answers, especially where it appears learners have this misconception.

Starter idea

nth term (2–5 minutes)

Resources: Mini whiteboards or notebooks

Description: This starter will remind learners of how to work out the nth term. Tell learners that you will write the first four terms of a sequence on the board. They should write down the term-to-term rule and the nth term rule for the sequence then show you their mini whiteboard with the answers on.

Write one sequence at a time, check answers and discuss any problems. Hopefully after the first two or three examples there will only be correct answers.

Sequences should be in the form of $n \pm a$ or an, for example:

$3, 4, 5, 6, \ldots [+1, n+2]$ 　　 $2, 4, 6, 8, \ldots [+2, 2n]$

$13, 14, 15, 16, \ldots [+1, n+12]$ 　　 $10, 20, 30, 40, \ldots [+10, 10n]$

$19, 20, 21, 22, \ldots [+1, n+18]$ 　　 $8, 16, 24, 32, \ldots [+8, 8n]$

$-2, -1, 0, 1, \ldots [+1, n-3]$

If the class are confident with giving the term-to-term rule and the nth term rule for these sequences, you could extend to include fractions, such as:

$3\frac{1}{2}, 4\frac{1}{2}, 5\frac{1}{2}, 6\frac{1}{2}, \ldots [+1, n+2\frac{1}{2}]$

$2\frac{1}{2}, 5, 7\frac{1}{2}, 10, \ldots [+2\frac{1}{2}, 2\frac{1}{2}n]$

$19\frac{2}{3}, 20\frac{2}{3}, 21\frac{2}{3}, 22\frac{2}{3}, \ldots [+1, n+18\frac{2}{3}]$

$1\frac{1}{3}, 2\frac{2}{3}, 4, 5\frac{1}{3}, \ldots [+1\frac{1}{3}, 1\frac{1}{3}n]$

Main teaching idea

Question 1 (3–5 minutes)

Learning intention: To help learners to visualise the answers to the first question, which covers many of the learning objectives of this unit.

Resources: Notebooks; Learner's Book

Description:

Ask learners to answer part **a**.

Draw/project the three patterns of the sequence on the board and write the number of squares beneath:

Pattern 1   Pattern 2   Pattern 3

  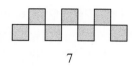

3   5   7

Allow self-marking.

Ask learners to answer part **b**.

Add to the drawing/projection:

Pattern 1   Pattern 2   Pattern 3

 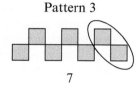

3   5   7

The term-to-term rule is **+2**

Allow self-marking.

Before learners answer part **c**, suggest learners copy Pattern 3 (add to your drawing/projection):

Pattern 1   Pattern 2

 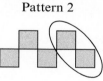

3   5

Pattern 3   Pattern 4

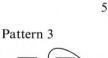 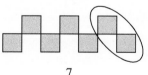

7

The term-to-term rule is **+2**.

Then, remind learners of the term-to-term rule while pointing at the previous two ovals showing the two added squares. Now let learners draw Pattern 4.

Ask learners to answer part **d**. Ask three or four learners to read out their explanations and discuss as a class the clearest way to explain how the sequence is formed.

Ask learners to copy the table from part **e** and to complete the first three rows.

Discuss/draw the answers and allow self-marking.

position number	1	2	3	4
term	3	5	7	9
2 × position number	2	4	6	8

Ask learners to complete the table.

Discuss/draw the answers and allow self-marking.

position number	1	2	3	4
term	3	5	7	9
2 × position number	2	4	6	8
2 × position number + 1	3	5	7	9

It may be appropriate here to remind learners that we write '**2 × position number + 1**' as '**$2n + 1$**'

Answers: Position-to-term rule is: term = 2 × position number + 1

> **Differentiation ideas:** This question can be used without using the help/checking as suggested. However, even confident learners will probably benefit from attempting this question with the step-by-step help/ checking. There are several very similar questions to Question 1 in this section without any visual assistance, which will be done faster, and with more confidence, once this question has been completed using the steps suggested here.

Plenary idea

Pattern sequence (3 minutes)

Resources: Mini whiteboards

Description: Draw or display the sequence on the board:

   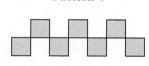

Ask learners to write out the term-to-term rule and to draw the next pattern in the sequence.

Answers: term-to-term rule $= +1\frac{1}{2}$, next pattern

> **Assessment ideas:** Learners can peer mark and discuss the methods they used.

Guidance on selected *Thinking and working mathematically* questions

Conjecturing and Convincing

Learner's Book Exercise 9.2, Question 8

By looking at a sequence of patterns, learners will make a conjecture about a later pattern in the sequence. They will need to justify their reasoning. This is quite difficult for many learners, unless they have remembered the methods used in similar questions.

When you assist them with this question, the first piece of advice should be for learners to set the problem out as ___, 5, ___, 13, . . . This may be enough help. If more help is required, suggest that the third term is halfway between 5 and 13, and ask 'What number is halfway between 5 and 13?' [9]

When learners have worked out that the third term is 9, they have ___, 5, 9, 13, ... Working *backwards* to get a sequence of 13, 9, 5, 1 by subtracting 4, it is straightforward for most learners to find the first term is 1.

Learners can now work out the number of trapezia in Pattern 18 [69] in a variety of ways: some learners will still prefer to repeatedly add 4 to the previous term; many will use the first term and the common difference $1 + 4 \times 17$ or use $13 + 4 \times 14$; while more confident learners will use $4n - 3$ to solve the problem.

Homework idea

As Section 9.2 will probably take more than one lesson, you can select questions from Workbook Exercise 9.2 at the end of each lesson. You can help learners to mark their homework at the start of the next lesson. This means you can address any problems before moving on.

Assessment idea

As learners are working, question individuals regularly. For example, you could ask: What methods are you using? What are you thinking when you look at a question? What is your plan for solving the question? Can you think of a quicker/better method for working out the answer?

9.3 Using the *n*th term

LEARNING PLAN

Framework codes	Learning objectives	Success criteria
8As.02	• Understand and describe *n*th term rules algebraically (in the form $n \pm a$, $a \times n$, or $an \pm b$, where *a* and *b* are positive or negative integers or fractions).	• Learners can give the *n*th term rules of increasing and decreasing linear sequences involving integers, fractions and decimals.

LANGUAGE SUPPORT

*n*th term: the general term of a sequence where *n* represents the position number of the term

Common misconceptions

Misconception	How to identify	How to overcome
Learners may not use the order of operation (BIDMAS) rules correctly with sequences such as $6 - 2n$.	Question 14.	Discussion during Question 14, checking answers for Question 15.

Starter idea

Work out the nth term (5 minutes)

Resources: Mini whiteboards or notebooks

Description: Put learners into pairs. Ask learners to work together to give the position-to-term rule, i.e. the nth term, for the following sequences:

3, 6, 9, 12, . . . [$3n$]   11, 22, 33, 44, . . . [$11n$]

101, 202, 303, 404, . . . [$101n$]   1, 2, 3, 4, . . . [n]

4, 5, 6, 7, . . . [$n+3$]   −3, −2, −1, 0, . . . [$n−4$]

3, 5, 7, 9, . . . [$2n+1$]   10, 13, 16, 19, . . . [$3n+7$]

2, 7, 12, 17, . . . [$5n−3$]

Depending on your class, you may wish to give them one or two sequences to work on at a time. Then check their answers and discuss errors in understanding before moving on. You could give them more sequences of your own if more practice is required.

Some learners find the fourth 'counting' sequence difficult and are surprised by the answer. Understanding this one is especially important as it forms the basis of the two questions that follow.

It is important that learners are confident with these types of sequences as they will build on them during this section. If learners struggle to find the nth term (the position-to-term rule) directly, encourage them to write down the term-to-term rule first.

Main teaching idea

Think like a mathematician, Question 7 (10 minutes)

Learning intention: To understand increasing and decreasing sequences and how to spot the difference between their nth terms.

Resources: Notebooks; Learner's Book Exercise 9.3

Description: Allow learners to answer part **a** individually. The answers to part **b** can be basic. Saying answers to **ai** and **aii** are both increasing is sufficient. Part **c** has many options for learners to group the cards. Hopefully the majority will follow on from part **b** and group them into increasing or decreasing sequences. Some may choose to group them by nth terms containing fractions/not containing fractions. If this occurs, ask which of the 'containing fractions' group had decreasing sequences. This is to check that these learners understand how to identify decreasing sequences.

Answers:

a i 16, 20, 24, 28   ii $1\frac{1}{4}, 1\frac{1}{2}, 1\frac{3}{4}, 2$

   iii 8, 4, 0, −4   iv $\frac{3}{4}, \frac{1}{2}, \frac{1}{4}, 0$

b Similar: in **ai** and **aii** – terms are increasing

   Similar: in **aiii** and **aiv** – terms are decreasing

   Different: in **ai** the terms are increasing and in **aiii** they are decreasing

   Different: in **aii** the terms are increasing and in **aiv** they are decreasing

c Group A – increasing terms,

   $3n+7, \frac{1}{2}n+12, \frac{1}{4}n−19$

   Group B – decreasing terms,

   $13−n, 9−5n, 15−\frac{2}{3}n, \frac{7}{8}−\frac{1}{8}n$

> **Differentiation ideas:** By now, most learners should be able to answer part **a** successfully. As the rest of the question relies on accuracy here, you could allow self-marking with a brief discussion of any errors before moving on to part **b**. You may decide to have a class discussion on how to identify whether an nth term will give an increasing or decreasing sequence. This will be especially useful if this point was not raised during discussions on part **b**.

Plenary idea

nth term rules for increasing sequences (3–5 minutes)

Resources: Mini whiteboards

Description: Answering the following questions successfully will show that your learners satisfy the learning objective 'Understand and describe nth term rules algebraically' for increasing sequences.

Write or display on the board:

1 Work out an expression for the nth term for each sequence.

   b −4, −1.5, 1, 3.5, . . .

   c $20\frac{1}{4}, 20\frac{1}{2}, 20\frac{3}{4}, 21, . . .$

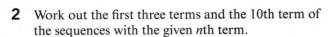

2 Work out the first three terms and the 10th term of the sequences with the given nth term.

a $n-2$ **b** $5n$ **c** $3n-1$

Answers:

1   **a** $2n+5$ dots   **b** $2.5n-6.5$,   **c** $\frac{1}{4}n+20$

2   **a** $-1, 0, 1, 8$ **b** $5, 10, 15, 50$ **c** $2, 5, 8, 29$

> **Assessment ideas:** These questions can be informally marked by self-marking or peer marking. Alternatively, you could mark them formally as proof of understanding part of the learning objective. You could use this information, together with information gained from the end-of-unit test, to help plan for future revision.

Guidance on selected *Thinking and working mathematically* questions

Conjecturing and Convincing

Learner's Book Exercise 9.3, Question 5

Many learners will be confident in answering this question correctly, spotting patterns and showing how they get the sequence from the nth term rule. This is the first time learners have seen a fraction before the n in an nth term expression, so this may cause some confusion. Others will need more convincing.

For any learners who struggle to understand, ask them to give the first four terms of a simpler sequence with

the nth term $2n+8$ [10, 12, 14, 16]. This should not be difficult for your learners. Once completed, ask 'What does the '$2n$' mean? [$2\times n$], 'So what do you think '$\frac{1}{2}n$' means? [$\frac{1}{2}\times n$ or $\frac{1}{2}$ of n].

Homework idea

As Section 9.3 will probably take more than one lesson, you can select questions from Workbook Exercise 9.3 at the end of each lesson. You can help learners to mark their homework at the start of the next lesson. This means you can address any problems before moving on.

Assessment ideas

At various times during Section 9.3, ask small groups of learners short, easy to answer questions that check knowledge. An easy method is to write at the edge of the board several nth terms such as:

$n-5$, $5n+1$, $\frac{1}{2}n+2$, $2n-1\frac{1}{2}$, $1.5n+3$, etc.

Ask questions without warning. Ask a group of three or four learners to write down the first term of one of the sequences whose nth term is on the board. Then ask for the second term of another sequence. Then ask for the tenth term of another sequence. Ask learners to compare answers and then compare methods. Later in the lesson, ask another group of three or four learners, and so on.

9.4 Representing simple functions

LEARNING PLAN		
Framework codes	**Learning objectives**	**Success criteria**
8As.03	• Understand that a function is a relationship where each input has a single output. Generate outputs from a given function and identify inputs from a given output by considering inverse operations (including fractions).	• Success with Questions 3 and 4 are required for this section. • Success with Question 5 shows good understanding of the learning objectives.

LANGUAGE SUPPORT

Algebraically: using algebra

Function: a relationship between two sets of numbers

Function machine: a method of showing a function

Input: a number that goes into a function machine

Map: the process of changing an input number to an output number using a function

Mapping diagram: a type of diagram that represents a function

One-step function: a function that has only one mathematical operation

Output: a number that comes out of a function machine

Reverse equation: the equation that does the opposite to the equation for the function machine

Two-step function: a function that has two mathematical operations

Common misconceptions

Misconception	How to identify	How to overcome
When given the output number, learners fail to reverse the function to work out the input number.	Question 4.	Discussion during Question 3 and checking answers and discussing errors during Question 4.
When using an inverse operation to find an input, learners may forget to check their answer by putting in the input they have found and showing they get the correct output.	Questions 4, 5 and 6.	Discussing this method of checking whenever a learner has given incorrect answers in these questions.

Starter idea

Stage 7 functions (5 minutes)

Resources: Electronic whiteboard; notebooks

Description: Display this question on the board:

Copy these function machines and work out the missing inputs and outputs.

Part a

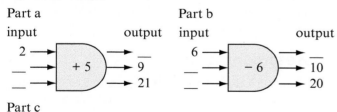

Part c

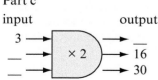

Ask learners to work individually. They should copy the function machines and work out the missing inputs and outputs. Once complete, move learners into pairs or small groups to compare answers, discussing any problems.

Answer: a inputs: 4, 16; output: 7 **b** inputs: 16, 26; output: 0 **c** inputs: 8, 15; output: 6

Main teaching idea

Find the inputs (10–15 minutes)

Learning intention: To invent their own questions, focusing on inverse operations.

Resources: Resource sheet 9.4 (you can download this resource from Cambridge GO)

Description: Let learners work in teams of about four. Give each team a copy of Resource sheet 9.4 and have a second copy ready to distribute when teams have completed the first sheet. Explain that learners will start by filling in the worksheet themselves. They will make up a function and work out the outputs. Explain that they will be getting an identical second sheet, on to which they should copy only the outputs. Then they will exchange sheets between teams and each team will try to work out the missing functions. Stress that, as other learners will have to work out their functions, they should make the function machines as difficult as possible for the opposing teams. Teams must fill in the functions and all the outputs, following the simple rules at the top of the sheet.

Give learners, still in teams, a second copy of the worksheet for them to write in only the outputs. Exchange worksheets among teams and record the time each team takes to complete the sheet they receive. When marking, add a one-minute penalty for each mistake. The winners are the team with the shortest overall time.

It is inevitable that some groups will not be able to work out some of the functions. This is an ideal opportunity to discuss methods used by others in solving similar problems. The key is to understand how to spot the patterns and relationships between the inputs and outputs.

> **Differentiation ideas:** To extend, use the blank function machine at the bottom of the resource sheet. Learners can write in their own inputs.

To extend further, allow integers and fractions throughout, but start with only allowing halves and, perhaps, quarters.

Plenary idea

Exit ticket (2 minutes)

Resources: Exit ticket 9.4 (you can download this resource from Cambridge GO)

Description: Give each learner a cut-out part of Exit ticket 9.4. Learners will complete it individually and hand it to you as they leave your class.

Answer:
Completed table:

x	4	**(6)**	7	(11)
y	(−1)	0	$\left(\dfrac{1}{2}\right)$	$2\dfrac{1}{2}$

Success with these questions shows a good level of understanding of the learning objectives. Any errors need to be discussed with individuals.

Guidance on selected *Thinking and working mathematically* questions

Specialising and Generalising

Learner's Book Exercise 9.4, Question 11

By considering numbers in a two-step function machine, learners will generalise to find the function itself. Most learners will use a trial and improvement method for this question. However, to encourage a deeper level of thinking, ask them to consider the term-to-term rules for x and y. [x goes up in 4s, but y goes up in 2s, which is half as much].

This should lead them to identify the first function must be $\times \dfrac{1}{2}$ (or $\div 2$). From this, they can reason that 9 has to be added in the second function box to give the y-value, so the answer is $y = \dfrac{1}{2}x + 9$. This process leads learners from specific values to a general rule.

Some learners may need a lot of convincing that this generalisation works. Ask them to check by substituting $x = 4$ and obtaining $y = 11$. Then they can repeat with values of x increasing by 4 to make sure the pattern is correct.

Homework idea

As Section 9.4 will probably take more than one lesson, you can select questions from Workbook Exercise 9.4 at the end of each lesson. You can help learners to mark their homework at the start of the next lesson. This means you can address any problems before moving on.

You could ask learners to make a mind map containing everything they think they need to remember for the end-of-unit test. The following lesson, it is important to share the mind maps in class, perhaps spread out over a few desks for everyone to look at. Discuss the different mind maps as a class. When the class agree that a point is important, that key point could be copied onto the board. Agree on as many key points as possible. Learners could then improve their individual mind maps if necessary. Learners could store their mind maps at home as a possible revision tool towards mid-term or end-of-year exams.

Assessment idea

Use Learner's Book Exercise 9.4, Question 4a as a hinge point question to assess whether learners are ready to move on. Learners must be able to work out how to fill in all eight empty cells in the tables before moving on. If necessary, encourage learners to explain methods to those that are struggling.

⟩ 10 Percentages

Unit plan

Topic	Approximate number of learning hours	Outline of learning content	Resources
Introduction and Getting Started	10–15 minutes		Learner's Book
10.1 Percentage increases and decreases	2	Write a change in value as a percentage. Increase or decrease a value by a given percentage.	Learner's Book Section 10.1 Workbook Section 10.1 ⤓ Additional teaching ideas Section 10.1
10.2 Using a multiplier	2	Use a multiplier to increase or decrease a value by a given percentage.	Learner's Book Section 10.2 Workbook Section 10.2 ⤓ Additional teaching ideas Section 10.2

Cross-unit resources
⤓ Language worksheet 10.1–10.2
⤓ End of Unit 10 test

BACKGROUND KNOWLEDGE

For this unit, learners will need this background knowledge:

- Recognise percentages, including percentages greater than 100 (Stage 7).

- Express one quantity as a percentage of another (Stage 7).

This unit extends the work to dealing further with percentage increases and decreases, introducing the concept of a multiplier.

TEACHING SKILLS FOCUS

Metacognition

Traffic Lights with three colours (red, yellow and green) are a simple way of encouraging learners to think about their own learning. This is what we mean by metacognition.

At an appropriate point in a lesson you can ask learners to indicate how they feel about an idea that you have been working on. You could give each learner three coloured slips of paper or card to hold up when you ask them to think about their learning:

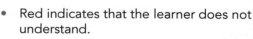

- Red indicates that the learner does not understand.
- Yellow means that the learner has some understanding of the idea but is not yet confident about using it.
- Green means that the learner feels confident about applying new knowledge.

Other suitable resources may be available from educational suppliers.

CONTINUED

Try using Traffic Lights as a regular part of your teaching. For example, when you introduce the idea of a multiplier in Section 10.2, you can use Traffic Lights to assess whether learners have understood the idea. Then, if necessary, you can go through another example or give extra support to some learners. You could also use Traffic Lights at the end of a lesson when learners have been working through an exercise. It will give you a quick overview of progress and encourage learners to take responsibility for their own learning.

10.1 Percentage increases and decreases

LEARNING PLAN

Framework codes	Learning objectives	Success criteria
8Nf.05	• Understand percentage increase and decrease, and absolute change.	• Learner can increase $360 by 15%.

LANGUAGE SUPPORT

Absolute change: the actual increase or decrease in the value of a number

Percentage decrease: the decrease in the value of a number, written as a percentage of the original value

Percentage increase: the increase in the value of a number, written as a percentage of the original value

Common misconceptions

Misconception	How to identify	How to overcome
A decrease of 80% means that the new value is 80% of the original.	Ask how to calculate a simple percentage decrease.	Complete the questions in Exercise 10.1 and check for errors, correcting them if necessary.

Starter idea

Previous knowledge (10 minutes)

Resources: Learner's Book 'Getting started' questions

Description: Set the questions and give learners a few minutes to complete them. If anyone finishes early they can compare their answers with a partner.

Go through the answers. Learners need to know how to do the following types of calculation:

- Write one number as a percentage of another. Learners will start with a fraction and multiply by 100%.
- Calculate a percentage of a particular value. Learners should start by changing the percentage to a decimal and then multiplying.

Learners are expected to use a calculator where appropriate throughout this unit. They should be aware of the fact that percentages can be more than 100%. Question 5 in particular gives a chance to emphasise this. If necessary, give learners some more simple examples to practise the skills required.

Main teaching idea

Percentage changes (10 minutes)

Learning intention: Learn to increase or decrease a value by a given percentage by first calculating the absolute change in value.

Resources: Calculators

Description: Describe the following situation: You have $200. This increases by 30%. How much do you have now? Learners should be able to see that 30% of $200 is $60, which is the absolute change, so you now have $200 + $60 = $260.

Now ask 'What if it was not an increase but a decrease of 30%?' They should be able to tell you that the amount is $200 − $60 = $140.

Finally, ask about an increase of 130%. Now the absolute change is an *increase* of $260 and the final amount is $460.

This first example uses simple numbers so that learners can see the idea more clearly without needing a calculator. Now use an example with more complicated numbers: You have $720 and this is increased by 63%. Ask learners to discuss this in pairs for a minute or two and then ask how to proceed. First 63% = 0.63 and so 63% of $720 = 0.63 × $720 = $453.60 This is the increase so now you have $720 + $453.60 = $1173.60.

Similarly for a *decrease* of 63% you have $720 − $453.60 = $266.40.

Finally try an increase of 142%. 142% = 1.42 and so 142% of $720 = 1.42 × $720 = $1022.40 and now you have $720 + $1022.40 = $1742.40.

⟩ **Differentiation ideas:** The idea of an increase of 130% may need more discussion for some learners. Diagrams like this can clarify the difference between an increase of 30% and an increase of 130%.

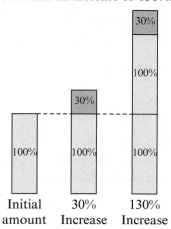

Emphasise the fact that the starting amount is 100%.

Plenary idea

Decreasing by more than 100% (10 minutes)

Resources: Learner's Book

Description: Learners must have already answered Learner's Book Exercise 10.1, Question 20.

Discuss the first part. Go through the calculation to show that savings of $500 reduced by 150% give a final amount of $500 − $750 = −$250. What does the negative number show? In this case Sofia has spent more money than she has. This means she has a *debt* of $250.

In the second case the calculation is the same but what does −250g of rice mean? Arun cannot cook more rice than he has. Perhaps he borrowed it from someone else?

Ask learners to think of other examples where a decrease of over 100% is possible and they should explain what it means. Also ask them to describe situations where a decrease of over 100% is not possible.

⟩ **Assessment ideas:** Ask learners to discuss their ideas for the final part in pairs. This gives the opportunity for peer assessment.

Guidance on selected *Thinking and working mathematically* questions

Conjecturing and Convincing

Learner's Book Exercise 10.1, Question 19

Learners are given three statements and are asked to decide which one is correct. They need to provide evidence to support their decision. This should take the form of calculations *and* explanation. So they could start by finding the result of a 20% increase and then using the result to do a further calculation. Encourage them to do more than just write down the calculation. They need to be able to convince someone reading the explanation.

Homework ideas

Exercise 10.1 in the Workbook has further questions. You could set all of them or a selection of questions.

If you use the Main teaching idea 'Price reductions', you could ask learners to complete the poster for homework. (You can download this resource from Cambridge GO.)

Assessment ideas

Learners need to be clear about the distinction between saying, for example, that $50 is 25% *more than* $40, and that $50 is 125% *of* $40. Learners have many opportunities to work through this idea in the exercise. Check their answers and also ask questions during whole class discussion to check their understanding where necessary.

10.2 Using a multiplier

LEARNING PLAN

Framework codes	Learning objectives	Success criteria
8Nf.05	• Understand percentage increase and decrease, and absolute change.	• Learner understands that multiplying by 0.85 decreases a quantity by 15%.

LANGUAGE SUPPORT

Multiplier: a number by which you multiply a given value

Common misconceptions

Misconception	How to identify	How to overcome
The multiplier for an increase or decrease of 25% is 0.25.	Ask how to calculate a particular increase/decrease to ensure that the multiplier is correct.	Learners should start by writing the value required as a percentage of the original value and use this to find the multiplier.

Starter idea

Recap of percentage increases and decreases (5 minutes)

Resources: The table in the description

Description: Display this table. Ask learners to copy it.

Percentage			100%			
Amount			$20			

Say that we are starting with $20 and that is 100%. You now write different percentages in the top row and ask them to put the corresponding amount in the bottom row. Check the answer each time before moving on to the next. Start by writing 50% in the second empty column. Fill in the answer below and then write 25% in the column to the left. Then go on to write 125%,

150% and 200% in the remaining blank columns. It will eventually look like this:

Percentage	25%	50%	100%	125%	150%	200%
Amount	$5	$10	$20	$25	$30	$40

If your learners need more practice, repeat the table with a different initial amount as 100%. You could also use different percentages but make them easy to calculate mentally.

Main teaching idea

Multipliers (10 minutes)

Learning intention: To show a more efficient way of calculating the result of a percentage increase or decrease.

Resources: Calculators

Description: Learners have practised calculating the result of a percentage increase or decrease in the previous section. In this activity you will show learners a more efficient method which they need to learn and practise in Exercise 10.2.

Start with this example: You want to increase $73 by 38%. Go through this argument, making sure learners are clear about each stage:

- $73 = 100%
- If you increase this by 38% you get
  $100\% + 38\% = 138\%$
- $138\% = 1.38$ and so 138% of
  $73 = 1.38 \times \$73 = \$100.74$

Ask, 'Why is this more efficient?' Learners should be able to say that it is quicker because you did not need to work out the absolute change separately. If learners are not convinced you could say that, in future, they will find this method better when they are doing more complicated problems. Examples include problems involving several successive percentage changes.

Go on to ask how to use this method to find the result of a 38% *reduction*. See if learners can make a similar argument:

- $73 = 100%
- If you *decrease* this by 38% you get
  $100\% - 38\% = 62\%$
- $62\% = 0.62$ and so 62% of $73 = 0.62 \times \$73 = \$45.26$

Finally ask how to find the result of an increase of 138%. In this case, learners need to find $100\% + 138\% = 238\%$ and $2.38 \times \$73 = \$173.74$.

The number to multiply by (1.38 or 0.62, etc.) is called the *multiplier* and this is the *multiplier method*. Emphasise that you want learners to practise this new method in Exercise 10.2 and not revert to the method they were using in the previous section.

Plenary idea

Check your progress (10 minutes)

Resources: Learner's Book Section 10.2, Check Your Progress

Description: Set the learners to answer the Check Your Progress questions, working in pairs. They should come

to an agreement on their answers. When they have all completed them, check the solutions are correct.

Ask the learners to describe the main points to be learnt from this unit. Their comments should cover two aspects:

- Using a multiplier to increase or decrease a given value by a given percentage.
- Calculating a multiplier in order to describe the increase or decrease between two given values as a percentage.

⟩ **Assessment ideas:** You are giving the opportunity for peer assessment and self-assessment by setting the task for learners to complete in pairs.

Guidance on selected *Thinking and working mathematically* questions

Conjecturing and Convincing

Learner's Book Exercise 10.2, Question 13

This gives learners a chance to look for patterns in real population data. The early parts of the question guide learners to focus on the percentage changes in separate periods. By looking at those, learners can make a judgement about how the population might change in the future. There is no exact answer to this. Learners should be able to make a convincing argument, based on the data, for why they have chosen a particular figure.

Homework ideas

There are more questions in Exercise 10.2 in the Workbook.

The extension challenge in Main teaching idea 'Increases and decreases' could be set as homework. (You can download this resource from Cambridge GO.)

Assessment ideas

You need to make sure that learners are using multipliers when they answer the questions in Exercise 10.2. You can do this by looking at their written work. Learners need to be showing their method in writing the answers. If individual learners are not doing so, question them and ask them to describe their method. Tell them to show their calculation in future.

> 11 Graphs

Unit plan

Topic	Approximate number of learning hours	Outline of learning content	Resources
Introduction and Getting Started	10–15 minutes		Learner's Book
11.1 Functions	2	Representing situations in words and with functions of the form $y = mx + c$.	Learner's Book Section 11.1 Workbook Section 11.1 ⬇ Additional teaching ideas Section 11.1
11.2 Plotting graphs	3	Constructing a table of values for a function and using it to plot a graph.	Learner's Book Section 11.2 Workbook Section 11.2 ⬇ Additional teaching ideas Section 11.2
11.3 Gradient and intercept	2	Plotting graphs of $y = mx + c$. Interpreting the values of m and c.	Learner's Book Section 11.3 Workbook Section 11.3 ⬇ Additional teaching ideas Section 11.3
11.4 Interpreting graphs	2	Interpreting real-life graphs with several components.	Learner's Book Section 11.4 Workbook Section 11.4 ⬇ Additional teaching ideas Section 11.4

Cross-unit resources

⬇ Language worksheet 11.1–11.4

⬇ Project Guidance: Straight line mix-up resource sheet A

⬇ Project Guidance: Straight line mix-up resource sheet B

⬇ End of Unit 11 test

BACKGROUND KNOWLEDGE

For this unit, learners will need this background knowledge:

- Represent situations by a function of the form $y = x + c$ or $y = mx$ (Stage 7).
- Use a table of values to plot a graph of $y = x + c$ or $y = mx$ (Stage 7).

- Recognise straight-line graphs parallel to the x-axis or y-axis (Stage 7).
- Interpret real-life graphs related to rates of change (Stage 7).

TEACHING SKILLS FOCUS

Language awareness

Language awareness is important in this unit. Suppose you are talking about a situation where the cost (c) of hiring a drill for d days is given by the function $c = 10d + 15$. Make sure you always say that d represents the *number* of days. Learners tend to shorten these phrases and say d stands for days which can sometimes be misleading. It represents a number, not a word.

Another important use of language occurs when learners are drawing graphs of functions. The function $c = 10d + 15$ can give rise to a table of values. These values provide coordinates for plotting points and drawing a straight line through them. We then talk about 'the line $c = 10d + 15$' and refer to $c = 10d + 15$ as the *equation* of the line. This means that $c = 10d + 15$ may be called a function or an equation, depending on the context. This use of the word 'equation' is different from the one learners are used to where they are given an equation with one variable and asked to solve it.

At the end of this unit, ask yourself: Do the learners understand and feel confident in using the correct terminology? Always use the correct terminology yourself and be alert for any confusion from the learners.

11.1 Functions

LEARNING PLAN

Framework codes	Learning objectives	Success criteria
8As.04	• Understand that a situation can be represented either in words or as a linear function in two variables (of the form $y = mx + c$), and move between the two representations.	• The cost of hiring a ladder is $10 plus $5 a day. Write this as a function involving the two variables, n and c, where n stands for the number of days, and c for the number of dollars.

LANGUAGE SUPPORT

Function: a relationship between two sets of numbers

Common misconceptions

Misconception	How to identify	How to overcome
Learners can confuse a fixed charge and a charge that depends on a variable such as time.	This will be apparent if learners transpose the values of m and c when writing a function.	Check the answers to questions in Exercise 11.1 and look for this error. Emphasise the difference when introducing the topic.

Starter idea

Prior knowledge (10 minutes)

Resources: Learner's Book Unit 11, 'Getting started' questions; Squared paper to draw the graphs (graph paper is not essential)

Description: Set the learners the 'Getting started' questions. This is revision material that should be familiar from Stage 7. When learners finish they should compare answers with another learner to assess their own work. Pay particular attention to the completion of the table in Question 3. Check that they know how to substitute values of x in the equation to calculate the values of y.

Learners should be able to draw the line. The most likely errors are not putting the numbers on the axes correctly or getting the coordinates the wrong way round.

Main teaching idea

Descriptions and functions (10 minutes)

Learning intention: Introduce learners to situations and functions where there are two parts to consider.

Resources: Learner's Book Section 11.1

Description: Learners are familiar with functions of the form $y = mx$ or $y = x + c$ where there is just one numerical value, m or c. In this section they will be introduced to the more general case $y = mx + c$ where two numerical values, m and c, are involved.

Read through the introductory text in Section 11.1 with the learners. Explain that the booking fee of $15 is the same however many hours are booked. Ask questions to ensure this is understood. For example: How much does it cost to hire the hall for 3 hours? [$135] How did you work that out? [$40 × 3 + $15].

Ask further questions of a similar type if necessary. Always ask learners for the method as well as the answer.

Now move on to finding a function. Suppose the cost for n hours is c. Then you can write this as a function $y = 40n + 15$. Make sure learners can see how the two numbers fit here. Emphasise with some numerical examples. If $n = 7$ then $y = 40 \times 7 + 15 = 295$; the cost for 7 hours is $295. The function just has numbers. (Do not insert the units in the function.)

Check learners' understanding by changing the numbers. For example, if the hourly charge is $30, how does the function change? If the function is $y = 25n + 33$, what do the numbers tell you?

Plenary idea

Finding a function (5 minutes)

Resources: Learner's Book Exercise 11.1, Question 15

Description: Question 15 gives the function $y = 20x + 15$ and asks learners to think of a real-life interpretation of this. Use the plenary as an opportunity to share ideas from individuals. They should already have had an opportunity for peer assessment so their examples should be good ones.

⟩ **Assessment ideas:** As learners share their ideas you can assess whether they are clear about the different roles played by the two numerical values (m and c in the function).

Guidance on selected *Thinking and working mathematically* questions

Specialising and Generalising

Learner's Book Exercise 11.1, Question 9

Parts **a** and **b** require learners to find answers for specific values of t. Then they use their results to make a generalised observation about what happens when the value of t is greater than 6. They should be able to observe that $3t > 18$ for all such values of t. So they can make a general rule that the value of r will always be negative when $t > 6$.

In part **c** the function $r = 18 - 3t$ represents the amount of petrol in a tank. In this context it follows that the value of t cannot be more than 6 because that will mean there is a negative amount of petrol in the tank. This is impossible. This highlights the fact that interpreting a function in a real-life situation depends on the circumstances. We can evaluate the function for any value of t but only certain values are valid in that context.

For more confident learners only, you could ask 'Can t be negative?' Suppose $t = -1$ then $r = 18 - 3 \times (-1) = 18 + 3 = 21$. What does this mean? If the journey began before the clock started, this would be the amount of petrol one hour earlier. However, the interpretation depends on the real-life circumstances.

Homework idea

Workbook Exercise 11.1 gives more questions of a similar type. You could set them all or a selection of questions.

Assessment idea

There are opportunities in Exercise 11.1 for peer assessment where learners look at the answers of a partner. However this can also lead to self-assessment if they realise there is a way to improve their own answer. This shows that peer assessment and self-assessment are often closely related.

11.2 Plotting graphs

LEARNING PLAN

Framework codes	Learning objectives	Success criteria
8As.05	• Use knowledge of coordinate pairs to construct tables of values and plot the graphs of linear functions, where y is given explicitly in terms of x ($y = mx + c$).	• Given the function $y = 4x - 5$, learners can construct a table of values and plot a graph.

LANGUAGE SUPPORT

Plot: put points on a graph in order to draw a line

Table of values: chart which can be used to determine the value of two or more variables

Common misconceptions

Misconception	How to identify	How to overcome
Learners may not be able to plot a graph correctly from a table of values.	Check whether graphs drawn by learners are straight lines.	Make sure learners know that the graphs should be straight lines. Tell them to self-assess by checking the numbering on their axes and the points they have plotted. If not all the points are on a straight line, check the calculation for the one(s) that look misplaced.

Starter idea

Finding pairs of values (10 minutes)

Resources: None

Description: Write down the following function: $y = 5x + 8$. Ask learners to work in pairs. They will write down six different values for x and the corresponding values for y. After one or two minutes ask for some suggestions from different pairs. Write the values in two rows like this:

x							
y							

After a few pairs of learners have made suggestions, ask questions to ensure you get a range of values. This will depend on the values you already have but here are some suggestions: Can you give me a pair of numbers where: x is negative? y is negative? x is a two-digit number? y is greater than 100? x is not an integer? This is just to get learners used to the idea of finding pairs of values. The Main teaching idea takes this further.

Main teaching idea

Plotting a graph (15 minutes)

Learning intention: From a function, produce a table of values and then plot a graph.

Resources: Squared paper for plotting a graph

Description: Write down the function $y = 2x - 1$ (this is the function used in Learner's Book Section 11.2).

Ask learners to give you possible values for x and y. When it is clear that learners know how to do this, ask them to copy this table.

x	−2	−1	0	1	2	3	4
y							

Ask learners to fill in the bottom row. They should get this:

x	−2	−1	0	1	2	3	4
y	−5	−3	−1	1	3	5	7

Ask how it will continue if more columns are added on the right. It should be like this:

x	4	5	6
y	7	9	11

and so on. How will it continue on the left? Like this:

x	−5	−4	−3	−2
y	−11	−9	−7	−5

Explain that the table gives pairs of coordinates: $(−2, −5)$, $(−1, −3)$, $(0, −1)$, $(1, 1)$, and so on. Tell learners to draw a pair of coordinate axes on squared paper and plot the points. They should find that the points are in a straight line. Tell them to draw this:

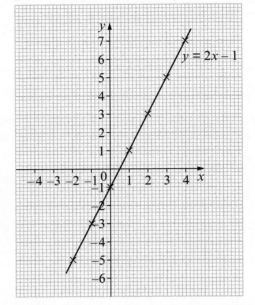

Tell them to check that it is a straight line. Ask learners to find and correct any errors if the points are not in a straight line. These are probably caused by incorrectly drawn axes or incorrectly plotted points. If they cannot find the error they can discuss it with a neighbour. Say that we call $y = 2x - 1$ the *equation of the line*.

Draw the line to cover as much of the grid as possible. The line segment they have drawn is part of a line that extends in both directions but is always straight. They should convince themselves that other pairs of points such as (6, 11) will also be on the line if it is extended.

⟩ **Differentiation ideas:** For more confident learners, ask them to consider points on the line that do not have integer coordinates, for example (2.5, 4). Show that these are also consistent with the equation, for example, $2 \times 2.5 - 1 = 4$.

Plenary idea

Review of the unit (5 minutes)

Resources: None

Description: Show learners this table:

x	−1	0	1	2	3	4	5
y		10	12	14		18	

Ask learners to use the pattern in the table to find the missing numbers [8, 16 and 20].

Ask them to explain how they did this. [The y-values are going up in 2s is the most likely explanation.] Say that the table shows the function $y = \ldots x + \ldots$ where two numbers are missing. What are they? By trying out suggestions learners should find that the function is $y = 2x + 10$.

More confident learners may point out the connection between the sequence of y values increasing by 2 and the fact that $m = 2$. Then ask them to predict what the line will be like if they draw it. Ask them to discuss this in pairs and then take suggestions from them. The terms 'y-intercept' and 'gradient' will be introduced in the next section. At this stage, learners should be able to describe a line passing through (0, 10) and sloping upwards from left to right.

› **Assessment ideas:** The discussion in pairs will give an opportunity for peer assessment. You can assess learners' understanding by asking them about the missing numbers, the function and the shape of the graph.

Guidance on selected *Thinking and working mathematically* questions

Characterising and Classifying

Learner's Book Exercise 11.2, Question 13

In this question, learners use information to select a correct line on a graph. This gives the link between the verbal description and the line. By interpreting this link in reverse, learners can then work from the other two lines to provide verbal descriptions. In this way they are showing the ability to identify particular properties and classify them.

Homework idea

There are similar questions in Workbook Exercise 11.2 which you can use for homework. You could use all the questions or a selection of them.

Assessment idea

Plotting graphs is an activity where self-assessment is appropriate and easy. Learners know that the line plotted should be straight. If it is not then they know that there is an error which they can look for. Learners sometimes draw a line of best fit which goes through some points but not all of them. Emphasise the fact that, in this section, all the points should fit exactly on a straight line.

If a learner asks for help when they find a graph is incorrect, tell them to check the numbering on their axes and the points they have plotted.

11.3 Gradient and intercept

LEARNING PLAN

Framework codes	Learning objectives	Success criteria
8As.06	• Recognise that equations of the form $y = mx + c$ correspond to straight-line graphs, where m is the gradient and c is the y-intercept (integer values of m).	• Correctly identify the gradient and y-intercept for a line such as $y = 4x + 9$ and relate them to the shape of the graph.

LANGUAGE SUPPORT

Coefficient: a number in front of a variable in an algebraic expression; the coefficient multiplies the variable

Equation of a line: when a function is used to draw a line, the function is called the equation of the line

Linear function: a function of the form $y = mx + c$ where m and c are numbers

x-intercept: the value of x where the graph of a line crosses the x-axis

y-intercept: the value of y where the graph of a line crosses the y-axis

Common misconceptions

Misconception	How to identify	How to overcome
Learners do not always identify m and c correctly but get them the wrong way round.	Ask learners to identify m and c for $y = 10 + 20x$ and $y = 2 - x$.	Check that learners can answer the questions in Exercise 11.3 correctly and find a y-intercept and a gradient from a table of values.

Starter idea

m and c (5 minutes)

Resources: Learner's Book Section 11.3

Description: Material in this starter is taken from the introduction to Section 11.3. Say that all the lines you have drawn in this unit are of the form $y = mx + c$ where m and c are numbers. The letters may not be x and y but there are always two letters. A function of the form $y = mx + c$ is called a *linear function* and the graph is always a straight line.

Write down these functions. Ask learners to write down m and c for each one. The answers are written in the table.

function	m	c
$y = 5x + 2$	5	2
$y = 3x - 4$	3	−4
$y = x + 10$	1	10
$y = 4x$	4	0
$y = -5x + 3$	−5	3
$y = -2x - 4$	−2	−4
$y = -x + 10$	−1	10
$y = 12$	0	12

Check that learners understand that m is the coefficient of x (the number in front of it) and $y = x + 10$ has $m = 1$

although this is not written in the equation. (In algebra we write $1x$ as simply x.) In a similar way, $y = -x + 1$ has $m = -1$.

Main teaching idea

Gradient and intercept (10 minutes)

Learning intention: Learners see the link between the equation of a straight line and the gradient and intercept of the line.

Resources: Squared paper for plotting a graph

Description: Write down the function $y = 3x + 4$ and a table of values for x between −3 and +5. Tell learners to copy the table and complete it. They should get this:

x	−3	−2	−1	0	1	2	3	4	5
y	−5	−2	1	4	7	10	13	16	19

Ask learners to describe the pattern in the table.

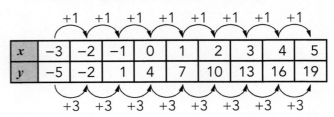

They need to see that, as x increases by 1, y increases by 3. This gives us the *gradient* (slope) of the graph.

Now ask learners to plot the points and then draw a graph. It should look like this:

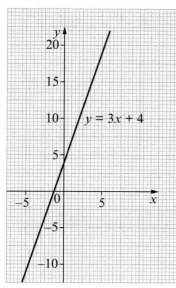

Ask learners to work in pairs and to check each other's graph to ensure that it is correct. They should check their choice of axes and the points they have plotted.

The graph crosses the y-axis at 4. Say that this is called the *y-intercept*. How can you find this from the table? [It is the y value when $x = 0$].

Look at the crosses.

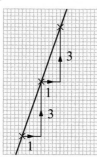

Imagine moving from one cross to the next one from left to right. For every one square you move across, you move up three squares so 3 is the *gradient*. It measures the steepness of the graph. Emphasise that you can find the y-intercept and the gradient from the table or from the graph.

> **Differentiation ideas:** For learners who struggle to draw the graph you may need to suggest a suitable scale.

Plenary idea

Properties of lines (5 minutes)

Resources: Learners should have completed Exercise 11.3 in the Learner's Book.

Description: Write down the function $y = 7x - 12$. Say that this is the equation of a line. Ask learners to write down the equations of three more lines that are parallel to this one. When they have finished they can show their answers to a partner to check. Make sure any disputes are settled. All the equations should be in the form $y = 7x + c$.

Then ask learners to write down the equations of three more lines that cross the y-axis at the same point as $y = 7x - 12$. They can ask a partner to check as before. All the answers should be of the form $y = mx - 12$.

> **Assessment ideas:** The description above includes opportunities for peer assessment.

Guidance on selected *Thinking and working mathematically* questions

Specialising and Generalising

Learner's Book Exercise 11.3, questions 1 and 2

Question 1 gives learners the opportunity to look at several examples to identify a pattern. In this case they see the connection between equations of parallel lines. Question 2 looks at equations of a different set of parallel lines. From these questions they can draw conclusions about the equations of parallel lines in general.

Homework ideas

There are similar questions in Exercise 11.3 in the Workbook.

You could set the task in the Plenary idea 'Summary' as homework. (You can download this resource from Cambridge GO.)

Assessment idea

Encourage self-assessment throughout Section 11.3. Learners should check that the information from their tables and graphs both indicate the same y-intercept and gradient. Learners should be confident in using both tables and graphs, so they can use one to check the other.

11.4 Interpreting graphs

LEARNING PLAN

Framework codes	Learning objectives	Success criteria
8As.07	• Read and interpret graphs with more than one component. Explain why they have a specific shape and the significance of intersections of the graphs.	• Able to answer questions by interpreting the points on a graph, such as those in Exercise 11.4.

Common misconceptions

Misconception	How to identify	How to overcome
Errors can occur if the scales on the axes are not interpreted correctly.	Ask learners to describe in detail what a graph with several components illustrates.	Complete the questions in Exercise 11.4 and check they are correct.

Starter idea

Recap (5 minutes)

Resources: None

Description: Write down this function $y = 15 + 20x$. Say that $\$y$ is the cost of hiring a bike for x days. Ask for the cost of 1, 2, 3, 7 days [\$35, \$55, \$75, \$155].

Ask what the numbers 15 and 20 represent. Learners should suggest that 15 is a fixed charge in dollars and 20 is a daily charge in dollars. Then ask them to imagine a graph of the function. How are 15 and 20 related to the graph? They should know that 15 is the y-intercept and 20 is the gradient. Make sure they get these the correct way round. If they are uncertain, put the values in an ordered table. They can see the gradient and intercept from this, as explained in the previous section. If there is still doubt, ask learners to draw the graph.

Main teaching idea

A graph with several sections (10 minutes)

Learning intention: Practise reading information from a graph.

Resources: Learner's Book

Description: Ask learners to look at this graph from Learner's Book Section 11.4, Worked example 11.4.

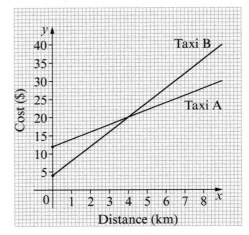

Explain that the graph shows the fare charged by two different taxis. Ask learners to complete a table of values for each taxi. They should get these values:

Distance (km)	0	1	2	3	4	5	6	7	8
Taxi A	12	14	16	18	20	22	24	26	28
Taxi B	4	8	12	16	20	24	28	32	36

Say that a journey of x km costs y dollars. Ask for the gradient and the y-intercept for taxi A. [2 and 12.] Make sure learners can see this from the table and from the graph. Ask for the equation of line A. [$y = 2x + 12$.]

Repeat the exercise for line B: Ask for the gradient and the y-intercept for taxi B. [4 and 4.] Ask for the equation of line B. [$y = 4x + 4$]

Ask what distance is the same cost for both taxis [4 km]. Ask how learners can see this both from the graph and from the table.

> **Differentiation ideas:** Learners may need to be reminded how to find the gradient from a table or from a graph. This was covered in the previous section so you can refer back to that.

Plenary idea

Check your progress (10 minutes)

Resources: Learner's Book Section 11.4

Description: Ask the learners to answer the Check Your Progress questions at the end of this unit. They should work in pairs. This way they can agree on the answers and have the opportunity for peer assessment. After they have done this, you can check for correct answers. Use Question 4 to emphasise the relationship between the equation, the gradient and the y-intercept.

> **Assessment ideas:** Paired work gives learners the opportunity for peer assessment.

Guidance on selected *Thinking and working mathematically* questions

Characterising and Classifying

Learner's Book Exercise 11.4, Question 10

In Question 10, learners can look at each graph and interpret its characteristics. Common to both graphs are

the initial value (which is linked to the y-intercept) and the rate of change (which is related to the gradient). By considering the abstract example of the line $y = mx + c$, learners can develop ideas that they can apply to this real-life example.

For liquid B the graph is not a straight line, but is made up of two straight line segments. Each segment has a rate of change (gradient).

If there is time, ask learners to look back at other graphs in this exercise. Ask them to interpret their characteristics in the same way.

Homework ideas

Workbook Exercise 11.4 gives further questions of a similar type. You can set all the questions or just a selection of them.

Ask learners to write a summary of the main things they need to remember from this unit.

Assessment idea

Peer assessment is particularly useful to give learners immediate feedback when they are drawing graphs.

PROJECT GUIDANCE: STRAIGHT LINE MIX-UP

Why do this problem?

In this problem, learners are invited to characterise the properties of a group of straight line graphs, and classify them according to their gradients and intercepts. To arrange the function cards, learners will need to reason about which combinations of properties are possible. They will also need to switch between graphical, algebraic and tabular representations of functions.

Possible approach

Draw a table on the board, like this one:

	The y intercept is positive	
Parallel to $y = 0$		*	

As an example, choose two properties like the ones in the table (one of which appears in the problem). Invite learners to suggest functions/graphs which could go in the cell marked *. Then set them the challenge of arranging the six property cards in the column and row headings. They need to find a place for all nine function cards in the grid.

While learners work in pairs, listen out for useful strategies and insights that can be shared with the whole class. For example, some learners might choose to sketch graphs so they can visualise the ones expressed as tables or equations. Other learners might write them all as equations then use what they know about $y = mx + c$ to classify them. Learners might also observe that some pairs of properties are mutually exclusive.

Once learners have successfully arranged all fifteen cards, finish off the lesson by discussing why there is essentially only one possible solution.

Key questions

Which cards could go in more than one place? Which cards can only go in one place?

Possible support

Learners could start with a smaller grid, using just four of the properties to start with.

Possible extension

Invite learners to choose their own functions and properties to create a table on a sheet of paper. They can cut it up and exchange with a partner to reassemble it.

> 12 Ratio and proportion

Unit plan

Topic	Approximate number of learning hours	Outline of learning content	Resources
Introduction and Getting Started	5–10 minutes		Learner's Book
12.1 Simplifying ratios	1–1.5	Use equivalence to simplify and compare ratios.	Learner's Book Section 12.1 Workbook Section 12.1 ⬇ Additional teaching ideas Section 12.1 ⬇ Resource sheet 12.1
12.2 Sharing in a ratio	1–1.5	Share an amount into a given ratio with two or more parts.	Learner's Book Section 12.2 Workbook Section 12.2 ⬇ Additional teaching ideas Section 12.2 ⬇ Resource sheet 12.2
12.3 Ratio and direct proportion	1	Understand and use the relationship between ratio and direct proportion.	Learner's Book Section 12.3 Workbook Section 12.3 ⬇ Additional teaching ideas Section 12.3 ⬇ Resource sheet 12.3

Cross-unit resources
⬇ Language worksheet 12.1–12.3
⬇ End of Unit 12 test

BACKGROUND KNOWLEDGE

For this unit, learners will need this background knowledge:

- Use knowledge of equivalence to understand and use equivalent ratios (same units) (Stage 7).

- Understand how ratios are used to compare quantities to divide an amount into a given ratio with two parts (Stage 7).

- Understand and use the unitary method to solve problems involving ratio and direct proportion in a range of contexts (Stage 7).

The focus of this unit is to increase learners' capability of using ratio and proportion. Learners will be familiar with simplifying ratios, sharing an amount to a given ratio and the unitary method. Learners will extend their knowledge of these skills in this unit.

TEACHING SKILLS FOCUS

Assessment for learning

A key aspect for assessment for learning is assessing prior knowledge. While the 'Getting started' exercise will help find weaknesses, much of this unit is built on previously learned skills. If any of those skills are weak or missing, it is important to revisit that area of the Stage 7 work.

You may need to adapt or stop the planned lesson if the required previous knowledge is missing. If only part of the class lacks a skill, then this is a great opportunity for you to get learners to help teach.

Show the skill required to all learners, set three or four basic questions, put learners in groups with one or two 'learners' with as many 'teachers' as possible.

Listen to the groups, ask that only one 'teacher' is speaking at any time. Regularly check with 'learners' that they understand and that the 'teacher' is giving good feedback to any questions they are asking.

Let learners self-mark their answers to the questions. Now give *slightly* harder questions to all learners, working in pairs. Arrange the pairs so that there is one 'learner' and one 'teacher' per pair if possible. Allow self-marking.

Now give one question for all learners to attempt, without help. Is there evidence of learning? Have the 'teachers' done a good job? Did the 'teachers' understand what they were teaching? Are there any aspects that you need to clarify?

At the end of Unit 12, ask yourself:

- Do you know what the learners know/knew about this topic?
- Have you asked questions to look for evidence of learning, of a depth of understanding of the topic that shows learners understand *how* the maths works, not just that they can get an answer to a question?

12.1 Simplifying ratios

LEARNING PLAN

Framework codes	Learning objectives	Success criteria
8Nf.10	• Use knowledge of equivalence to simplify and compare ratios (different units).	• Learners can simplify and compare ratios in a variety of situations including those with quantities in different units.

LANGUAGE SUPPORT

Adapt: change to make suitable for a new situation

Common factor: a number that is a factor of two or more different numbers

Highest common factor: the largest number, and/or letters, that is a factor of two or more other numbers or expressions

Ratio: an amount compared to another amount, using the symbol :

Simplify (a ratio): divide all parts of the ratio by a common factor

Common misconceptions

Misconception	How to identify	How to overcome
Learners may reverse the numbers in a ratio problem.	Question 1 parts d, e and f.	Check answers are in the correct order, e.g. part d, 6 : 1 and not 1 : 6.
Learners may simplify a ratio, but not to its simplest form.	Question 1 parts e, f, k or l.	Discuss incorrect answers.

Starter idea

Getting started (5–10 minutes)

Resources: Notebooks; Learner's Book Section 12.1, 'Getting started' questions

Description: Learners should have little difficulty with the 'Getting started' material. Before they attempt the questions, discuss what they remember about converting metric units, e.g. 100 cm = 1 m, 10 mm = 1 cm. They also need to know that 1 tonne = 1000 kg, 1 kg = 1000 g, 1 litre = 1000 ml and 1 km = 1000 m.

A few learners may need prompting with Question 3. Remind learners that sharing in a ratio is always the same method. Perhaps they remember setting out their workings like this:

   number of parts = ...

   each part = ...

   and then multiplying to work out the value of each side of the ratio.

Remember that this is not a test. It is designed to help learners cope with Unit 12. It is good practice to allow learners to attempt the questions individually, but to discuss their answers or any problems in pairs or small groups.

Main teaching idea

Side length: diagonal (5–10 minutes)

Learning intention: To use ratio in a practical setting.

Resources: Notebooks; Learner's Book; squared paper or Resource sheet 12.1 (you can download this resource from Cambridge GO)

Description: Set this activity after learners have completed Learner's Book Exercise 12.1.

Ask learners to draw five squares of different sizes. To achieve a satisfactory final outcome, they must measure these squares accurately. Make sure they use squared or graph paper and a sharp pencil.

Ask learners to measure, as accurately as they can, the side length and the diagonal length of each of their squares. For each square, learners should now find the ratio side length : diagonal length then simplify each ratio into its lowest terms.

Ask learners to discuss what they notice about these ratios. [All ratios should be approximately the same, but there will inevitably be differences, depending on measuring/drawing skills. The exact ratio is $1 : \sqrt{2}$. Learners should get approximately 5 : 7, although some may get 10 : 14 if they don't simplify it.]

Ask what ratio they think represents the class average ratio best. Ask whether that ratio is the same for very large and for very small squares. The learners themselves might give a reason why all squares seem to have the same ratio of side length to diagonal length [the squares are enlargements of each other, so are similar]. At this stage, it is enough for learners to discover that this ratio is always the same, without necessarily knowing why.

> **Differentiation ideas:** To enable all learners to use the same set of accurate squares, distribute copies of Resource sheet 12.1.

Plenary idea

Mistakes (5 minutes)

Resources: Mini whiteboards

Description: Write on the board

'Simplify 50 minutes : 2.5 hours'.

Ask learners to write down the mistakes that someone might make when trying to answer this question.

> **Assessment ideas:** Once completed, put learners into pairs. Ask them to compare answers and write down any mistakes that only one of the pair had noted. Hold a

class discussion about these less common mistakes. Can all learners see what has been done in each case, and why it is incorrect?

Some possible mistakes: 50 minutes = 0.5 hour; 2.5 hours = 250 minutes; 2.5 hours = 2 hours 50 minutes = 170 minutes; × both by 10, giving 500 minutes : 25 minutes or 50 hours : 25 hours, etc.

Guidance on selected *Thinking and working mathematically* questions

Conjecturing and Convincing

Learner's Book Exercise 12.1, Question 8

This is an example of what could be a complex question if attempted in certain ways. The easiest method is first to work out the correct ratio carefully [by simplifying 250 ml of white to 750 ml of red to 1.2 litres of yellow, getting 5 : 15 : 24]. Then learners can use this information to convince someone of whether or not Marcus or Sofia is correct. Learners often don't want to work out the question in this way as the question asks for the reasoning after asking if either person is correct. However, this is a valid method.

Homework idea

As Section 12.1 will probably take more than one lesson, you can select questions from Workbook Exercise 12.1 at the end of each lesson. Only set questions that can be answered using skills and knowledge gained from that lesson. You can help learners to mark their homework at the start of the next lesson. This means you can address any problems before moving on.

Assessment idea

Use Question 7 as an extended hinge point question. It can help you to decide whether learners are ready to move on. Ask learners to close their Learner's Books and give them mini whiteboards (or similar) to show you their answers and workings. Write one question at a time on the board. Give learners a set time to answer (e.g. 30 or 40 seconds) then ask them to show their boards.

Just using this method for the first two or three parts of Question 7 will tell you if learners need more help. If they do, you could give them examples similar to Question 2 or Question 5. Then you could ask them to finish Question 7 in their notebooks.

12.2 Sharing in a ratio

LEARNING PLAN		
Framework codes	**Learning objectives**	**Success criteria**
8Nf.11	• Understand how ratios are used to compare quantities to divide an amount into a given ratio with two or more parts.	• Learners can share an amount in a given ratio with three parts.

LANGUAGE SUPPORT	
Profit: a gain in money. You make a profit if you sell something for more than you paid for it	**Share:** to split up into parts

Common misconceptions

Misconception	How to identify	How to overcome
For a ratio such as 3 : 5 : 2, some learners will think that there are three parts, rather than the actual 10.	Question 2.	Checking answers, e.g. if answers for part a are $30, $30, $30 there is misunderstanding.

Starter idea

The method (2 minutes)

Resources: None

Description: After working through Learner's Book Worked example 12.2, emphasise the method to learners. Whenever they have to share (or divide) an amount in a given ratio, the method is always the same:

1 add the parts of the ratio,

2 divide the amount by the number of parts to find the value of one part,

3 multiply to work out the final answer.

Suggest to learners that the shortest way to set their work out is as follows. Write or display on the board:

> Number of parts = __ + __ …
> Each part = __ ÷ __
>
> A gets: __ × __
> B gets: __ × __
> Smallest part: __ × __
> etc.

Encourage learners to check that the total of all the shares is the same as the initial amount to be shared.

Main teaching idea

Jigsaw puzzle (10–15 minutes)

Learning intention: To practise simplifying ratios and sharing in a ratio.

Resources: Resource sheet 12.2 (you can download this resource from Cambridge GO)

Description: Set this activity after learners have completed Exercise 12.2.

Distribute copies of Resource sheet 12.2 and ask learners to cut out the triangles. Let learners work individually or in groups. If they work as a group, learners can compare their answers before placing a triangular piece of the jigsaw puzzle.

In completing this jigsaw, learners practise simplifying ratios and sharing in a ratio. The aim is to put the triangles together to make a hexagon. Sides of adjacent triangles that meet must match one another. Either they will be an answer and a question or a pair of equivalent ratios with one in its simplest form. Those pieces with a blank side go around the edge of the finished hexagon.

Answers:

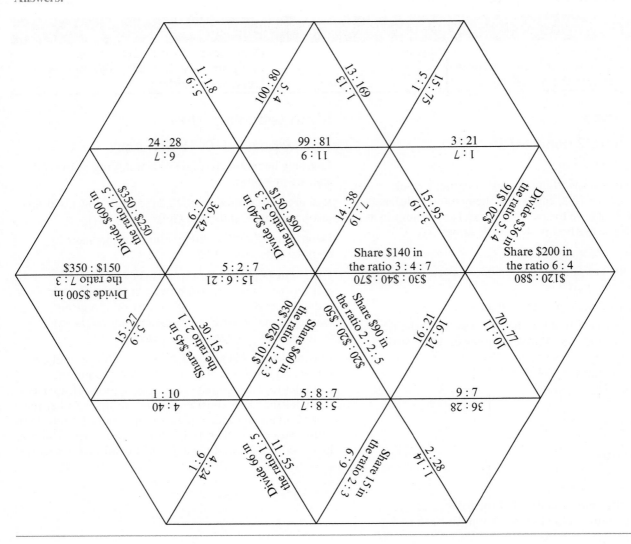

> **Differentiation ideas:** Working in larger groups will help learners who are working at a slower pace.

Plenary idea

1 : 2 : 3 : 4 (5 minutes)

Resources: Mini whiteboards or notebooks

Description: Put learners into pairs. Learners to be named **A** and **B**.

Ask learner **A** to work out the smallest share when $1000 is shared in the ratio of 1 : 2 : 3 : 4.

Ask learner **B** to work out the smallest share when $200 is shared in the ratio of 1 : 4 : 6 : 9.

Until now, learners have only shared an amount in a ratio with two or three parts, but the method is identical. Learners who have difficulty with this question after discussing it will need one-to-one help.

> **Assessment ideas:** Learner **A** explains to **B** how they answered their question, showing working and the answer [$100].

Then learner **B** explains to **A** how they answered their question, showing working and the answer [$10].

This is followed by a brief class discussion: Were methods the same? Were workings similar? Did it matter that there were four parts to the ratio rather than two or three as before?

Guidance on selected *Thinking and working mathematically* questions

Conjecturing and Convincing

Learner's Book Exercise 12.2, Question 11

Learners will say what they notice in this question then explain their reasoning. There are several ways learners can make mistakes with this type of question:

- they may be confused by the context,
- they may only share the money in the ratio for this year,
- they may only share the money in the ratio for two years' time,
- they may work out the ratios for both years but forget to work out the difference.

Suggest that learners work out how much each child will get this year, and then ask 'How old will the children be in two years' time?' When learners realise that they need to share the $300 in a new ratio, they usually succeed.

You may, however, need to make sure that learners go on to show how much less the oldest child receives in the second ratio.

Homework idea

As Section 12.2 will probably take more than one lesson, you can select questions from Workbook Exercise 12.2 at the end of each lesson. Only set questions that can be answered using skills and knowledge gained from that lesson. You can help learners to mark their homework at the start of the next lesson. This means you can address any problems before moving on.

Assessment idea

Use Question 2 as a hinge point question. It is essential that learners can confidently answer this straightforward question. If there are learners struggling to answer this question, consider giving them a few questions from Stage 7 Unit 12. This only uses two parts to the ratio. Alternatively ask other learners to explain the method to them.

Allowing a calculator will help learners to concentrate on the method rather than worrying about accuracy in their division or multiplication.

12.3 Ratio and direct proportion

LEARNING PLAN

Framework codes	Learning objectives	Success criteria
8Nf.09	• Understand and use the relationship between ratio and direct proportion.	• Learners can convert a ratio into fractions for making comparisons.

LANGUAGE SUPPORT

Comparison: to look at how things are the same or different

Justify: give a reason for your decision

Proportion: amount compared to the whole thing, usually written as a fraction, decimal or percentage

Shade: a colour which is lighter or darker than a similar colour

Common misconceptions

Misconception	How to identify	How to overcome
To use the numbers in the ratio as the numerator and denominator of the fraction, instead of using the total as the denominator, e.g. with a ratio of 3 : 7 using a fraction of $\frac{3}{7}$ rather than $\frac{3}{10}$.	Question 3.	Discussions during Worked example 12.3 and questions 1 and 2.

Starter idea

Fraction of an amount (3–5 minutes)

Resources: Mini whiteboards

Description: Write or display on the board:

1. What is $\frac{1}{2}$ of 20? **2.** What is $\frac{1}{2}$ of 24?

3. What is $\frac{1}{3} \times 24$? **4.** What is $\frac{1}{6} \times 24$?

5. What is $\frac{1}{12} \times 24$? **6.** What is $\frac{2}{3} \times 24$?

7. What is $\frac{5}{6} \times 24$? **8.** What is $\frac{3}{8} \times 24$?

Answers:
1. 10,   **2.** 12,   **3.** 8,   **4.** 4,   **5.** 2,
6. 16,   **7.** 20,   **8.** 9

Ask learners to try one question at a time and show you their answers.

Ask successful learners their method for answering the question.

Main teaching idea

Think like a mathematician, Question 12 (5 minutes)

Learning intention: To be able to understand other approaches to the same problem.

Resources: Notebooks; Learner's Book Exercise 12.3

Description: There are many possible methods of answering this question:

- compare fractions
- cancel both ratios down to simplest form then compare as fractions
- cancel both ratios down to simplest form then compare as decimals
- compare as percentages

- change the 40 : 840 into 25 : ?
- change the 25 : 535 into 40 : ?
- convert to equivalent ratios, either both into 5 : ? or both into 1 : ?

Learners' choice of method will usually be partly personal preference and partly not realising they have so many options. If learners do not have access to a calculator for converting both ratios into 5 : ?, the easiest options are using HCF or possibly changing the 40 : 840 into 25 : ?

Plenary idea

Purple paint (3 minutes)

Resources: Mini whiteboards

Description: Write or display on the board:

Royal purple paint is made by mixing red and blue paint in the ratio 2 : 3.

a What fraction of the royal purple paint is red?

b 10 litres of royal purple paint is mixed. How much blue paint was used?

Answers:

a $\frac{2}{5}$,   **b** 6 litres

> **Assessment ideas:** A quick scan of learners' boards will show you their errors. Look out for the answer $\frac{2}{3}$ in part **a** as this shows a particular lack of understanding.

Guidance on selected *Thinking and working mathematically* questions

Conjecturing and Convincing

Learner's Book Exercise 12.3, Question 9

In this question, learners will use ratios to make a comparison and justify their choice. This type of question can often be confusing for some learners.

The first common mistake is with the fractions. Any learner seen writing $\frac{2}{3}$ or $\frac{3}{7}$ instead of $\frac{2}{5}$ or $\frac{3}{10}$ will need extra guidance.

The second, more commonly occurring problem, is with misunderstanding part **b**. Some learners, even when they have the correct fractions of $\frac{2}{5}$ and $\frac{3}{10}$, are confused as to the next step.

You could start by asking learners how best to compare the two fractions. The learner needs to understand that the easiest way to compare the two fractions is to convert them to a common denominator, in this case 10. Now that learners have $\frac{4}{10}$ and $\frac{3}{10}$ they will be able to answer the question.

They also need to understand that, as the fractions refer to the amount of white, the larger the fraction the lighter the colour.

Homework ideas

As Section 12.3 will probably take more than one lesson, you can select questions from Workbook Exercise 12.3 at the end of each lesson. Only set questions that can be answered using skills and knowledge gained from that lesson. You can help learners to mark their homework at the start of the next lesson. This means you can address any problems before moving on.

You could ask learners to make a summary containing everything they think they need to remember for the end-of-unit test. The following lesson, it is important to share their summaries in class, perhaps spread out over a few desks for everyone to look at. Discuss the different summaries as a class. When the class agree that a point is important, that key point could be copied on to the board. Agree on as many key points as possible. Learners could then improve their individual summary if necessary. Learners could store their summary at home as a possible revision tool towards mid-term or end-of-year exams.

Assessment idea

Use Learner's Book Exercise 12.3, Question 10 as an extended hinge point question. It can help you decide whether learners are ready to move on.

If learners need further support with converting ratios to fractions then comparing them, show them Worked example 12.3 again. Then set Learner's Book Exercise 12.3, Question 11 under test conditions. It is important that learners understand the method. Once completed, it may be useful for learners to have a brief discussion in small groups or as a class. They should be able to explain to each other *why* the method works.

> 13 Probability

Unit plan

Topic	Approximate number of learning hours	Outline of learning content	Resources
Introduction and Getting Started	10–15 minutes		Learner's Book
13.1 Calculating probabilities	3	Calculate the probability of an event by first finding the probability of the complementary event, or by listing all the possible outcomes in a systematic way.	Learner's Book Section 13.1 Workbook Section 13.1 ⬇ Additional teaching ideas Section 13.1
13.2 Experimental and theoretical probabilities	2	Compare the results of an experiment to estimate probabilities, with the probabilities obtained from equally likely outcomes.	Learner's Book Section 13.2 Workbook Section 13.2 ⬇ Additional teaching ideas Section 13.2

Cross-unit resources

⬇ Language worksheet 13.1–13.2

⬇ Project Guidance: High fives resource sheet

⬇ Spreadsheet simulation

⬇ End of Unit 13 test

BACKGROUND KNOWLEDGE

For this unit, learners will need this background knowledge:

- Use language associated with probability such as fair, unfair, equally likely, random, bias, outcome, event (Stage 7).
- Understand that probabilities range from 0 to 1 and can be written as fractions, decimals or percentages (Stage 7).
- Recognise when outcomes are mutually exclusive and equally likely (Stage 7).
- Use equally likely outcomes to find probabilities (Stage 7).

TEACHING SKILLS FOCUS

Active learning

Traffic Lights with three colours (red, yellow and green) are a useful active learning technique.

Each learner is given three cards or slips of paper that are coloured red, yellow and green. The learner uses them to indicate how confident they are about a particular idea, technique or explanation. Ask learners to hold up the appropriate colour:

- green if they are feeling confident,
- red if they are not at all confident,
- yellow if they have some understanding but need a bit more help.

You could use something else instead of cards. Suitable resources may be available from educational suppliers.

Traffic Lights are a simple way to get learners to reflect on their own progress. They are easy to use. Learners are more willing to use these than to say that they do not understand. It also gives you instant feedback. You will know whether you need to do more teaching in response to the replies or whether you can move on to the next topic.

13.1 Calculating probabilities

LEARNING PLAN

Framework codes	Learning objectives	Success criteria
8Sp.01	• Understand that complementary events are two events that have a total probability of 1.	• Given the probability that a team will win a match, find the probability of not winning.
8Sp.02	• Understand that tables, diagrams and lists can be used to identify all mutually exclusive outcomes of combined events (independent events only).	• Show the outcomes of throwing two fair dice using a suitable diagram.
8Sp.03	• Understand how to find the theoretical probabilities of equally likely combined events.	• Use a sample space diagram to find the probabilities of a total of 10 or doubles when two unbiased dice are thrown.

LANGUAGE SUPPORT

Complementary event: two events are complementary if exactly one of them must happen

Sample space diagram: a way of showing all the possible outcomes of combined events

---

CONTINUED

For example, 'winning a match' and 'not winning a match' are complementary events. Either one event or the other must happen. The sum of their probabilities is 1. Note that 'winning a match' and 'losing a match' are *not* complementary because there is a third option of a draw. Be careful with the use of language. The key word for the complementary event is 'not'.

Notice the spelling of the word complementary. A word with the same pronunciation but different spelling and meaning is complimentary.

A sample space diagram can show the 36 possible outcomes when two fair dice are thrown. That is 1 to 6 on each dice. The outcomes are mutually exclusive.

Common misconceptions

Misconception	How to identify	How to overcome
Learners sometimes say 'either it will happen or it won't, so the probability is 50%'.	Say that a spinner can show either red or white and ask for the probability it shows red. The answer is 50% only if the areas are the same size.	Use this question with the whole class and throughout Exercise 13.1 where learners calculate the probability of a complementary event.
Lack of understanding of what constitutes equally likely outcomes.	Ask about the probabilities of 0, 1 or 2 heads when two coins are thrown. See if learners think that each event has a probability of one third.	Use diagrams in different contexts to show equally likely outcomes and use these to calculate probabilities of events.

Starter idea

Ready to start (10 minutes)

Resources: Learner's Book 'Getting started' questions

Description: Set the questions and give the learners 5 minutes to finish them. Allow learners to discuss the questions in pairs if they are stuck. They can also peer assess each other's work when they finish.

Check that all learners can calculate simple probabilities based on equally likely outcomes (questions 1 and 2), that they know when the probabilities sum to 1 (Question 3), and they can calculate an experimental probability (Question 4). All these concepts should have been covered in Stage 7.

Main teaching idea

Combined events (15 minutes)

Learning intention: Understand different ways to identify outcomes for combined events, such as throwing two fair dice.

Resources: Two unbiased dice of different colours (for example red and blue)

Description: Say that a fair dice is thrown. Ask learners for probability outcomes for 'a 2', 'a 3', 'an even number', . . . Ask learners to justify their answers. Look for the term 'equally likely' in their answers.

Now hold up the two dice, one red and one blue, and ask for the outcomes when these are thrown together. How many outcomes are there and what are they? Ask learners to discuss this in pairs for a couple of minutes then take answers. They should be able to see that any possible pair of numbers can occur. Make sure they see that pairs such as 3 and 5 can be obtained in 2 ways: red 3 and blue 5, or red 5 and blue 3.

Ask learners to list all the outcomes. They might get muddled doing this. Encourage them to be systematic. For example, start with 1 on the red dice: (1, 1), (1, 2), . . . then (2,1), (2, 2), . . . , etc. Do not spend too long on this before showing them a more efficient method, using a diagram like this:

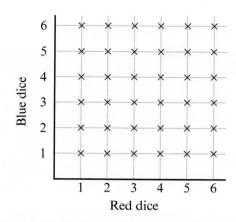

This is sometimes called a possibility diagram but learners do not need to remember that term.

Ask questions to ensure that learners can interpret particular crosses correctly.

Ask for the probability of any particular pair. There are 36 outcomes so this is $\frac{1}{36}$.

Ask which points show the same number on each dice.

There are 6 of them so the probability is $\frac{6}{36} = \frac{1}{6}$

Try other examples such as a total of 8 or a total of more than 8. These are, respectively, $\frac{5}{36}$ and $\frac{10}{36} = \frac{5}{18}$.

Illustrate them with loops on the diagram.

Say that if you are interested in the total of the two dice then a table is useful. This is also known as a sample space diagram.

Blue dice						
6	7	8	9	10	11	12
5	6	7	8	9	10	11
4	5	6	7	8	9	10
3	4	5	6	7	8	9
2	3	4	5	6	7	8
1	2	3	4	5	6	7
	1	2	3	4	5	6

Red dice

The previous answers can be found easily from this table. Learners can now answer questions in Exercise 13.1 of the Learner's Book.

> **Differentiation ideas:** The material in this activity is also covered in Worked example 13.1b. You can use that as well if learners need more support. They could copy both types of diagram in their books as reinforcement and for use in the exercise.

Plenary idea

Reflection (5 minutes)

Resources: Learner's Book Exercise 13.1, Question 11

Description: Give the learners a short time to look at Learner's Book Exercise 13.1, Question 11 if they have not already done so. Then ask what methods they have used to find outcomes. They should mention or describe possibility diagrams, 2-way tables, tree diagrams and listing systematically. They may have a preference for a particular method. Point out that the most useful method can depend on the situation. They need to be able to work with them all.

> **Assessment ideas:** Peer assessment is useful with tree diagrams and when making lists of outcomes. One learner can look at the work of another. They can compare it with their own work and check that it is correct.

Guidance on selected *Thinking and working mathematically* questions

Characterising and Classifying

Learner's Book Exercise 13.1, Question 12

Learners list all the ways of making numbers in several different situations. Doing this systematically involves a type of classifying. If they just randomly write down numbers, it is easy to miss one or duplicate another.

One systematic way is to list the numbers in order of magnitude. So if you are finding 3-digit numbers from 2, 4, 5, 8, the list starts 245, 248, 254, and so on.

An alternative way is to leave out one number at a time and make all possible numbers with the other three. So if you leave out the 2, you have six possibilities: 458, 485, 548, 584, 845, 854. Similarly for leaving out each of the other three digits.

Homework idea

Exercise 13.1 in the Workbook has further questions. You could set them all or select questions for learners to practise particular skills.

Assessment idea

Peer assessment is particularly useful in this section. A learner will get feedback much more quickly this way. They will be able to correct misconceptions and errors. This will be evident from their lists of outcomes and correctly drawn tree diagrams.

13.2 Experimental and theoretical probabilities

LEARNING PLAN

Framework codes	Learning objectives	Success criteria
8Sp.04	• Design and conduct chance experiments or simulations, using small and large numbers of trials. Compare the experimental probabilities with theoretical outcomes.	• Design and carry out an experiment to test whether a coin is being spun fairly.

LANGUAGE SUPPORT

Experimental probability: a probability resulting from an experiment involving a large number of trials

Theoretical probability: probability calculated on the basis of equally likely outcomes

Probabilities in Stage 7 were mainly theoretical ones. Also introduced in Stage 7 was the idea of using an experiment when equally likely outcomes could not be used. In this section, the emphasis is on a comparison between the theoretical and experimental probabilities. Usually when we just say 'probability' we mean theoretical probability.

Common misconceptions

Misconception	How to identify	How to overcome
Not distinguishing clearly between experimental and theoretical probability.	Ask if all numbers are equally likely when you throw a fair dice or whether some are more likely than others.	The questions in Exercise 13.2 will help to clarify the distinction. Stress that theoretical probability is based on the assumption that events are equally likely. Experimental probability is based on experience.

Starter idea

Experimental probability (5 minutes)

Resources: A box of drawing pins

Description: Learners should be familiar with relative frequency as an estimate of probability. This will remind them of that idea.

Empty the box of drawing pins on your desk. They can land point up or point down. Tell learners the number of each, point up or point down.

Ask learners to work out the experimental probability of point up. Learners should know this is the relative frequency, (number point up)/(total number). Ask for the answer as a decimal (use a calculator). It will probably need to be rounded.

Then repeat the experiment. The numbers should be different this time (if they are not do it again!) and so

the experimental probability will be different. That is the point to make here. The experimental probability can vary from one experiment to another.

We cannot find a theoretical probability in this case because the outcomes are not equally likely. However if we could, it would have just one value. It does not vary.

Main teaching idea

Comparing experimental probabilities (15 minutes)

Learning intention: Learners will start to think about the effect of the number of trials on an experimental probability.

Resources: Each learner needs a fair dice

Description: Ask each learner to throw their dice 10 times and record whether it is even or odd. Then find the experimental probability of an even number. Record all their results on the board in a tally chart.

Experimental probability	Tally
0.1	
0.2	
0.3	
0.4	
0.5	
0.6	
0.7	
0.8	
0.9	
1.0	

Briefly discuss the distribution of values. You should see a range of values with some outliers and the majority clustered around 0.5. Remind them that 0.5 is the theoretical probability if the dice is fair.

Now ask each learner to throw the dice another 10 times. Use the 20 throws to find another experimental probability. Make a second tally chart of the results. This time there could be decimals with a second digit (0.45, 0.55, 0.65, etc.), which they should round to one d.p.

Compare the two tally charts. It is likely that the values of the second chart are clustered more closely around 0.5, with fewer outliers. Learners should also appreciate that more intermediate values are possible, not just 0.4 or 0.5 and so on but also 0.45 or 0.55 and so on.

Finally ask learners what they think will happen if they throw the dice more times. They should appreciate that the likelihood of it being close to 0.5 increases as the number of throws increases.

> **Differentiation ideas:** More confident learners can be encouraged to work together to pool their results and get a larger number of trials. They can find the experimental probability and see if it is close to 0.5.

You could also ask more confident learners to draw a diagram to illustrate the two sets of experimental probabilities. A bar chart is the most likely choice.

Learners who find this difficult could work in pairs with one person throwing the dice and the other person recording the results.

Plenary idea

Reflection (10 minutes)

Resources: None

Description: Say that a spinner has a number of sectors, all equally likely, numbered 1, 2, etc. Say that the spinner is spun a number of times and the experimental probability of 1 is found. Show the learners this table but only put numbers in the first column (20 spins). $P(1)$ means the experimental probability of getting a 1.

Spins	20	50	100	200	500
P(1)	0.45	0.3	0.26	0.22	0.210

Ask how many sectors they think there are. Since the probability is 0.45 they are like to say 2 (theoretical probability 0.5) or 3 (theoretical probability 0.333).

Now add the second column (50 spins). What do they think now? Does anyone want to change their mind? Other theoretical probabilities are 0.25 for 4 sectors and 0.2 for 5 sectors.

Repeat this with the last 3 columns, adding them one at a time and asking each time if anyone wants to change their mind. By the end most learners will probably have decided there are 5 sectors.

Emphasise the fact that you cannot be sure. The way the values are changing as the number of spins increases makes 5 sectors a sensible *conjecture*.

You could end the plenary at that point. If learners are interested you could show them these results for a second set of spins.

Spins	20	50	100	200	500
P(1)	0.3	0.32	0.31	0.29	0.24

What do learners think now?

And here is a third set.

Spins	20	50	100	200	500
P(1)	0.15	0.14	0.13	0.16	0.174

What do learners think now?

Note: the results in the three tables were obtained from computer simulations. The author has chosen not to reveal the number of sectors in the simulation so you cannot be absolutely sure you are correct.

> **Assessment ideas:** You will be able to see if there are learners who cannot decide about a likely value for the

number of sectors. Ask a learner who has decided on the value to explain their decision and to try to convince the others.

Guidance on selected *Thinking and working mathematically* questions

Conjecturing and Convincing

Learner's Book Exercise 13.2, Activity 13.2

Learners design an experiment to answer a question. They will need to make a conjecture and then decide how to collect evidence to test it with experimental probabilities. Planning this before starting is an important skill. Questions that simply give learners instructions on how to do a task would not develop this skill.

Homework ideas

Workbook Exercise 13.2 has extra questions. You could use all the questions or a selection.

Learners may have access to a computer spreadsheet at home. In that case it may be possible to set questions from Learner's Book Exercise 13.2 as a homework. It would be a good idea to show learners in the classroom how they can start. For some guidance, see 'A spreadsheet simulation' (you can download this resource from Cambridge GO).

Assessment idea

The traffic light assessment idea described in the Teaching skills focus for Unit 13 is one that can easily be used in many situations. It is a simple form of self-assessment and gives you, the teacher, instant feedback to help you plan your future teaching.

PROJECT GUIDANCE: HIGH FIVES

Why do this problem?

In this problem, learners are invited to explore the distribution of the larger of a pair of random numbers. They will also critique experimental and theoretical approaches to calculating probabilities. Learners can use sample space diagrams. These will help them notice patterns, make conjectures and generalise for cases that are too large to explore experimentally.

Possible approach

This problem offers a great opportunity to do some work with spreadsheets. Learners could use the random number function to generate a set of 100 pairs of random numbers. Then they could find the larger of the two random numbers and plot a graph showing the distribution. Alternatively, learners could generate random numbers using spinners, dice or counters.

Invite learners to imagine spinning two 1 to 5 spinners and writing down the higher of the two numbers. If they did this lots of times, how often would they expect to write each of the numbers from 1 to 5? Give them a short time to think and then discuss with a partner, before sharing ideas. Learners may intuitively realise that 5 will appear much more often than 1. They may not have a sense of the proportions of each number.

Introduce the experiment. Give learners time to perform or simulate 100 trials. Ask them to represent their results, perhaps as a bar chart. Then share with learners the idea that mathematicians often use theoretical probabilities as a way to explain and understand experimental data. As a class, fill in the sample space diagram for two 1–5 spinners. Invite learners to reflect on any patterns they see.

Next, invite learners to picture what the sample space diagram might look like for: two 1–6 spinners, two 1–7 spinners, two 1–20 spinners or even two 1–100 spinners. Can they work out how many times each number will appear on each sample space diagram?

One way to finish off the lesson could be to simulate a large number of trials for a 1–10 spinner. See how closely the distribution from the simulation matches the prediction from the sample space diagram.

Key questions

What needs to happen on the two spinners in order for me to write down a 1?

If I get a 4 on the first 1 to 5 spinner, how likely is it that I will write down a 4?

Where do the 1s appear in the sample space diagram? The 2s? The 3s? . . .

How many times will each number appear?

Possible support

Learners could start by exploring spinners with fewer numbers and work up to a spinner showing 1 to 5.

Possible extension

In the sample space diagrams, each number appears an odd number of times. Learners could explore why the sequence of odd numbers always adds up to a square number.

> 14 Position and transformation

Unit plan

Topic	Approximate number of learning hours	Outline of learning content	Resources
Introduction and Getting Started	15 minutes		Learner's Book
14.1 Bearings	0.5–1	Understand and use bearings.	Learner's Book Section 14.1 Workbook Section 14.1 ⬇ Additional teaching ideas Section 14.1 ⬇ Resource sheet 14.1A ⬇ Resource sheet 14.1B
14.2 The midpoint of a line segment	1	Use coordinates to find the midpoint of a line segment.	Learner's Book Section 14.2 Workbook Section 14.2 ⬇ Additional teaching ideas Section 14.2
14.3 Translating 2D shapes	1	Translate points and 2D shapes using vectors.	Learner's Book Section 14.3 Workbook Section 14.3 ⬇ Additional teaching ideas Section 14.3 ⬇ Resource sheet 14.3
14.4 Reflecting shapes	1–1.5	Reflect 2D shapes and points in a given mirror line. Identify a reflection and its mirror line.	Learner's Book Section 14.4 Workbook Section 14.4 ⬇ Additional teaching ideas Section 14.4 ⬇ Resource sheet 14.4A ⬇ Resource sheet 14.4B
14.5 Rotating shapes	1	To be able to rotate shapes and describe rotations on a coordinate grid.	Learner's Book Section 14.5 Workbook Section 14.5 ⬇ Additional teaching ideas Section 14.5 ⬇ Exit ticket 14.5 ⬇ Resource sheet 14.5A ⬇ Resource sheet 14.5B

Topic	Approximate number of learning hours	Outline of learning content	Resources
14.6 Enlarging shapes	1–1.5	Enlarge 2D shapes using a centre of enlargement. When given an object and its image, work out the scale factor.	Learner's Book Section 14.6 Workbook Section 14.6 ⬇ Additional teaching ideas Section 14.6 ⬇ Resource sheet 14.6A ⬇ Resource sheet 14.6B ⬇ Resource sheet 14.6C

Cross-unit resources

⬇ Resource sheet 14.6 Key words

⬇ Language worksheet 14.1–14.3

⬇ Language worksheet 14.4–14.6

⬇ End of Unit 14 test

BACKGROUND KNOWLEDGE

For this unit, learners will need this background knowledge:

- Use knowledge of 2D shapes and coordinates to find the distance between two coordinates that have the same x or y coordinate (Stage 7).

- Translate 2D shapes, identifying the corresponding points between the original and the translated image, on coordinate grids (Stage 6).

- Reflect 2D shapes on coordinate grids, in a given mirror line (x- or y-axis), recognising that the image is congruent to the object after a reflection (Stage 7).

- Rotate shapes 90° and 180° around a centre of rotation, recognising that the image is congruent to the object after a rotation (Stage 7).

- Understand that the image is mathematically similar to the object after enlargement. Use positive integer scale factors to perform and identify enlargements (Stage 7).

Learners will deepen their knowledge and extend their use of reflection, rotation and translation from Stage 7. Bearings are also introduced as a measure of direction.

TEACHING SKILLS FOCUS

Language awareness

To help you to highlight and concentrate on language awareness it is a good idea, before the lesson, to be aware of the key words learners will meet during this unit. Make sure you are clear in your understanding of the key words before the lesson. Use the Glossary if necessary.

Give all learners a copy of Resource sheet 14.6 Key words. (You can download this resource from

Cambridge GO.) Read out each word in turn. Afterwards, ask learners 'Do you know what any of these key words mean?' Discuss any ideas learners have. Emphasise that by the end of the unit they will know the meaning of all of these key words. Refer to the worksheet as you work through the unit. Encourage learners to fill in the meaning of a word in the list when they meet each one in the unit, including an example too.

CONTINUED

During each section, refer to the key words as often as possible and encourage learners to use the key words during any classroom discussions. When the opportunity arises, e.g. when one learner has used a key word, ask another learner what the key word means. If you do this throughout the unit, you could give learners a copy of Resource sheet 14.6 Key words as a class test at the end of Section 14.6.

Alternatively, you could introduce the resource sheet at the end of the unit.

When you reach the end of Section 14.6, ask yourself: Do the learners understand and feel confident in using the key words? If the answer is yes, then this work has been successful. If the answer is no, then think how you can change the way you approached discussing and using the key words.

14.1 Bearings

LEARNING PLAN

Framework codes	Learning objectives	Success criteria
8Gp.01	• Understand and use bearings as a measure of direction.	• Learners understand that a bearing is measured from <u>north</u> in a <u>clockwise</u> direction.

LANGUAGE SUPPORT

Bearing: an angle measured clockwise from north

North in these types of questions will always be vertically up the page.

Common misconceptions

Misconception	How to identify	How to overcome
Some learners may measure the acute angle when inappropriate.	Worked example discussions and almost all questions.	Remind the class repeatedly that a bearing is *always* measured from north and *always* measured clockwise.
Learners not measuring accurately due to incorrect usage of a protractor.	Questions 1 and 2.	Ensure thorough checking of these answers to ensure all learners are using their protractors correctly.
Some learners may not know what 'north' refers to.	Introduction.	A brief discussion about the four points of the compass and how that is used for direction finding.

Using copies of Resource sheet 14.1A can help learners who might struggle to use a protractor on the book. The diagrams are larger than those in the book and this will help some learners. (You can download this resource from Cambridge GO.)

Starter idea

Getting started (15 minutes)

Resources: Notebooks; Learner's Book Section 14.1, 'Getting started' questions

Description: A few learners may need help with Question 1. Ask learners to measure the angle [it is 30°]. Check that learners' answers are no more than 2° in error [i.e. answer between 28° and 32°]. Any more than 2° error usually indicates some mistake in positioning the protractor or in reading it.

It is probably best to ask learners to answer one question then check their answers. You can deal with any misunderstanding before moving on to the next question. Remember that this is not a test but it is designed to help learners cope with Unit 14. It is good practice to allow learners to attempt the questions as individuals. Depending on the question, they can then discuss their answers or any problems in pairs, small groups or as a whole class.

Note how well learners copy and use their diagrams from Questions 4, 5 and 6. This will help you decide whether or not to use copies of diagrams in Resource sheet 14.1A.

Main teaching idea

Going for a walk (5 minutes)

Learning intention: Using bearings in real-life situations.

Resources: Notebooks; Learner's Book; Resource sheet 14.1B (you can download this resource from Cambridge GO)

Description: Learners can attempt this activity at any time after they have followed through Worked example 14.1. It will be most beneficial after they have at least worked beyond Question 3. Learners should work individually. Each learner requires a copy of Resource sheet 14.1B.

These are the questions on Resource sheet 14.1B [with answers in brackets]:

1   Alan is walking on a bearing of 135° and meets Birra who is walking on a bearing of 170°. They stop for a chat. On what bearing must Elise walk to meet with Alan and Birra? [072° ± 2°]

2   Chan is walking on a bearing of 265° and meets Dillan who is walking on a bearing of 315°. They stop for a chat. On what bearing must Freddie walk to meet with Chan and Dillan? [158° ± 2°]

The starting positions of all the people mentioned in the questions are given on the sheet.

Learners should draw bearings as accurately as possible in order to answer the two questions.

> **Differentiation ideas:** The activity can be extended by asking similar questions based on the same sheet. For example:

1   Alan is walking on a bearing of 165° and meets Elise who is walking on a bearing of 050°. They stop and talk. On what bearing must Birra walk to meet Alan and Elise? [192° ± 2°]

2   Chan is walking on a bearing of 005° and meets Freddie who is walking on a bearing of 095°. They stop for a chat. On what bearing must Dillan walk to meet with Chan and Freddie? [038° ± 2°]

Extend the activity further by asking learners to make up their own questions, based on Resource sheet 14.1B. They can exchange sheets with a partner and answer each other's questions.

Plenary idea

A from B (2 minutes)

Resources: Mini whiteboards

Description: Sketch or display on the board:

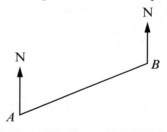

Ask learners to write down the bearing of A from B when the bearing of B from A is 040° [220°].

> **Assessment ideas:** If anyone shows a bearing of any other number, ask a successful learner to explain how they got the answer. If needed, give another value for the bearing of B from A, e.g. 070°, and ask for the bearing of A from B [250°]. Repeat this process until all learners are correct.

Guidance on selected *Thinking and working mathematically* questions

Conjecturing and Convincing

Learner's Book Exercise 14.1, Question 3

Learners will say what they notice and explain it. They are likely to check the angle first [32°]. At this point some learners will be confused and think they have read the question incorrectly. They may try to measure the bearing of A from B. Other learners will think that Freya is correct as the angle is 32° as she has said. It is useful to have a class discussion of learners' answers to deal with these misunderstandings. They need to remember that bearings are always written with three digits. So, Freya is correct that the angle is 32°, but incorrect that the bearing is 32°. The bearing is written as 032°.

Homework idea

As Section 14.1 will probably take more than one lesson, you can select questions from Workbook Exercise 14.1 at the end of each lesson. Only set questions that can be answered using skills and knowledge gained from that lesson. You can help learners to mark their homework at the start of the next lesson. This means you can address any problems before moving on.

Assessment idea

This can be used at or near the end of exercise 14.1.

Learners studied compass points [cardinal (N, E, S and W) and ordinal (NE, SE, SW and NW)]

in Stage 4. Many learners may have forgotten these lessons, but a diagram will help. Draw or display on the board:

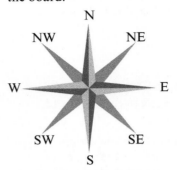

Ask learners for the bearing of

- east [090°]
- south [180°]
- south-east [135°] Check carefully that learners have the correct answer. Ask successful learners to explain how they got their answer if necessary.
- west [270°]
- north-west [315°] Again check carefully that learners have worked this out correctly.

Say to learners 'Ali is driving south-west. In his rear-view mirror he sees a building directly behind him. What is the three figure bearing of the building from his current position?' [045°].

Say 'Billar is walking in a north-west direction. She turns right, 90°. What is the three figure bearing of her direction now?' [045°].

Say 'Cathy is facing north east. How many degrees does she have to turn clockwise to face south?' [135°].

14.2 The midpoint of a line segment

LEARNING PLAN		
Framework codes	**Learning objectives**	**Success criteria**
8Gp.02	• Use knowledge of coordinates to find the midpoint of a line segment.	• Learners can find the midpoint of a line segment given any two integer coordinates.

LANGUAGE SUPPORT

Line segment: a part of a straight line between two points

Midpoint: the centre point of a line segment

Common misconceptions

Misconception	How to identify	How to overcome
When adding x and y coordinates and dividing by two to find midpoints, learners may forget to include any negative signs in their calculations.	Question 8.	Check answers to Question 8 carefully. Look out for answers of (3.5, 4), (3.5, 2.5) or (8.5, 7.5) indicating this error. Use starter idea 'Horizontal or vertical' (you can download this resource from Cambridge GO).

Starter idea

Halfway between (5 minutes)

Resources: Mini whiteboards

Description: Ask learners to work out the number which is halfway between:

2 and 4 [3], 2 and 6 [4], 4 and 6 [5], 4 and 10 [7].

Ask learners for the methods they used to work out the answer. Discuss which are most efficient or easiest methods.

Ask, 'What is halfway between . . .':

2 and 3 [2.5], 3 and 6 [4.5], 5 and 10 [7.5], 2 and 13 [7.5].

Ask learners for the methods they used to work out the answer. Were they the same as before? Have learners changed their method?

Ask learners to work out the number which is halfway between 2 and −4 [−1]. Check answers immediately, discuss as a class the best method.

Ask learners to work out the number which is halfway between:

5 and −10 [−2.5], 4 and −12 [−4], 10 and −10 [0]. Ask again about methods. Ask if any learners have changed their method.

Ask learners to work out the number which is halfway between:

−2 and −4 [−3], −2 and −6 [−4], −4 and −6 [−5], −4 and −11 [−7.5]. Only discuss methods here if learners are making mistakes.

Main teaching idea

Think like a mathematician, Question 7 (5 minutes)

Learning intention: To understand a possible error when using a new method.

Resources: Notebooks; Learner's Book Exercise 14.2

Description: The mistake made by Shen is a common one. Shen has added the negative numbers incorrectly in both coordinates. Tell learners that this is the type of simple error which even occurs in exams. They should always take care when dealing with negative numbers.

Part **b** may require a class discussion. We know that $2 + 3$ and $3 + 2$ give the same answer (as do $4 − 5$ and $−5 + 4$, etc). For the same reason, adding two coordinates together in either order gives the same answer.

⟩ **Differentiation ideas:** Learners who find this difficult should carefully work out the midpoint themselves. Then they can compare their answer with the two options. This is usually the easiest method of spotting errors.

Plenary idea

Online midpoints (5–10 minutes)

Resources: Mini whiteboards

Description: Type 'transum.org, coordinates' into a search engine. When directed to the page, learners will complete the level 5 material. This material changes every time it is clicked on, so no two sessions are the same.

This is a free resource and learners can access this too. They may wish to practise at home so make sure they write down the web address of this resource. There are many other similar resources available. If you use an electronic whiteboard, all learners see the same questions. If you use a suite of computers or tablets, learners will see different questions.

If learners struggle to answer, it is often because they are too far from the grid to count accurately. Learners using their own computer or tablet don't have this issue. If using an electronic whiteboard, allow learners to come to the board where they can count the horizontal and vertical distances between points. Then they can halve the values and count on the grid to the position of the midpoint.

> **Assessment ideas:** Ask learners in turn for an answer then you type the answer. (Alternatively, you could put learners into pairs or small groups first and ask each pair or group in turn.) Ask the rest of the class if they agree. If learners disagree, they should not just say the correct answer. You should ask them to explain what mistake may have been made. Check using the button below the questions. Then either get learners to try again (if incorrect) or congratulate them and continue.

Guidance on selected *Thinking and working mathematically* questions

Conjecturing and Convincing

Learner's Book Exercise 14.2, Question 11

Some learners will need to draw a grid and plot the points. You should discourage this unless it is essential for the learner to achieve success. If it is required,

encourage a quick sketch rather than an accurate diagram. Preferably, learners should think through the problem. They should realise that the two line segments (diagonals) are (−2, 1) to (5, 2) and (0, 4) to (1, −1). From this they can work out that the midpoints are (1.5, 1.5) and (0.5, 1.5) respectively. So they can use their thinking to convince someone that the diagonals do not have the same midpoint.

Homework idea

As Section 14.2 will probably take more than one lesson, you can select questions from Workbook Exercise 14.2 at the end of each lesson. Only set questions that can be answered using skills and knowledge gained from that lesson. You can help learners to mark their homework at the start of the next lesson. This means you can address any problems before moving on.

Assessment idea

Use Question 6, part **a** as a hinge point question to help you decide whether learners are ready to move on. It is essential that learners understand this method, as it will be the method they use from now on. Ask learners to answer part **a**, then to work with a partner to compare their method and answer. Any pair with either a different method or answer should ask you to check. The method can be flexible, depending on the ability of the learner, but obviously the answer must be (10, 4). If there have been mistakes, repeat this process for part **b**.

14.3 Translating 2D shapes

LEARNING PLAN		
Framework codes	**Learning objectives**	**Success criteria**
8Gp.03	• Translate points and 2D shapes using vectors, recognising that the image is congruent to the object after a translation.	• Learners can translate shapes on a coordinate grid using vectors.

LANGUAGE SUPPORT

Column vector: two numbers, placed vertically, that describe a translation of a point or shape; the top number describes the horizontal movement, while the bottom number describes the vertical movement

Congruent: identical in shape and size

Image: a shape after a transformation

Object: a shape before a transformation

Translate: transform a shape by moving each part of the shape the same distance in the same direction

---

Common misconceptions

Misconception	How to identify	How to overcome
Thinking the column vector $\begin{pmatrix} 2 \\ 5 \end{pmatrix}$ means move 5 units right and 2 units up.	Worked example and all questions.	Question 1 is designed to stop this error.

Lack of accuracy causes the most problems. The most common issue is drawing the shape itself on to a grid. Using Resource sheet 14.3 can eliminate the need for learners to copy diagrams in Exercise 14.3, Questions 2, 3, 6 and 10. It will also save a great deal of time in the classroom. (You can download this resource from Cambridge GO.)

Starter idea

Translation (3–5 minutes)

Resources: Mini whiteboards or notebooks

Description: Ask learners to quickly sketch a coordinate grid with each axis from 0 to 5.

Ask learners to follow each of these steps in turn:

a Draw a clear dot at the coordinate (2, 3) and label the point A.

b Translate point A 2 units right and 2 units up. Label the point P.

c Translate point A 2 units right and 1 unit down. Label the point Q.

d Translate point A 1 unit left and 2 units down. Label the point R.

e Translate point A 1 unit left and 1 unit up. Label the point S.

f Name the quadrilateral PQRS [parallelogram, vertices at (4, 5), (4, 2), (1, 1) and (1, 4)].

Main teaching idea

Online vector problems (5–10 minutes)

Learning intention: To attempt a variety of vector problems.

Resources: Mini whiteboards or access to computer/tablet

Description: Use this idea at or near the end of Exercise 14.3.

Type 'transum.org, transformations' into a search engine. When directed to the page, learners will complete the level 2 material. This material changes every time it is clicked on, so no two sessions are the same. This is a free resource and learners can access this too. They may wish to practise at home so make sure they write down the web address of this resource. There are many other similar resources available. Remember that the questions tend to get harder further down the page. You should think about which question to ask which learner. If you use an electronic whiteboard, all learners see the same questions. If you use a suite of computers or tablets, learners will see different questions.

Ask learners in turn for an answer. Alternatively you can put them into pairs or small groups first and ask each pair or group in turn. Ask the rest of the class if they agree. If learners disagree, ask them to explain what mistake may have been made. Check using the button below the questions. Then either get them to retry (if incorrect) or congratulate them and continue.

If each learner has individual access to the site you may wish to limit the time taken on the activity. It may help to have two learners per computer or tablet. This will lead to differentiation by outcome, but hopefully all learners will be successful and practise a valuable skill.

> **Differentiation ideas:** Working together and having the answer checker freely available helps almost all learners gain some level of success.

Plenary idea

Translate the point (3–5 minutes)

Resources: Mini whiteboards

Description: Ask learners to draw a horizontal line halfway down their boards and a vertical line halfway across their boards. Next, ask learners to plot using an 'x' where they think the point (5, 2) would be on their grid.

Ask learners to translate their point using the column vector:

$\begin{pmatrix} -6 \\ 1 \end{pmatrix}$, then label the point ①.

$\begin{pmatrix} 2 \\ 2 \end{pmatrix}$, then label the point ②.

$\begin{pmatrix} -5 \\ -5 \end{pmatrix}$, then label the point ③.

$\begin{pmatrix} 1 \\ -4 \end{pmatrix}$, then label the point ④.

> **Assessment ideas:** Ask learners to compare boards with a partner and discuss any differences. You may be asked to decide whose board is correct. This is usefully done on an individual basis. Note the quadrant where each point lies, even though the exact position of their original point is not known.

You could draw or display:

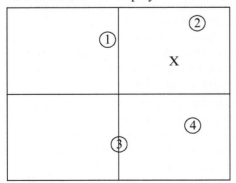

Guidance on selected *Thinking and working mathematically* questions

Specialising and Generalising

Learner's Book Exercise 14.3, Question 6

In this question, learners will work with particular triangles then generalise later. Most or all learners should be able to complete parts **a** and **b** successfully. You could allow learners to use the diagram on Resource sheet 14.3 to speed up **a**. It may also lead to better accuracy with part **b** if some learners have difficulty with accurate copying. (You can download this resource from Cambridge GO.)

The main idea of this question is to confirm what learners should already know: the object and image are congruent after a translation. It is important to discuss learners' answers to part **c**. You can reinforce the idea that the object and image are congruent. Learners can discuss the reasons why they are congruent.

Homework idea

As Section 14.3 will probably take more than one lesson, you can select questions from Workbook Exercise 14.3 at the end of each lesson. Only set questions that can be answered using skills and knowledge gained from that lesson. You can help learners to mark their homework at the start of the next lesson. This means you can address any problems before moving on.

Assessment idea

Write/display on the board:

Object coordinate	translation vector
(5, 5)	$\begin{pmatrix} 2 \\ 4 \end{pmatrix}$
(4, 7) (3, 4)	
(−3, −3) (−5, 0)	$\begin{pmatrix} 0 \\ 1 \end{pmatrix}$ $\begin{pmatrix} -2 \\ 5 \end{pmatrix}$
(0, 0)	

In this game, the winner is the person who is quickest at saying the coordinates of the image.

Put learners into pairs. Point to a coordinate then a vector. The first learner to say the correct image coordinate is the winner. Then move on to the next pair, and give them a different coordinate and vector. Repeat this process until all learners have had a turn.

Next put 'winners' into pairs and repeat the process. (They do not need to move next to each other.) Then put these 'winners' into pairs and repeat until you have one final winner.

If this is a fast game, try it several times, hopefully with a different winner. Learners will almost certainly get a different question to answer.

14.4 Reflecting shapes

LEARNING PLAN

Framework codes	Learning objectives	Success criteria
8Gp.04	• Reflect 2D shapes and points in a given mirror line on or parallel to the x- or y-axis, $y = \pm x$ on coordinate grids. Identify a reflection and its mirror line.	• Learners can reflect a shape on a coordinate grid in the lines $x =$ 'a number', $y =$ 'a number', $y = x$ and $y = -x$. • Learners can identify a reflection and describe its mirror line.

LANGUAGE SUPPORT

Equation: a way of labelling a line on a grid

Mirror line: a line dividing a diagram into two parts, each being a mirror image of the other

Reflect: to draw the image of a shape as seen in a mirror

Common misconceptions

Misconception	How to identify	How to overcome
Learners may use the wrong mirror line, for example, reflecting in $x = 4$ instead of $y = 4$.	Questions 1 to 5.	Regularly refer to Section 14.4 Introduction and Worked examples.
Learners often make mistakes reflecting shapes in the $y = \pm x$ line. The image may look as though it has been reflected in a vertical or horizontal line rather than a diagonal one.	Questions 6 and 9.	Encourage learners to rotate their notebooks so that the line of symmetry appears vertical. Most learners will quickly identify any mistake they have made.

If you use Resource sheet 14.4A, learners will not need to copy diagrams in Questions 1, 2, 3, 4, 5, 6, 8, 9, 10 or Activity 14.4. It will save a great deal of time in the classroom. (You can download this resource from Cambridge GO.)

Starter idea

Reflections (5 minutes)

Resources: Resource sheet 14.4B (you can download this resource from Cambridge GO)

Description: Distribute copies of the two diagrams on Resource sheet 14.4B. Ask learners to complete both drawings, using reflection to position the triangles. Each grid will require learners to draw three reflected triangles. Once completed, learners could check each other's drawings with a partner. When they have finished, discuss:

- which drawing was easier,
- why the other one was more difficult,
- which methods seemed to make the more difficult one a little easier.

Main teaching idea

Activity 14.4 (5–10 minutes)

Learning intention: To reflect accurately a rectangle in both the lines $y = x$ and $y = -x$. To check images drawn by others.

Resources: Learner's Book Exercise 14.4, Activity 14.4; squared paper

Description: Tell learners that their rectangle can be of any size, but it must fit within the shaded area shown. Vertices of the rectangle can, if desired, be located on the 45° diagonal lines. Display an example grid to the class to illustrate what you mean:

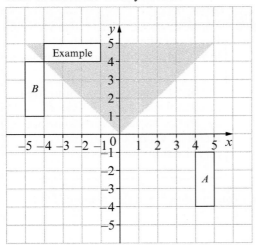

> **Differentiation ideas:** To extend, ask learners to draw a triangle on their diagram using the coordinates (3, 3), (−1, 3) and (−1, 4). Ask them to reflect the triangle in the lines $y = x$ and $y = -x$. Learners can then compare answers with a partner to check accuracy. You could also ask learners to use their rules from questions 7 and 9 to check the coordinates.

Answers: Extension: $y = x$ reflection has coordinates (3, 3), (3, −1) and (4, −1); $y = -x$ reflection has coordinates (−3, −3), (−3, 1) and (−4, 1).

Plenary idea

Online reflection check (5–10 minutes)

Resources: Mini whiteboards or access to computer or tablet

Description: Type 'transum.org, transformations' into a search engine. When directed to the page, learners will complete the level 1 material. This material changes every time it is clicked on, so no two sessions are the same. This is a free resource and learners can access this too. They may wish to practise at home so make sure they write down the web address of this resource. There are many other similar resources available. Remember that the questions tend to get harder further down the page. You should think about which question to ask which learner. If you use an electronic whiteboard, all learners see the same questions. If you use a suite of computers or tablets, learners will see different questions.

Ask learners in turn for an answer. Alternatively you could put them into pairs or small groups first and ask each pair or group in turn. Ask the rest of the class if they agree. If learners disagree, ask them to explain what mistake may have been made. Check using the button below the questions. Then either get them to try again (if incorrect) or congratulate them and continue.

If each learner has individual access to the site you may wish to limit the time taken on the activity. This will lead to differentiation by outcome, but hopefully all learners will be successful and practise a valuable skill.

> **Assessment ideas:** If you do this as a class activity, you can mark the answers with the class. If learners have access to their own computers or tablets, they should mark each shape as they complete it. If learners are working on their own computers or tablets, move about the class and note learners who find this work very easy. When they finish, these learners could help explain the required skills to other learners.

Guidance on selected *Thinking and working mathematically* questions

Specialising and Generalising

Learner's Book Exercise 14.4, Question 9

This question is closely linked with Question 7 as the skills needed are the same. Learners will draw a table to show coordinates. They will notice the way that the x and y coordinates change when an object has been reflected in the line $y = -x$. Then they will generalise by putting those thoughts into words.

Depending on the ability of your class, you may decide to allow learners to work in pairs or small groups to write the rule. As with Question 7, discuss the various ways that learners have tried to explain the 'rule'. Write a few of their rules on the board. That may help learners to see the similarities. Decide as a class the clearest rule and ask all learners to write it in their notebooks. The exact wording of the rule is not particularly important but learners must think how to express it. Saying that the values of the x and y coordinates swap over and change sign is enough.

Homework idea

As Section 14.4 will probably take more than one lesson, you can select questions from Workbook Exercise 14.4

at the end of each lesson. Only set questions that can be answered using skills and knowledge gained from that lesson. You can help learners to mark their homework at the start of the next lesson. This means you can address any problems before moving on.

Assessment ideas

With so many diagrams, this is an excellent opportunity for peer marking. If learners regularly exchange books to check, it helps them to focus on the important aspects of the work. With practice, learners should become better assessors of their own and other's work. You could ask them to work in pairs or groups.

Ask if any learners have made a mistake but know what they did wrong. Ask them if they know how to get that type of question correct next time. These are active learners who need encouraging with a 'well done'.

Also ask if learners have made a mistake but do not know what they have done wrong or how to correct it. Depending on the question, and the learner, it may be worth helping that learner separately. Alternatively you could ask learners near them to explain or you could hold a class discussion on that particular question or skill.

14.5 Rotating shapes

LEARNING PLAN

Framework codes	Learning objectives	Success criteria
8Gp.05	• Understand that the centre of rotation, direction of rotation and angle are needed to identify and perform rotations.	• Learners can describe rotations and rotate shapes on a coordinate grid.

LANGUAGE SUPPORT

Anticlockwise: turning in the opposite direction to the hands of a clock

Centre of rotation: the point that remains still when a shape is turned

Clockwise: turning in the same direction as the hands of a clock

Common misconceptions

Misconception	How to identify	How to overcome
Lack of accuracy will cause the majority of problems. This may be with drawing the shape or with placing the point of the pencil on the centre of rotation when using tracing paper.	Almost all questions in this section require accuracy.	Practice. You can use Resource sheet 14.5A so that copying grids or shapes inaccurately will not be part of the problem.

Use Resource sheet 14.5A so that learners do not need to copy diagrams. It will also save a great deal of time in the classroom. (You can download this resource from Cambridge GO.)

Tracing paper should be available for all learners for this section.

Starter idea

Online rotations (5–10 minutes)

Resources: Electronic whiteboard or suite of computers/tablets

Description: Type 'transum.org, rotation' into a search engine. When directed to the page, learners attempt level 3, but only the first seven questions. They should not attempt the last five questions (which use rotations of 270°).

If this is a class exercise using the electronic board, ask learners to give coordinates of vertices. Ask other learners if they agree and then check. If learners have their own computer tablet, be aware that the page may be different for each learner. The shapes and the rotations are the same but the location of the shape on the grid changes. As with other pages of this type, learners mark the vertices of the rotated shape and can then check using the button at the bottom of the questions. This is a free resource and learners can access this too. They may wish to practise at home so make sure they write down the web address of this resource. There are many other similar resources available.

Ask 'Without tracing paper, what methods have you used to help you work out where the vertices of the image will be?'

Main teaching idea

Rotation (5–10 minutes)

Learning intention: To be able to describe a variety of rotations.

Resources: Notebooks; Learner's Book; Resource sheet 14.5B (you can download this resource from Cambridge GO); tracing paper

Description: To be used after completing Exercise 14.5. Split the class into teams of three or four learners. Each team will need a copy of Resource sheet 14.5B. The winner is the first team to give the correct information for rotating each shape 1 onto its image, shape 2.

Access to tracing paper is important here. This will help with accuracy and careful checking of answers. It is expected that tracing paper is used in questions of this type in examinations.

Even after completing Questions 7, 8 and 9 from Exercise 14.5 some learners will find this activity quite difficult. Most learners will tackle it with a trial and improvement method. With practice, however, the number of trials will decrease. They will become more familiar with this type of question, recognising more easily how to find the centre of rotational symmetry.

Answers:
Learners should identify the rotations as:
a rotation 90° anticlockwise, centre (2, 4)
  or rotation 90°, clockwise centre (4.5, 6.5)
b rotation 180°, centre (3, 4)
c rotation 180°, centre (4, 4)
d rotation 90° anticlockwise, centre (4, 3)
e rotation 180°, centre (5, 4)
f rotation 90° anticlockwise, centre (0.5,5)
  or rotation 90° clockwise, centre (4, 1.5)

> **Differentiation ideas:** If learners struggle with this topic, revisit Question 7. Emphasise how to work out the centre of rotation using tracing paper.

Plenary idea

Exit ticket (3–4 minutes)

Resources: Tracing paper; exit ticket for each learner (cut these out from Exit ticket 14.5. You can download this resource from Cambridge GO)

Description: On the sheet, there are two types of exit tickets. Give half of the class one version, the other half the other version. Ask learners to complete their exit ticket and give it to you at the end of the lesson.

> **Assessment ideas:** A key aspect of understanding what learners have understood, and how to help them, is to read what learners *think* they have learned. It will also help you to clarify teaching points for individual learners or the class for future lessons. [Coordinates for the image are (−1, 2), (−1, 4), (0, 4), (1, 3) and (1, 2). Description of the rotation: 90° rotation clockwise, centre (3, 1)]

Guidance on selected *Thinking and working mathematically* questions

Characterising and Classifying

Learner's Book Exercise 14.5, Question 8

Some learners will try to answer this question without writing down the rotation for each card. However, very few learners can keep that amount of information in their head at once. Encourage all learners to write down

a description of each of the rotations. Then they can use their notes to classify the cards into groups using one property of the rotations.

Homework idea

As Section 14.5 will probably take more than one lesson, you can select questions from Workbook Exercise 14.5 at the end of each lesson. Only set questions that can be answered using skills and knowledge gained from that lesson. You can help learners to mark their homework at the start of the next lesson. This means you can address any problems before moving on.

Assessment idea

Use the initial work done by learners for Question 8 as a class 'test'. Learners must describe the rotation that transforms one 'flag' to another. There are several types of rotations to understand. Completing this part of the question correctly means that learners understand how to 'describe rotations on a coordinate grid'. Their notes will show evidence of their success at this learning objective.

14.6 Enlarging shapes

LEARNING PLAN

Framework codes	Learning objectives	Success criteria
8Gp.06	• Enlarge 2D shapes, from a centre of enlargement (outside or on the shape) with a positive integer scale factor. Identify an enlargement and scale factor.	• Learners can enlarge shapes from a centre of enlargement.

LANGUAGE SUPPORT

Centre of enlargement: the fixed point of an enlargement (COE)

Enlargement: a transformation that increases or decreases the size of a shape to produce a mathematically similar shape

Scale factor: the ratio by which a length is increased (or decreased)

Common misconceptions

Misconception	How to identify	How to overcome
The most common error is that learners enlarge the shape but ignore the centre of enlargement.	Question 1.	Asking learners to compare diagrams in small groups for Question 1 will highlight any learners with this misconception.
Measuring from the object to draw the image rather than measuring from the centre of enlargement to draw the image.	Starter idea 'Enlargement'.	Discussions on the Starter.

Use Resource sheet 14.6A so that learners do not need to copy diagrams from the Learner's Book. It will also save a great deal of time in the classroom. (You can download this resource from Cambridge GO.)

Starter idea

Enlargement (2–5 minutes)

Resources: Resource sheet 14.6B (you can download this resource from Cambridge GO)

Description: Use this starter before Section 14.6.

Let learners work individually. Give each learner a copy of Resource sheet 14.6B to complete.

Once completed, put learners into small groups to carefully compare their drawings, especially the last diagram. Now draw or display the answers:

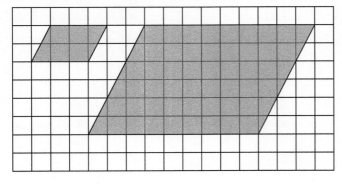

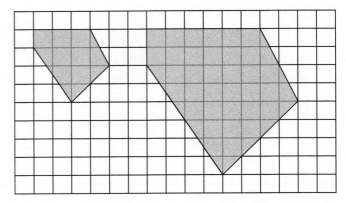

Allow learners to mark their own work. Discuss the dimensions of the images with the class, especially the last diagram. Focus especially on the sloped sides.

Main teaching idea

Initials (5–10 minutes)

Learning intention: To enlarge more complex shapes.

Resources: Centimetre-squared paper

Description: Set this activity at any time after learners have completed Question 5. Give learners centimetre-squared paper. Ask learners to draw their initials in stylised capital letters on the lines of the squared paper. Suggest they use only two letters, at least on their first attempts. There are many possible ways of drawing initials within a grid. Here are some examples for Greg Byrd drawing his initials GB [display to board].

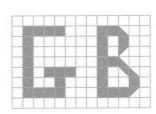
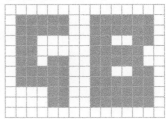

Ask learners to enlarge their letters by a scale factor of 2 several times, placing the centre of enlargement in different positions, anywhere on the perimeter of one of the two letters. Learners can continue this work as a homework.

> **Differentiation ideas:** Extend this activity by suggesting that learners use a variety of scale factors of enlargements.

Extend the activity further by asking learners to pick a point for their centre of enlargement between their two letters. Ask them to draw the image when their letters are enlarged by a scale factor of, e.g. 2.

Although fractions will not be dealt with until Stage 10, they could pose an interesting discussion point for more confident learners. You could ask them what they think an enlargement of $1\frac{1}{2}$ would look like. Is it possible to draw an image with an enlargement of $2\frac{1}{2}$? What about having a scale factor of $\frac{1}{2}$?

Plenary idea

Online enlargement check (5–10 minutes)

Resources: Mini whiteboards or access to computer or tablet

Description: Type 'transum.org, transformations' into a search engine. When directed to the page, learners will complete the level 4 material. This material changes every time it is clicked on, so no two sessions are the same. This is a free resource and learners can access this too. They may wish to practise at home so make sure they write down the web address of this resource. There are many other similar resources available. If you use an electronic whiteboard, all learners see the same questions. If you use a suite of computers or tablets, learners will see different questions.

Note: Some of the questions have the centre of enlargement inside the shape. Ignore these questions as this aspect of enlargement will be covered in Stage 9.

Point out to learners that the grids are not numbered – they will need to carefully count to locate the centre of enlargement. Learners will need to plot points around their enlarged shape in order. Ask learners in turn for an answer. Alternatively, you could put them into pairs or small groups first and ask each pair or group in turn. Ask the rest of the class if they agree. If learners disagree, ask them to explain what mistake may have been made. Check using the button below the questions.

Then either get learners to try again (if incorrect) or congratulate them and continue.

If each learner has individual access to the site you may wish to limit the time taken on the activity. This will lead to differentiation by outcome, but hopefully all learners will be successful and practise a valuable skill.

> **Assessment ideas:** Either marked with the class or, if learners have access to their own computer/tablet, they should mark as each shape is completed.

Guidance on selected *Thinking and working mathematically* questions

Conjecturing and Convincing

Learner's Book Exercise 14.6, Question 2

In this question, learners will say what they notice and explain it. Using a vertex of an object as a centre of enlargement is a surprisingly common mistake. This is particularly true when the centre of enlargement is on the right hand side of the object. Here, the centre of enlargement has been placed to encourage that mistake. The image would be correct if the centre of enlargement were actually at the lower left vertex.

The question states that a mistake has been made, so most learners will see the error. Once learners have had time to complete part **a**, discuss their answers before allowing them to draw the correct enlargement. After completion, ask learners to compare their answers with a partner or within a group.

Homework ideas

As Section 14.6 will probably take more than one lesson, you can select questions from Workbook Exercise 14.6 at the end of each lesson. Only set questions that can be answered using skills and knowledge gained from that lesson. You can help learners to mark their homework at the start of the next lesson. This means you can address any problems before moving on.

You could ask learners to make a poster containing everything they think they need to remember for the end-of-unit test. The following lesson, it is important to share their posters in class, perhaps spread out over a few desks for everyone to look at. Discuss the different posters as a class. When the class agree that a point is important, that key point could be copied onto the board. Agree on as many key points as possible. Learners could then improve their individual poster if necessary. Learners could store their poster at home as a possible revision tool towards mid-term or end-of-year exams.

Assessment idea

Use Learner's Book Exercise 14.6, Question 3 as an extended hinge point question. It is important for all learners to be able to use the basic skills required for this question in order to be successful with the rest of the section. Give learners Resource sheet 14.6A to speed up their answering of the question. It will also remove a potential source of error. (You can download this resource from Cambridge GO.)

Once completed, ask learners to mark their work or peer mark. Only give them the coordinates of the image: (4, 4), (10, 4), (4, 7). Any learner making mistakes needs help to understand their error, either from you or other learners. If necessary, ask learners to repeat the question using (3, 1) as the centre of enlargement [image coordinates are (0, 4), (0, 7) and (6, 4)].

> 15 Distance, area and volume

Unit plan

Topic	Approximate number of learning hours	Outline of learning content	Resources
Introduction and Getting Started	5–10 minutes		Learner's Book
15.1 Converting between miles and kilometres	1–1.5	Know that distances can be measured in miles or kilometres, and that a kilometre is approximately $\frac{5}{8}$ of a mile and a mile is $\frac{8}{5}$ or 1.6 kilometres.	Learner's Book Section 15.1 Workbook Section 15.1 ⬇ Additional teaching ideas Section 15.1 ⬇ Resource sheet 15.1
15.2 The area of a parallelogram and trapezium	1–1.5	Derive and use the formulae for the area of parallelograms and trapezia.	Learner's Book Section 15.2 Workbook Section 15.2 ⬇ Additional teaching ideas Section 15.2 ⬇ Resource sheet 15.2A ⬇ Resource sheet 15.2B
15.3 Calculating the volume of triangular prisms	1	Derive and use the formula for the volume of a triangular prism.	Learner's Book Section 15.3 Workbook Section 15.3 ⬇ Additional teaching ideas Section 15.3 ⬇ Exit ticket 15.3
15.4 Calculating the surface area of triangular prisms and pyramids	1	Calculate the surface area of cubes, cuboids, triangular prisms and pyramids.	Learner's Book Section 15.4 Workbook Section 15.4 ⬇ Additional teaching ideas Section 15.4 ⬇ Resource sheet 15.4

Cross-unit resources

⬇ Language worksheet 15.1–15.4

Project Guidance: Biggest cuboid resource sheet

⬇ End of Unit 15 test

BACKGROUND KNOWLEDGE

For this unit, learners will need this background knowledge:

- Know and use the formula for the area of rectangles, squares and triangles (Stage 7).
- Derive and use a formula for the volume of a cube or cuboid (Stage 7).

- Use knowledge of area, and properties of cubes and cuboids, to calculate their surface area (Stage 7).

Learners' knowledge of area and volume will be extended to several new shapes. Learners will learn to convert between miles and kilometres.

TEACHING SKILLS FOCUS

Active learning

Throughout the four sections of Unit 15, if learners do not understand or they continue to get the same type of question incorrect, ask another learner to help them. It is important that you also listen to the explanation given by another learner. You need to be able to confirm that the help is of good quality.

Active learning helps to establish good learning patterns and practice. When a learner can explain well, it shows that they really understand what they are doing and know how to improve. Also, learners often feel more confident speaking to other learners. By asking more targeted questions, they become more active learners themselves. As learners get more used to explaining concepts or asking for specific, targeted help from other learners, these discussions can happen without

you being present. Remind learners that the key to being successfully involved in this type of learning is that there is no judgement. The learner asking for help and the learner giving help are both learning and improving.

At the end of Unit 15, ask yourself:

- Did learners have useful discussions that solved issues one of them was having?
- Are all learners that require help getting it?
- In what other ways could you get learners to explain more to others, e.g. a learner could take your place by saying the answers and encouraging other learners to explain their methods. You can correct them and help them if necessary.

15.1 Converting between miles and kilometres

LEARNING PLAN

Framework codes	Learning objectives	Success criteria
8Gg.03	• Know that distances can be measured in miles or kilometres, and that a kilometre is approximately $\frac{5}{8}$ of a mile or a mile is 1.6 kilometres.	• Learners can convert between miles and kilometres and vice versa.

LANGUAGE SUPPORT

Kilometre: measure of distance, and approximately $\frac{5}{8}$ of a mile

Mile: measure of distance, approximately $\frac{8}{5}$ of a kilometre

Common misconceptions

Misconception	How to identify	How to overcome
Using the wrong conversion factor, e.g. 8 miles = 5 km (using $\times\frac{5}{8}$ instead of $\times\frac{8}{5}$).	Question 5.	Constantly asking learners for the method (i.e. $\times\frac{5}{8}$ or $\times\frac{8}{5}$) of either converting from miles to kilometres or from kilometres to miles.

Starter idea

Getting started (3–5 minutes)

Resources: Notebooks; Learner's Book 'Getting started' questions

Description: Learners should have little difficulty with the 'Getting started' material. Before learners attempt the questions, discuss what they remember about formulae for area and volume of shapes.

Main teaching idea

Free Mumbai! (5–10 minutes)

Learning intention: Real life use of km/mile conversion using large numbers.

Resources: Notebooks; Resource sheet 15.1 (you can download this resource from Cambridge GO)

Description: Set this activity after learners have completed Learner's Book Exercise 15.1. Let learners work individually, in pairs or in groups, depending on ability levels. Distribute copies of the map from Resource sheet 15.1.

Explain that Adirake is an international salesman who lives in Bangkok. He travels abroad once a month for a meeting. Each time he buys a return flight on his credit card, he gets rewarded with 1 'air mile' for every 10 km he travels. So far this year, he has flown to Hong Kong, New York, London, Kolkata and Buenos Aires. Adirake wants to use his 'air miles' to take his wife to visit his cousin in Mumbai. Has he earned enough air miles for them both to travel free of charge?

Answers:
Yes [13 929 km > 12 040 km or 8745 air miles > 7525 air miles]

> **Differentiation ideas:** Help some learners by reminding them that the distances on the map are the 'one way' distances, in kilometres. Adirake bought return flights, so each journey was twice as far as is shown on the map. Encourage learners to work out the total distance he flew in kilometres. Then they can divide by 10 to work out his 'air miles'. Learners will need to convert the air miles to kilometres before working out whether he has enough for two *return* flights to Mumbai.

Plenary idea

Online converting (5–10 minutes)

Resources: Mini whiteboards or computer/tablet; calculators

Description: Type 'transum.org, Mileometer' into a search engine. When directed to the page, learners will see a self-marking quiz. Many of the questions change when the page is opened but questions 6, 9, 10 and 12 are always the same. This is a free resource and learners can access this too. They may wish to practise at home so make sure they write down the web address of this resource. There are many other similar resources available. If you use an electronic whiteboard, all learners see the same questions. If you use a suite of computers or tablets, learners will see different questions.

Remember that the questions get harder further down the page. You should not only think about which learner to ask which question, but whether all of the questions are suitable. The last question is only for the most confident learners.

If you work as a class, ask all learners to work out each question in turn. Ask a learner to show their answer, type it into the answer box and press 'Check'. If their answer is correct, congratulate them and move on. If their answer is incorrect, ask other learners what mistake they might have made. Encouraging the initial learner to make another attempt. Check again.

If each learner has individual access to the site you may wish to limit the time taken on the activity. For most learners, being in a pair or small group may be helpful. Encourage learners to write down their methods, especially after completing the first five questions. This may lead to differentiation by outcome, but hopefully all learners will be successful and practise a valuable skill.

> **Assessment ideas:** Use the 'Check' button after each question has been answered. This applies whether you are using an electronic whiteboard or a suite of computers or tablets.

Guidance on selected *Thinking and working mathematically* questions

Conjecturing and Convincing

Learner's Book Exercise 15.1, Question 11

This is a typical multistep, real-life question. In later years of the course, this type of question may be presented as a single problem rather than split into parts **a** and **b**. At first glance, this question looks difficult

to many learners. It contains large numbers, kilometres, miles, money and lots of words. Encourage learners to read through the whole question first. Then they can focus on one part at a time and not rush. Learners must plan the necessary calculations to answer the questions and explain their answers convincingly.

To answer part **a**, they must work out the number of miles travelled [870] and convert that to kilometres [1392].

Part **b** requires learners to multiply the km by 20 cents. Look out for the learners who multiply by 20 and give the answer as $27 840 rather than 27 840 cents or $278.40. If this occurs, remind them that 20 cents is $0.20. So they need to multiply by 0.2 (or $\frac{1}{5}$ if they prefer working with fractions).

Homework idea

As Section 15.1 will probably take more than one lesson, you can select questions from Workbook Exercise 15.1 at the end of each lesson. Only set questions that can be answered using skills and knowledge gained from that lesson. You can help learners to mark their homework at the start of the next lesson. This means you can address any problems before moving on.

Assessment idea

Use Learner's Book Exercise 15.1, Question 9 parts **a** and **b** as a class 'test'. If learners can answer these two basic questions, they obviously understand how to convert between kilometres and miles. If they struggle with either of these two questions, they will need you to identify their misconception and to help them overcome it.

15.2 The area of a parallelogram and trapezium

LEARNING PLAN		
Framework codes	**Learning objectives**	**Success criteria**
8Gg.04	• Use knowledge of rectangles, squares and triangles to derive the formulae for the area of parallelograms and trapezia. Use the formulae to calculate the area of parallelograms and trapezia.	• Learners can derive and use the formula for the area of a parallelogram and a trapezium.

LANGUAGE SUPPORT

Trapezia: plural of trapezium

Common misconceptions

Misconception	How to identify	How to overcome
Learners may halve both the bracketed terms and the height of the trapezium and then multiply these values.	Question 9.	Starter idea $\frac{1}{2} \times (a+b) \times h$ on Cambridge GO, discussion during Worked example part **b**, Question 2.

Starter idea

Area of a parallelogram (5–10 minutes)

Resources: Mini whiteboards; notebooks; Resource sheet 15.2A (you can download this resource from Cambridge GO); scissors

Description: Use this starter before working through the introduction to Learner's Book Section 15.2.

There are seven pairs of parallelograms on Resource sheet 15.2A. Each pair of parallelograms needs to be neatly cut out from the resource sheet. Each learner or group needs a pair of identical parallelograms. One of the parallelograms is to be cut in two, with the cut *perpendicular* to the base of the parallelogram, e.g. the position shown.

Learners can then move one of the cut pieces to form a rectangle, e.g.

It would be useful for each learner to glue their parallelogram and its equal area rectangle in their notebooks. One pair of parallelograms per learner is ideal. Alternatively, you may only wish to use the parallelograms to help learners visualise while they derive the formula for the area. In this case, they will only need one pair of parallelograms per group.

Now discuss as a class what the two shapes show about the area of the rectangle and parallelogram [they are the same]. Ask them what that means regarding the formula for the area of a parallelogram [it is the same as the formula for the area of a rectangle, [$b \times h$].

Main teaching idea

Rank and check (10 minutes)

Learning intention: To make their own measurements and to work out the area of parallelograms and trapezia.

Resources: Notebooks; Resource sheet 15.2B (you can download this resource from Cambridge GO)

Description: Set this activity after learners have completed Exercise 15.2. Let learners work individually or in groups. Distribute copies of Resource sheet 15.2B to each individual or group.

Ask learners to rank the shapes on the resource sheet in order of size, starting with the smallest. This is an estimation exercise, so no rulers are allowed!

Now ask learners to make any necessary measurements and to work out the area of each parallelogram and trapezium.

Once completed, ask them again to rank the shapes in order of size, starting with the smallest. How accurate were they?

Answers:
Areas, in order: $F = 18.2 \, \text{cm}^2$, $A = 18.3 \, \text{cm}^2$, $D = 18.4 \, \text{cm}^2$, $B = 19.425 \, \text{cm}^2$, $C = 19.53 \, \text{cm}^2$, $E = 21.33 \, \text{cm}^2$

> **Differentiation ideas:** When learners measure the trapezia and parallelograms, ask them to draw in any line that they measure. This will help if learners make mistakes. You will be able to see if they have measured appropriate lengths, especially the *perpendicular height*.

Plenary idea

Online trapezia (10–20 minutes)

Resources: Mini whiteboards or suite of computers or tablets; calculators

Description: Type 'transum.org, Area of a trapezium' into a search engine. When directed to the page, learners will complete the level 1 material. This is a free resource and learners can access this too. They may wish to practise at home so make sure they write down the web address of this resource. There are many other similar resources available. This material changes every time it is clicked on, so no two sessions are the same. If you use an electronic whiteboard, all learners see the same questions. if you use a suite of computers or tablets, learners will see different questions.

Remember that the questions get harder further down the page, so you should think about which learner to ask which question.

Ask learners to work out the area of each trapezium in turn. When working as a class, ask a learner to show their answer. Discuss as a class whether the answer is probably correct or not. If learners think it is correct, type it into the answer box and check. If it is not correct, discuss possible errors and then retry.

If each learner has individual access to the site you may wish to limit the time taken on the activity. This will lead to differentiation by outcome, but hopefully all learners will be successful and practise a valuable skill.

> **Assessment ideas:** Answers are checked online. Alternatively, learners could use part of the level 1 material as a test to be answered in their notebooks.

This would be appropriate when learners are near the end of Learner's Book Exercise 15.2.

Use questions 3, 4 and 5 from this exercise as the test material. Once completed, this can be self or peer marked (using the 'Check' button). Or you could collect in learners' notebooks and mark them. This would give you a more formal analysis of learners' ability to work out the area of a trapezium.

Guidance on selected *Thinking and working mathematically* questions

Conjecturing and Convincing

Learner's Book Exercise 15.2, Question 7

As with other 'what mistake has been made' questions, learners are likely to answer the question themselves first. Then they will compare their answer with Zalika's homework, spot the difference and explain convincingly what her mistake was. If learners focus solely on the numbers, they will end up with the same answer. They will only be able to find the mistake when they realise that the units are not the same for both shapes. If learners cannot understand what the error is, allow another learner to explain.

Homework idea

As Section 15.2 will probably take more than one lesson, you can select questions from Workbook Exercise 15.2 at the end of each lesson. Only set questions that can be answered using skills and knowledge gained from that lesson. You can help learners to mark their homework at the start of the next lesson. This means you can address any problems before moving on.

Assessment idea

While learners are working through Exercise 15.2, regularly ask individual learners to recite the formula for both the parallelogram and the trapezium.

15.3 Calculating the volume of triangular prisms

Framework codes	Learning objectives	Success criteria
8Gg.06	• Use knowledge of area and volume to derive the formula for the volume of a triangular prism. Use the formula to calculate the volume of triangular prisms.	• Learners can derive and use the formula for the volume of a triangular prism.

LANGUAGE SUPPORT

Cross-section: the 2D face formed by slicing through a solid shape

Prism: a solid 3D shape that has the same cross-section along its length

Common misconceptions

Misconception	How to identify	How to overcome
Learners may use incorrect units, e.g. cm or cm^2 instead of cm^3.	Question 2.	Discussion during Worked examples and Question 1.
Forgetting to use the $\frac{1}{2}$ when dealing with a triangular prism.	Question 2.	Discussion during Worked examples and questions 1 and 3.

Starter idea

Formula for the volume of a triangular prism (5 minutes)

Resources: Mini whiteboards; notebooks

Description: Use this starter before working through the introduction to Learner's Book Section 15.3.

Sketch or display a cuboid on the board:

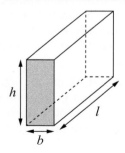

Ask learners for methods of working out the volume of the cuboid. In Stage 7, learners used

$$volume = length \times width \times height$$

If necessary, guide learners to the formula $volume = b \times h \times l$ and then to

$volume = area\ of\ cross\text{-}section \times length.$

Write on the board:

$volume\ of\ cuboid = end\ area \times length$

$$= b \times h \times length$$

Now alter your drawing or display:

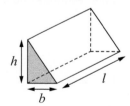

Ask learners for methods of working out the volume of the triangular prism. Ensure that learners have suggested and written:

Volume of triangular prism = area of cross section × length

$$= \frac{1}{2} \times b \times h \times \text{length}$$

Now work through the introduction and Worked example.

Main teaching idea

Question 7 (5–10 minutes)

Learning intention: To understand different methods of working out the volume of a compound shape.

Resources: Notebooks; Learner's Book

Description: Ask learners to sketch the compound shape **a**, ensuring they include measurements. Have a brief class discussion on possible methods of how to work out the volume of the shape. It is possible that both methods will be thoroughly discussed and understood, but if not, sketch the following:

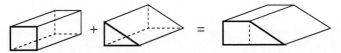

Briefly discuss that working out the volume of each simple shape then adding those volumes together is a good method for working out the volume of the compound shape. Ask how many learners think they might have used this method.

Tell learners that another method is one using area first, rather than volume. Sketch the following on the board:

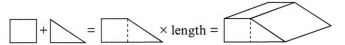

Discuss that volume can be calculated using the end area of a shape multiplied by its length. Some more confident learners may prefer to work out the area of a trapezium rather than a rectangle and a triangle, giving the diagram as:

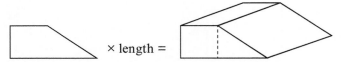

Now discuss the three options. Explain that all three are equally good. Ask learners to say which method they will use and why. Emphasise that it doesn't matter which they use. Leaving your diagrams on display, ask learners to work out the answer to part **a**. Allow peer marking, asking learners to decide if the work they are marking is easily understood as well as having the correct answer.

Repeat with part **b**. Note that there are just two options with part **b**, as the rectangle and triangle of the cross section do not make another common shape.

Answers:
a 81 m³   **b** 1980 mm³

⟩ **Differentiation ideas:** If learners cannot decide for themselves which option to choose, suggest they work out the volume of the cuboid (using area of cross section × length), then the volume of the triangular prism (using area of cross section × length) and then add their answers to get the volume of the compound shape.

Plenary idea

Exit ticket (3–5 minutes)

Resources: Exit ticket 15.3 (you can download this resource from Cambridge GO)

Description: Towards the end of the lesson, give one exit ticket to each learner.

⟩ **Assessment ideas:** Note different methods of working, especially if the answer is incorrect [150 cm³].

Reading what learners *think* they have learned is a key aspect of their learning. Looking at the completed exit tickets will help you to clarify teaching points for individual learners or the class as a whole. You will know better how to help them in the next lesson.

Guidance on selected *Thinking and working mathematically* questions

Conjecturing and Convincing

Learner's Book Exercise 15.3, Question 11

This is an example of a multistep question. Because of the large numbers, learners may find a calculator useful. Planning their approach may require some guidance, preferably from another learner. Any calculations they do should enable them to explain convincingly whether or not Jan is correct.

They will first need to work out the volume of the triangular prism [4500 mm³]. They will then need to know the volume of one of the cubes [512 mm³]. Dividing the volume of the prism by the volume of one cube gives 8.789. . . Some learners will stop at this point, thinking they have answered the question. They have not read the question carefully enough. Learners need to explain that there is only enough silver to make eight whole cubes (with some silver left over). So Jan is not correct.

Homework ideas

As Section 15.3 will probably take more than one lesson, you can select questions from Workbook Exercise 15.3 at the end of each lesson. Only set questions that can be answered using skills and knowledge gained from that lesson. You can help learners to mark their homework at the start of the next lesson. This means you can address any problems before moving on.

Assessment idea

First ask learners to work through Learner's Book Exercise 15.3, questions 1 and 2 **a**. Then check their answers. After this, you can use Question 2**b** as a class 'test'. If learners can answer this question, they understand how to calculate the volume of a triangular prism. This question can also act as a hinge point question. If learners do not fully understand this basic question, they need your help before they are ready to move on to more complicated questions.

15.4 Calculating the surface area of triangular prisms and pyramids

LEARNING PLAN

Framework codes	Learning objectives	Success criteria
8Gg.08	• Use knowledge of area, and properties of cubes, cuboids, triangular prisms and pyramids to calculate their surface area.	• Learners can calculate the surface area of triangular prisms and pyramids.

LANGUAGE SUPPORT

Net: a flat diagram that can be folded to form a 3D shape

Surface area: the total area of the faces of a 3D shape

Common misconceptions

Misconception	How to identify	How to overcome
Learners may not include the bottom face of the pyramid if working without a net.	Question 4 and Activity 15.4.	Encourage learners always to use a net.

Starter idea

Nets of a cube and a cuboid (5 minutes)

Resources: Mini whiteboards

Description: Sketch a cube on the board:

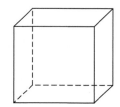

Ask learners to sketch the net of a cube. If a learner does not know how to start, ask another learner to explain what is required. If none of your learners can remember what a net is, you will need to help them imagine a cube's net. You could say that, if the cube was made like a cardboard box, cutting along some of the edges would mean that it could be folded flat. Once learners have completed their nets, ask a learner to sketch theirs on the main board. The most commonly drawn tend to be:

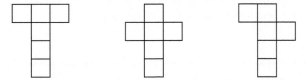

There are, however, a total of 11 different nets of a cube. Ask learners with other shaped nets to draw them on the board. If you or the class are interested in the possible nets, use the internet to find an image of all 11 of them.

Next sketch a cuboid on the board:

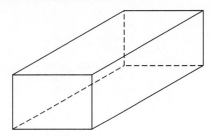

Ask learners to sketch the net of a cuboid. Again, ask to see different nets drawn on the board. Avoid asking for all possible nets as there are 54 possibilities! Although the nets are just sketches, they should be reasonably accurate. Learners should try to ensure that edges that would meet, when the net is cut out and folded, should be approximately the same length.

Display these nets and discuss them:

correct net

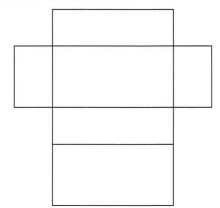

incorrect net

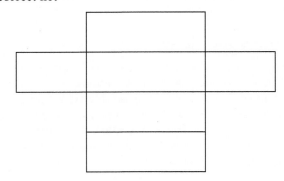

Main teaching idea

The Great Pyramid of Giza, Egypt (5–10 minutes)

Learning intention: Using maths to be amazed at the oldest of the Seven Wonders of the Ancient World.

Resources: Notebooks; calculators

Description: When it was first built more than 4500 years ago, the Great Pyramid was 146.7 m high. It had a square base of side length 230.3 m. The perpendicular height of each triangular face of the pyramid was 186.5 m. Now, due to stone robbing and erosion, it is only 138.8 m high. The base is still the same size. The perpendicular height of each triangular face of the pyramid is now 180 m.

Work out the *reduction* in surface area since the pyramid was first built (to the nearest square metre) [2994 m²].

› **Differentiation ideas:** Some learners will be confused by the different height measurements. Point out that 146.7 m, is the vertical height of the original pyramid, but the 186.5 m is the sloped measurement of the triangular face of the pyramid. Tell learners that it is this sloped measurement that they will need to use to work out the surface area of the pyramid. To speed up some learners, point out that as the base has stayed the same size.

Plenary idea

What's the difference? (5–10 minutes)

Resources: Notebooks

Description: Draw or display these two shapes on the board:

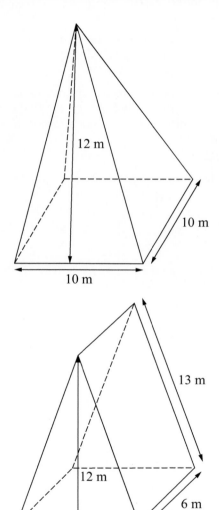

Work out the difference between the surface areas of the two shapes.

⟩ **Assessment ideas:** This can be self-marked. The answer is $4\,m^2$ (the two surface areas are 340 and $336\,m^2$). Any learner with an incorrect answer could compare their working with a successful learner's work. This will help them to decide what their mistake might have been. For

learners with an incorrect answer, the first thing you can check is whether their net of each solid has the correct lengths written on it.

Guidance on selected *Thinking and working mathematically* questions

Conjecturing and Convincing

Learner's Book Exercise 15.4, Activity 15.4

In this activity, learners will use a diagram to solve a problem logically so that they can convince a partner. The key point here is that learners recognise that all four triangles are identical. This should lead them to divide the surface area by four to work out the area of one face. Some learners might need guidance to write $\frac{1}{2} \times b \times h = 62.4$, substitute for b and solve for h.

Once learners have completed the question, ask them to exchange answers with a partner. Encourage learners to look carefully at their partner's work. They should check that no working is missing and that each step is clear.

Homework ideas

As Section 15.4 will probably take more than one lesson, you can select questions from Workbook Exercise 15.4 at the end of each lesson. You can help learners to mark their homework at the start of the next lesson. This means you can address any problems before moving on.

You could ask learners to make a list of worked examples containing everything they think they need to remember for the end-of-unit test. The following lesson, it is important to share the lists in class. Perhaps you could spread them out over a few desks for everyone to look at. Discuss the different worked examples as a class. When the class agree that a point is important, you or a learner could copy that key point on to the board. Agree on as many key points as possible. Learners could then improve their individual list if necessary. Learners could store their list at home as a possible revision tool towards mid-term or end-of-year exams.

Assessment idea

There are fewer questions in this section but they are fairly complex. Allow learners to compare answers regularly. They should look for unclear, confusing or incorrect working. Learners should point out any steps that they don't understand in a partner's work. If a partner's work is particularly clear, they can use this to improve their own work.

PROJECT GUIDANCE: BIGGEST CUBOID

Why do this problem?

This task offers learners the opportunity to apply their knowledge of volume and surface area. It also challenges them to improve upon their initial solutions as they try to find an optimal arrangement.

Possible approach

Learners may need squared paper.

Show the diagram of the six rectangles. Invite learners to consider how the rectangles could be arranged to form a cuboid and what the dimensions of the cuboid would be.

Point out that there is a variety of different cuboids that could be made by cutting rectangles from a 12 by 12 square. Challenge learners to find some examples.

As the lesson progresses, invite learners to share the volumes of the cuboids they have found. Challenge them to find the maximum possible volume that can be made.

You could also invite them to try to make a cuboid with a surface area of exactly 144 cm² (which uses all of the paper).

Key questions

If one of the rectangles has dimensions 3 cm and 4 cm, what must be true about the dimensions of the other rectangles?

How many different ways can you arrange six rectangles on the paper?

Possible support

Learners could start with a smaller square of paper, such as 8 cm by 8 cm.

Possible extension

Learners could investigate the largest volume of cuboid that can be made from rectangular paper of different dimensions, keeping one dimension fixed. For example:

12 cm by 2 cm

12 cm by 4 cm

12 cm by 6 cm and so on.

> 16 Interpreting and discussing results

Unit plan

Topic	Approximate number of learning hours	Outline of learning content	Resources
Introduction and Getting Started	10 minutes		Learner's Book
16.1 Interpreting and drawing frequency diagrams	1–1.5	Record, organise and represent categorical, discrete and continuous data.	Learner's Book Section 16.1 Workbook Section 16.1 ⬇ Additional teaching ideas Section 16.1 ⬇ Resource sheet 16.1
16.2 Time series graphs	0.5–1.5	Use time series graphs to record, organise and represent continuous data.	Learner's Book Section 16.2 Workbook Section 16.2 ⬇ Additional teaching ideas Section 16.2 ⬇ Resource sheet 16.2
16.3 Stem-and-leaf diagrams	1–1.5	Use stem-and-leaf diagrams to record, organise and represent discrete and continuous data.	Learner's Book Section 16.3 Workbook Section 16.3 ⬇ Additional teaching ideas Section 16.3 ⬇ Exit ticket 16.3 ⬇ Resource sheet 16.3
16.4 Pie charts	1–1.5	Use pie charts to record, organise and represent categorical, discrete and continuous data.	Learner's Book Section 16.4 Workbook Section 16.4 ⬇ Additional teaching ideas Section 16.4 ⬇ Resource sheet 16.4
16.5 Representing data	1–1.5	Record, organise and represent categorical, discrete and continuous data. Choose and explain which representation to use in a given situation.	Learner's Book Section 16.5 Workbook Section 16.5 ⬇ Additional teaching ideas Section 16.5 ⬇ Resource sheet 16.5A ⬇ Resource sheet 16.5B

Topic	Approximate number of learning hours	Outline of learning content	Resources
16.6 Using statistics	1–1.5	Use mode, median, mean and range to compare two distributions.	Learner's Book Section 16.6 Workbook Section 16.6 ⬇ Additional teaching ideas Section 16.6 ⬇ Resource sheet 16.6 Key words

Cross-unit resources

⬇ Resource sheet 16.6 Key words

⬇ Language worksheet 16.1–16.6

⬇ End of Unit 16 test

⬇ End-of-year test

BACKGROUND KNOWLEDGE

For this unit, learners will need this background knowledge:

- Know how to draw and interpret bar charts (Stage 6) and frequency diagrams (Stages 5, 6 and 7).
- Understand how to plot points on a graph (Stage 7).
- Know how to draw and interpret a pie chart (Stage 7).

Learners already know how to draw bar charts using discrete and grouped discrete data. This knowledge is now extended to frequency diagrams with continuous data using ≤, < for continuous data intervals. Learners' use of pie charts will be extended to comparing pie charts which represent different totals. Learners will practise deciding how best to represent different types of data.

TEACHING SKILLS FOCUS

Language awareness

To help you to highlight and concentrate on language awareness, it is a good idea to be aware of the key words learners will meet during this unit. Make sure you are clear in your understanding of the key words before the lesson. Use the Glossary if necessary.

Give all learners a copy of Resource sheet 16.6 Key words. (You can download this resource from Cambridge GO.) Read out each word in turn. Afterwards, ask learners 'Do you know what any of these key words mean?' Discuss any ideas learners have. Emphasise that by the end of the unit learners will know the meaning of all of these key words. Refer to the worksheet as you work through the

unit. Encourage learners to fill in the meaning of a word in the list when they meet each one in the unit, including an example too.

During each section, refer to the key words as often as possible and encourage learners to use the key words during any classroom discussions. Many of the activties ask learners to write their own questions, giving them plenty of opportunity to practise using the correct vocabulary. When the opportunity arises, e.g. when one learner has used a key word, ask another learner what the key word means. If you do this throughout the unit, you could give learners a copy of Resource sheet 16.6 Key words as a class test at the end of Section 16.6.

CONTINUED

Alternatively, you could introduce the resource sheet at the end of the unit.

When you reach the end of Section 16.6, ask yourself: Do the learners understand and feel confident in using the key words? If the answer is yes, then this work has been successful. If the answer is no, then think how you can change the way you approached discussing and using the key words.

16.1 Interpreting and drawing frequency diagrams

LEARNING PLAN

Framework codes	Learning objectives	Success criteria
8Ss.03	• Record, organise and represent categorical, discrete and continuous data: Tally charts, frequency tables and two-way tables.	• Learners can draw and interpret frequency diagrams.

LANGUAGE SUPPORT

Class interval: the width of a group in a grouped frequency table/diagram

Classes: the groups used for recording data in a grouped frequency table/diagram

Continuous data: data that can take any value within a given range

Discrete data: data that can only take exact values

Frequency diagram: any diagram that shows frequencies

Grouped data: where data values are recorded into groups rather than individual values

Common misconceptions

Misconception	How to identify	How to overcome
Not understanding the differences between discrete and continuous data.	All questions.	Ask learners what type of data they are dealing with at the start of each part of Worked example 16.1 and throughout the exercise.
Learners may forget the difference between < and ≤, and so place a value in the wrong group.	Question 3.	When working through Worked example 16.1, part b, ask learners which group someone would go in, e.g. a teacher of mass 80 kg. Ask how they know they are correct.
Choosing to have too many or too few classes when forming their own frequency table.	Question 3.	Tell learners that they should have four, five, six or seven classes unless there is a good reason not to.

Starter idea

Getting started (10 minutes)

Resources: Notebooks; Learner's Book 'Getting started' questions

Description: Learners should have little difficulty with 'Getting started' Question 1. As they may find some of the other questions more difficult, it is sensible to ask them to answer one question at a time. Then you can check their understanding and deal with any misconceptions as they arise.

Question 2 will probably cause some confusion. Ask learners to answer part **a**, then discuss what type of diagram, graph or chart they have chosen and ask for their reasons. Discussing which diagram, graph or chart *not* to use (and why) will help learners with the rest of the question.

For Question 3, some learners may not recall how to use an angle in a pie chart to calculate percentages, e.g. $\frac{90}{360} \times 100 = 25\%$ or $\frac{1}{4} \times 100 = 25\%$. They may not remember how to work out the basic fraction, e.g. train $= \frac{30}{360} = \frac{1}{12}$. Ask other learners to explain the method.

In Question 4 part **a**, check for learners who have worked out, e.g. the median, but called it the mode. During discussions, ensure that all learners understand the reasons why the median is probably the best option and why the mean and the mode are less helpful.

Main teaching idea

Your own questions (5–10 minutes)

Learning intention: To invent questions using a frequency diagram.

Resources: Notebooks; Learner's Book; Resource sheet 16.1 (you can download this resource from Cambridge GO)

Description: Set this activity before learners have completed Exercise 16.1 but after going through Worked example 16.1, part **a**. Let learners work in groups. Give each group a copy of Resource sheet 16.1 which shows a frequency diagram.

The task for each group is to make up five questions that could be answered using the information in the frequency diagram. Other learners will answer their questions. They can make the questions as difficult as

they like, but they must be able to answer the questions themselves. Make sure that the members of a group discuss both questions and answers before writing them down.

When the groups have written their questions, exchange sheets among the groups. Ask learners to answer the questions on the sheet that they have received. Instruct learners to give full answers.

When they have answered the questions, exchange sheets among groups again (not necessarily back to the group who created the questions). Ask learners to check the answers given by the previous group.

Use this as the basis for a class discussion about the questions that were asked: How many were the same? How difficult were they to answer? How many mistakes were made? What seemed to be good answers? How was the working set out? It is likely that most groups devised the same or very similar questions. This is not surprising since, for this type of frequency diagram, the options are fairly limited.

› **Differentiation ideas:** Learners can make their questions as complicated as they want. Some learners will write questions that are more easily answered. Ensure that these learners do not receive the questions from a group of more confident learners.

Plenary idea

Frequency diagrams (10 minutes)

Resources: Notebooks or grid paper

Description: Tell learners that the two tables, A and B, show the results of a tree frog survey. Tree frogs were counted and some were caught and weighed.

Table A

Mass, m (g)	Frequency
$60 < m \le 70$	3
$70 < m \le 80$	8
$80 < m \le 90$	6
$90 < m \le 100$	4

Table B

Number of tree frogs counted	Frequency
$60-69$	3
$70-79$	8
$80-89$	6
$90-99$	4

Ask learners to draw suitable diagrams for each table.

› **Assessment ideas:** Draw or display the answers on the board and allow peer marking.

Diagram A

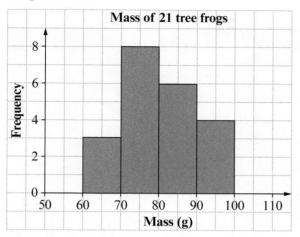

Diagram B

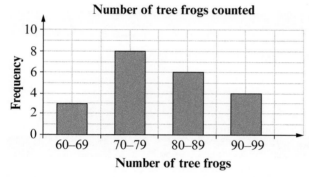

Discuss what information each diagram can show. Discuss what looks similar and what looks different about the two graphs. Ask learners to think about why differences in the graphs arise as a result of using discrete or continuous data.

Guidance on selected *Thinking and working mathematically* questions

Conjecturing and Convincing

Learner's Book Exercise 16.1, Question 2

In this question, learners will say what they notice and explain what it means. Use the frequency diagrams from Worked example 1 and Question 1 to help learners if they are not sure how to draw a diagram. Once learners have completed part **a**, discuss as a class the appearance of the 'correct' diagram. Both axes should be correctly labelled, there should be the same sized gaps between the 'bars' and bars should all be the same thickness, with heights marked accurately. The diagrams also need a title.

Learners should first look at the type of data in order to decide which month the data represents. If learners need guiding, ask if the number of cups of coffee sold gives a clue to the month. Unfortunately, the number of cups of coffee sold give no real clue to the month. (If you observed a large increase in Christmas trees sold, of sewayian sweets sold, of coloured dye powder sold in India or lanterns sold in Japan, you would be able to deduce which month it was.)

The next logical step is to work out the total number of days for which data was collected. In this case, the total is 28. The *only* month with 28 days is February. Learners need to make sure they show their logic and give a brief explanation of how they arrived at their answer.

Homework idea

As Section 16.1 will probably take more than one lesson, you can select questions from Workbook Exercise 16.1 at the end of each lesson. Only set questions that can be answered using skills and knowledge gained from that lesson. You can help learners to mark their homework at the start of the next lesson. This means you can address any problems before moving on.

Assessment idea

Throughout most of Learner's Book Exercise 16.1, encourage peer marking. Ask learners to check each other's work carefully. They should use the key words from the key word list to help identify clear answers as well as areas for improvement.

16.2 Time series graphs

LEARNING PLAN

Framework codes	Learning objectives	Success criteria
8Ss.03	• Record, organise and represent categorical, discrete and continuous data: Time series graphs.	• Learners can draw and interpret time series graphs.
8Ss.05	• Interpret data, identifying patterns, trends and relationships, within and between data sets, to answer statistical questions. Discuss conclusions, considering the sources of variation, including sampling and check predictions.	• Learners can interpret data, identify trends and draw conclusions.

LANGUAGE SUPPORT

Time series graph: a series of points, plotted at regular time intervals, joined by straight lines

Trend: a pattern in a set of data

Common misconceptions

Misconception	How to identify	How to overcome
Drawing graphs which are too small to be useful or with a scale that means not all data can be plotted.	Questions 4 and 5.	Encourage learners to think carefully about the scales on their axes before they start drawing graphs. They should always make the most of the available space.
Some learners may plot the points but not join them with a line.	Questions 4 and 5.	This should be a talking point for learners when discussing each other's graphs in questions 4 and 5.
When asked for a trend, learners may give a very short answer, e.g. 'It goes up'. A more comprehensive answer is required, e.g. 'In the first four years the value increased by between 5 and 6, but in the fifth year it decreased by 3.'	Most questions.	Checking, through discussion, that learners' descriptions are clear and concise.

Starter idea

Bamboo growth (5 minutes)

Resources: Mini whiteboards

Description: Use this Starter idea before working through the introduction to Section 16.2.

Write or display on the board:

Addis measures the height of a new bamboo shoot as it grows. This is the data.

Time (hours)	1	2	3	4	5	6	7	8
Height (mm)	3	7	8	12	18	22	30	38

Ask learners what scale they would use on their x-axis (time) and y-axis (length) if they had to plot this data on a grid. Tell learners that the grid is 10 squares by 10 squares.

Once completed, discuss learners' choices. Hopefully all learners would use one square to one hour for the *x*-axis. There is a choice of either 4 or 5 mm per square for the *y*-axis. Both are acceptable, but learners must understand that choosing 4 mm per square will use more of the grid. Many learners may find that using 5 mm per square seems easier to count.

Now ask learners what scale they would use on their *x*-axis (time) and *y*-axis (length) if they had to plot this data on a grid which is 20 squares by 20 squares.

Once completed, discuss the options. The main error would be if learners still used one square to one hour for the *x*-axis. This would only use half of the grid. Hopefully all learners would use 2 mm per square for the *y*-axis.

Main teaching idea

Think like a mathematician, Question 3

Learning intention: Understanding some of the limitations of a time series graph.

Resources: Notebooks; Learner's Book Exercise 16.2

Description: Ask learners to work individually answering Question 3. Once completed, ask learners to compare their answers in small groups.

Answers: Learners' discussions and answers. Example: Sofia is correct. You cannot tell from the graph in which year the average price of crude oil was at its highest. This is because it only shows the price every 10 years and does not show any intermediate values. It does, however, show that the overall trend is that the price is going up.

After this, display the following data on the board:

This list shows the yearly average oil price from 2006 to 2018.

2006	$58.30	2013	$91.17
2007	$64.20	2014	$85.60
2008	$91.48	2015	$41.85
2009	$53.48	2016	$36.34
2010	$71.21	2017	$43.33
2011	$87.04	2018	$58.15
2012	$86.46		

Ask learners to look at the list and decide if they would like to change any of their answers. Discuss as a class the different information now available and how this more accurate list alters the graph in Question 3.

> **Differentiation ideas:** You may need to point out that the graph uses a ten-yearly average, which does not seem suitable if you want to determine any intermediate values. Discuss with learners the fact that the gaps between the values is large. It is so large that no one could give an accurate answer about oil costs for any of the other years on the graph.

Plenary idea

Silver time series graph (5 minutes)

Resources: Grid or graph paper

Description: The following table is from Question 5:

Year	1990	1994	1998	2002
Average price of silver ($)	4.80	5.30	5.50	4.60
Year	2006	2010	2014	2018
Average price of silver ($)	11.60	20.20	19.10	15.70

Ask learners to draw the time series graph to show the data from the table. Remind learners to use as much of the grid or graph paper as possible. Also make sure they give the graph a title and label the axes.

> **Assessment ideas:** Allow peer marking. Note that axes may be labelled differently depending on the type of grid or graph paper being used. Display this example graph for checking:

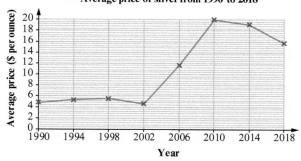

Average price of silver from 1990 to 2018

Guidance on selected *Thinking and working mathematically* questions

Conjecturing and Convincing

Learner's Book Exercise 16.2, Question 7

In this question, learners will say what they notice on the graph and then explain what it means. Question 7 is different from any of the other questions in this exercise. Learners may say that the trend is that shirt sales are falling, with sales of Scarlets rugby shirts falling faster. In reality, the Scarlets sales are actually increasing. The sales of Dragons rugby shirts are slowly decreasing. Ask learners to answer part **a**. Check to make sure learners have understood the graph properly. Once learners realise that the lines show the amount of stock left in the shop, the rest should be straightforward.

Homework idea

As Section 16.2 will probably take more than one lesson, you can select questions from Workbook Exercise 16.2 at the end of each lesson. You can help learners to mark their homework at the start of the next lesson. This means you can address any problems before moving on.

Assessment idea

Use Learner's Book Exercise 16.2, Question 2 as a class 'test'. If learners can answer this question, they obviously understand how to 'interpret a time series graph', even if it is a very simple one. Extend this question by asking how certain learners are of their answers to part **e**. The actual values could be very different from the estimates. If learners realise that these two answers are only estimates, they clearly understand this time series graph.

16.3 Stem-and-leaf diagrams

LEARNING PLAN

Framework codes	Learning objectives	Success criteria
8Ss.03	• Record, organise and represent categorical, discrete and continuous data: Stem-and-leaf diagrams.	• Learners can draw and interpret stem-and-leaf diagrams.

LANGUAGE SUPPORT

Mean: an average of a set of numbers, found by adding all the numbers and dividing the total by how many numbers there are in the set

Median: the middle number when a set of numbers is put in order

Mode: the most common number in a set of numbers

Range: the difference between the largest and smallest numbers in a set

Stem-and-leaf diagram: a way of displaying data like a horizontal bar graph but with sets of digits, in order of size, forming the bars

Common misconceptions

Misconception	How to identify	How to overcome
Learners often forget to include a key with their diagram.	Question 2.	Regularly remind learners that they must include a key every time they draw a stem-and-leaf diagram. Emphasise that, without this, the information it contains is meaningless.

Misconception	How to identify	How to overcome
Learners often try (and fail) to draw an ordered stem-and-leaf diagram without first drawing a stem-and-leaf diagram displaying the data in its original order.	Question 3.	Encourage learners always to start by drawing a stem-and-leaf diagram displaying the data in its original order. Then they should redraw it, putting the numbers in order, to produce an ordered stem-and-leaf diagram. This will make it easy to check that they have included all the numbers.
Learners may forget to check that the number of pieces of data is the same as the number of 'leaves' in their stem-and-leaf diagram.	Question 3.	Ask them to check during discussions.

Starter idea

A quicker way (5 minutes)

Resources: Mini whiteboards or notebooks

Description: Use this starter before working through the introduction to Section 16.3. Write or display these numbers on the board:

33, 23, 26, 35, 22, 41, 38, 33, 39, 28, 39, 43, 26, 26, 40, 31

Ask learners to write out the list in order of size, starting with the smallest. Once completed, ask learners to write the ordered list again. This time, they should write the 20s on one line, the 30s on the next line and the 40s on the last line. Write or display the list on the board:

22, 23, 26, 26, 26, 28

31, 33, 33, 35, 38, 39, 39

40, 41, 43

Tell learners that, not surprisingly, there is a shorter way to write the same list. Tell them it is called a stem-and-leaf diagram, and would look like this: (Write or display the stem-and-leaf diagram on the board)

2	2 3 6 6 6 8
3	1 3 3 5 8 9 9
4	0 1 3

Tell learners, while pointing at the numbers, that 2|2 means 22, 2|3 means 23 and 2|6 means 26.

You can extend this discussion to include the key, as covered in the introduction and Worked example.

Main teaching idea

How far? (10 minutes)

Learning intention: To invent questions relating to a stem-and-leaf diagram.

Resources: Notebooks; Learner's Book; Resource sheet 16.3 (you can download this resource from Cambridge GO)

Description: Set this activity after learners complete Exercise 16.3.

Let learners work in groups. Give each group a copy of Resource sheet 16.3. This shows an ordered stem-and-leaf diagram of distances travelled by different cars using 5 litres of fuel.

Ask learners to make up five questions that can be answered from the stem-and-leaf diagram. Other learners will answer their questions. They can make the questions as difficult as they like, but they must be able to answer the questions themselves.

When the groups have written their questions, exchange sheets among the groups. Ask learners to answer the questions on the sheet that they have received. Instruct learners to give full answers.

When they have answered the questions, exchange sheets among groups again (not necessarily back to the group who created the questions). Ask learners to check the answers given by the previous group.

Use this as the basis for a class discussion about the questions that were asked: How many were the same? How difficult were they to answer? How many mistakes were made? What seemed to be good answers? How was the working set out?

> **Differentiation ideas:** Learners can make their questions as complicated as they want. Some learners will write questions that are more easily answered. Ensure that these learners do not receive the questions from a group of more confident learners.

Plenary idea

Drawing a stem-and-leaf diagram (5–10 minutes)

Resources: Mini whiteboards

Description: Ask learners to draw a stem-and-leaf diagram representing the following data:

167, 159, 159, 169, 171, 167, 162, 157, 172, 160, 167, 158

> **Assessment ideas:** Peer marking. Write or display the correct stem-and-leaf diagram on the board.

Key: 15 | 7 means 157

```
15 | 7  8  9  9
16 | 0  2  7  7  7  9
17 | 1  2
```

Ask learners to check that the work they are marking has:

- the numbers in order of size from smallest to largest,
- a key to explain the numbers,
- all the numbers in line vertically and horizontally.

Guidance on selected *Thinking and working mathematically* questions

Conjecturing and Convincing

Learner's Book Exercise 16.3, Question 3

In this question, learners will spot patterns in the data and use them to answer questions. Ask learners to answer parts **a** and **b** and then compare answers with a partner. It might be useful to display the answers after a minute:

Answers: a Key: 10 | 1 means 101 kB   b 10

```
10 | 1  3  8  9
11 | 0  7  7  7
12 | 5  5  8
13 | 0  0  1  5  9  9
14 | 0  5  8
15 | 1  2  4  5  8
16 | 0  2  5  6  8
```

Now ask learners to answer parts **c** and **d**. If some learners do not start immediately you can prompt them. Suggest that, to answer part **c**, they first must work out the mode [117 kB] and the median [137 kB].

Once completed, discuss learners' answers to part **c**. Ask three or four learners to read out exactly what they have written. Discuss as a class the important points. For example, the mode is too close to the smallest value (or too far from the largest value) to be representative. The median would be best as it is in the middle of the data. To extend the questioning, ask if the mean would be a good way to represent the data. Why or why not? [Yes, it is a good way. There is quite a lot of data and the data is evenly spread out with no extreme values.]

Ask a learner for the answer to part **d**, check others have the same answer and ask them to self-mark. Discuss the possible error made [second largest number is 166, and 166 − 101 = 65].

Homework ideas

As Section 16.3 will probably take more than one lesson, you can select questions from Workbook Exercise 16.3 at the end of each lesson. Only set questions that can be answered using skills and knowledge gained from that lesson. You can help learners to mark their homework at the start of the next lesson. This means you can address any problems before moving on.

Assessment idea

Give each learner a ticket cut out from Exit ticket 16.3 (you can download this resource from Cambridge GO). Learners should complete the exit ticket just before leaving your class. Allow them 2–3 minutes to complete it.

Ask learners to put their names on their exit tickets. Alternatively you could ask only learners who would like some specific help to put their name on their exit ticket. Or you could ask them to be anonymous as this often leads to more honest reflection. When reading their answers, you will see what learners *think* they have learned. This will give you ideas about how you might help them further. It should clarify teaching points for the next lesson.

16.4 Pie charts

LEARNING PLAN

Framework codes	Learning objectives	Success criteria
8Ss.03	• Record organise and represent categorical, discrete and continuous data: Pie charts.	• Learners can draw and interpret pie charts
8Ss.05	• Interpret data, identifying patterns, trends and relationships, within and between data sets, to answer statistical questions. Discuss conclusions, considering the sources of variation, including sampling and check predictions.	• Learners can interpret data, identify relationships between two pie charts and answer statistical questions.

LANGUAGE SUPPORT

Pie chart: a circle divided into sectors, each sector represents its share of the whole

Proportions: fractions (or percentages) of the whole

Common misconceptions

Misconception	How to identify	How to overcome
Learners may fail to consider the total frequencies when comparing two pie charts. They may think that a bigger sector in one of them automatically means a greater frequency.	Question 3d.	Discussion during Worked example 16.4, part b.

Starter idea

Drawing pie charts (5 minutes)

Resources: Mini whiteboards or notebooks

Description: Copy or display the table below onto the board.

Type of holiday	Number of people
activity	32
beach	27
city break	24
other	7

Ask learners to write down the angle representing 'other' in a pie chart. They must show their working. Once completed, ask learners to compare answers. Probably a number of learners will have forgotten this example from Stage 7. You could ask successful learners to remind the others about the method. Make sure that learners explain that the total number of people on the four types of holiday is 90. A whole pie chart has angles adding to 360° and 360° ÷ 90 = 4°, so each person is represented by 4° in the pie chart. 'Other' has 7 people, so $7 \times 4° = 28°$. Different methods, e.g. $\frac{7}{90} \times 360 = 28°$ are equally valid.

Main teaching idea

Pie chart questions (10–15 minutes)

Learning intention: To invent questions based on information in a pie chart.

Resources: Notebooks; Learner's Book; calculators; Resource sheet 16.4 (you can download this resource from Cambridge GO)

Description: Set this activity after learners have completed at least the first three questions from Exercise 16.4. Let learners work in groups. Give each group a copy of Resource sheet 16.4 which shows a pie chart about the number of text messages received by a class.

Ask learners to make up five questions that can be answered from the pie chart. Other learners will answer their questions. They can make the questions as difficult as they like, but they must be able to answer the questions themselves.

When the groups have written their questions, exchange sheets among the groups. Ask learners to answer the questions on the sheet that they have received. Instruct learners to give full answers.

When they have answered the questions, exchange sheets among groups again (not necessarily back to the group who created the questions). Ask learners to check the answers given by the previous group.

Use this as the basis for a class discussion about the questions that were asked: How many were the same? How difficult were they to answer? How many mistakes were made? What seemed to be good answers? How was the working set out?

> **Differentiation ideas:** Learners can make their questions as complicated as they want. Some learners will write questions that are more easily answered. Ensure that these learners do not receive the questions from a group of more confident learners.

Many questions will be quite similar. This is not surprising since, for this type of pie chart, the options are limited.

> **Differentiation ideas:** To extend this work, tell learners that the pie chart represents a total of 90 text messages. Then repeat the activity.

Plenary idea

Avocado (3–5 minutes)

Resources: Mini whiteboards or notebooks

Description: Draw or display the pie charts, information and questions on the board.

Children who had eaten avocado

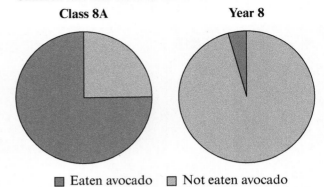

■ Eaten avocado   ■ Not eaten avocado

1   Which group had the higher proportion of children who had eaten avocado? Explain your answer.

2   Which group had the higher number of children who had eaten avocado? Explain your answer.

Answers:
1   Class 8A as, of the two pie charts, it has a larger proportion of dark grey.
2   Cannot say. The number of children represented by each pie chart is not given.

> **Assessment ideas:** Peer mark. Ask learners to exchange answers with a partner and discuss them. If their answers are not clear, learners should explain them to their partner.

Guidance on selected *Thinking and working mathematically* questions

Conjecturing and Convincing

Learner's Book Exercise 16.4, Question 7

In this question, learners will compare data from pie charts and use it to support their explanation. Learners should notice that the 30° for black rice can be used as a multiplier. It enables them to work out all of the other amounts of rice in the table in part **a**. If any learner starts to work out masses using a calculator, make sure you help them to see the link.

Completing the table in part **b** is more complex. 12 kg of red rice is represented by 30°. You might need to suggest to some learners that they use this to work out the mass represented by 10°. This is usually enough guidance for completing the table.

In part **c**, many learners would think Sofia's statement is true. However, the question tells them it is incorrect. Once learners have written their answers it is worth spending some time in a class discussion. In the pie chart for shop A, the angle for red rice is twice as big as for shop B. Try to ensure that all learners understand what this means. Since the amount of red rice is the same, each degree must represent half as much red rice.

Homework ideas

As Section 16.4 will probably take more than one lesson, you can select questions from Workbook Exercise 16.4 at the end of each lesson. Only set questions that can be answered using skills and knowledge gained from that lesson. You can help learners to mark their homework at the start of the next lesson. This means you can address any problems before moving on.

Assessment idea

With learners giving such a large number of explanations and showing their working, this is a good exercise for learners to peer mark. Having learners regularly exchange books (in pairs or groups) for checking and marking helps them to focus on the important aspects of their work. Learners will need to read explanations very carefully to determine whether they are easy to understand as well as correct. This process helps all learners to become clear and concise writers. It will take some learners more time and practice than others.

16.5 Representing data

LEARNING PLAN

Framework codes	Learning objectives	Success criteria
8Ss.03	• Record, organise and represent categorical, discrete and continuous data. Choose and explain which representation to use in a given situation: Venn and Carroll diagrams; tally charts, frequency tables and two-way tables; dual and compound bar charts; pie charts; line graphs and time series graphs; scatter graphs; stem-and-leaf diagrams; infographics.	• Learners can choose and explain which representation to use depending on the type of data.

LANGUAGE SUPPORT

Justify: give a reason for your decision

Common misconceptions

Misconception	How to identify	How to overcome
Learners may choose an inappropriate way to display the data.	Most questions.	Practice and discussions throughout this exercise.

Starter idea

Worked example 16.5 (5–10 minutes)

Resources: Learner's Book

Description: After a brief class discussion on the meaning of 'justify', read the question and answer of part **a**. Ask how learners think a time series graph allows them to see how the value of gold changes over time. This may be difficult to articulate for many learners, so help the discussion by projecting this graph onto the board:

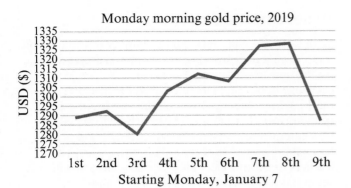

Monday morning gold price, 2019

Even a quick sketch of this will probably be enough to allow more clarity in the learners' discussion:

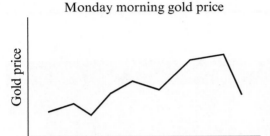

Monday morning gold price

Make sure learners explain that the graph shows the values, so it is easy to spot any trends in how the data changes over time. Explain that there are other options of data display, such as bar charts, but time series graphs are quicker to draw and show any trends more clearly.

Next, read the question and answer for part **b**. Ask learners why compound bar charts are easy to compare. Make sure learners understand that the two salad dressings must have the same volume so that the individual ingredients can be compared. Explain that there are, again, other options of data display, such as a dual bar chart or a pie chart, but both are usually harder and more time-consuming to draw unless using spreadsheet software such as Excel®. As with almost any data, you could also use an infographic to display the information on the two salad dressings.

Finally, read the question and answer for part **c**. Ask learners why it is useful to see the exact data. Learners should remember that this will allow for comparisons across age groups, but it also allows you to work out other statistics, such as mean, median, mode and range if you need to.

Discuss with learners that, if you used grouped data (for example, $10 \leq a < 20$, $20 \leq a < 30$, etc.), you could display the data using a bar chart or a pie chart, but much of the useful information will be lost by grouping the data.

Main teaching idea

The Amazon Rainforest (10–20 minutes)

Learning intention: To decide what data to display and how to display it.

Resources: Large sheet of paper for each pair of learners; Resource Sheet 16.5A or 16.5B (these are both available from Cambridge GO and contain the same information, but in Resource Sheet 16.5B the text has been broken into smaller amounts of text).

Description: Learners work in pairs to make a poster. It is important to read through the information headed 'The Amazon rainforest'. Learners need the chance to ask if there is something they don't understand. Then read part **a**, making sure that all learners have understood the instruction 'You do not need to show *all* of the information.'

Once learners have completed their posters, you could spread them out over a few desks so that all learners get to see all the posters. Alternatively, you could put two or three pairs of learners together to discuss each other's posters.

Discuss as a class how they can clearly display certain data. This is an important way to reinforce much of the work done in this exercise.

> **Differentiation ideas:** Some pairs of learners might be a little overwhelmed with the amount of data in the article. Help them to break down the data into smaller amounts that are more easily displayed. Suggest a method of representing the data. You could point out that some people might think it is important to know who owns the Amazon. For these people, the data 'Brazil has 60%, Peru has 13%, Columbia has 10%, Bolivia has 7%, and the remaining 10% is shared between five other countries' might be worth displaying. A compound bar chart or an ordinary bar chart could be a good way to display this data easily. Learners could then discuss whether they want to display this data and, if so, how to display it.

Plenary idea

Diagram, graph or chart? (3–5 minutes)

Resources: Notebooks

Description: Write or display on the board:

Which type of diagram, graph or chart do you think is best to display the data? Justify your choice.

a The percentage of teachers at two schools who use a black, white, red, blue or other coloured vehicle to get to school.

b The mass and the height of people at a sports centre.

c The mark, out of 20, scored by 100 learners in a history exam.

d The mass of peppers picked at a farm each week.

Ask learners not to look at the Learner's Book or previous pages in their notebooks as they answer the questions.

> **Assessment ideas:** Either take in notebooks for a formal assessment or ask learners to peer mark. Include discussions to clarify the answers if needed.

Answers: Examples:

a Dual bar chart – to compare two sets of discrete data. Allow pie chart or compound bar chart as these are also good ways to compare proportions (percentages).

b Scatter graph – to plot two data points for each person and see if there is any relationship between mass and height.

c Stem-and-leaf diagram – you can see the actual scores as well as the grouping of the scores.

d Time series graph – you can clearly see how the mass of the peppers picked changes over time.

Guidance on selected *Thinking and working mathematically* questions

Characterising and Classifying

Learner's Book Exercise 16.5, Question 2

In this question, learners will examine the data and decide which type of diagram, graph or chart is best suited to it. Learners may be confused with which type of representation to use. They have probably not used Venn diagrams for more than a year. The example in the table in the introduction shows only two interlocking circles. In this question there are three science subjects to display.

For learners who cannot start this question, it may be useful to work in pairs or a small group. Ask them to look at the table in the introduction. Then read out the 'When do I use it?' for the first row.

Ask learners to decide if they want to sort data into groups that have some common features [Yes].

Ask learners to decide if a Venn diagram has to have two circles [It could have three].

Suggest that learners try to represent the data using a Venn diagram. If they need help with placing the numbers, ask a successful learner to help them. They could show them how to write in just one number and explain why it should go in that place on the Venn diagram.

Homework ideas

As Section 16.5 will probably take more than one lesson, you can select questions from Workbook Exercise 16.5 at the end of each lesson. You can help learners to mark their homework at the start of the next lesson. This means you can address any problems before moving on.

Assessment idea

In this game, the winner is the fastest person to write down two facts about a diagram, graph or chart: How many sets of data can it represent? [1 or 2] Do we use it for discrete [D] or continuous [C] data or either [E]?

Put learners into groups of three. Say the name of a diagram, graph or chart, e.g. 'bar chart'. The first learner to write '**1 D**' is the winner [1 set of data, discrete data]. Then the next group of three has a go with a different diagram, graph or chart. Repeat the process until all learners have had a go.

Next put winners into pairs or groups of three, depending on the numbers in your class and repeat the process. (They do not need to move next to each other.)

Then put these winners into pairs and repeat the process until you have one final winner.

Some diagrams, graphs or charts may be harder to characterise, e.g. compound bar charts can show discrete or grouped continuous data. Leave these more complex diagrams, graphs or charts until later in the game or select more confident learners to work together on these.

Answers:

Bar chart	1 D
Dual bar chart	2 D
Compound bar chart	2 E
Frequency diagram	1 C
Time series graph	1 E
Scatter graph	2 E
Pie chart	1 E
Stem-and-leaf diagram	1 E

16.6 Using statistics

LEARNING PLAN

Framework codes	Learning objectives	Success criteria
8Ss.04	• Use knowledge of mode, median, mean and range to compare two distributions, considering the interrelationship between centrality and spread.	• Learners can compare two distributions using mode, median, mean and range.

LANGUAGE SUPPORT

Mean: an average of a set of numbers, found by adding all the numbers and dividing the total by how many numbers there are in the set

Median: the middle number when a set of numbers is put in order

Mode: the most common number in a set of numbers

Range: the difference between the largest and smallest numbers in a set

Common misconceptions

Misconception	How to identify	How to overcome
Learners may forget to use the 'frequency' part of a frequency table when working out an average.	Question 8.	Discussion after completion of Question 8, especially if the answers include 'no mode', median of 2.5 or working out the mean by either $15 \div 6$ or $15 \div 5$.

Starter idea

Mode, median, mean and range (5 minutes)

Resources: Mini whiteboards

Description: Before working through the introduction of Section 16.6, write or display on the board:

Here are the times, in minutes, Sofia waits in line for lunch on 20 different days:

2, 5, 3, 8, 5, 2, 10, 7, 8, 8, 4, 7, 2, 2, 3, 6, 10, 3, 4, 7

a Work out

 i the mode **ii** the median **iii** the mean time.

b Which average best represents this data? Give a reason for your choice of average.

c Work out the range in her waiting times.

Once completed, discuss the answers as a class and clarify any misunderstandings. This discussion will allow you to note who has remembered these basics from Stage 7 and who might require more help later in this section. If any learners have wrong answers, it may be worth first checking their rewritten list:

2 2 2 2 3 3 3 4 4 5 5 6 7 7 7 8 8 8 10 10

Answers:
a **i** 2 minutes **ii** 5 minutes **iii** 5.3 minutes
b Either the median or the mean (not the mode). Nine of the times are above 5 minutes and nine are below 5 minutes. Both 5 (median) and 5.3 (mean) are in the middle of the data so both are suitable.
c 8 minutes

Main teaching idea

Heads? (10 minutes)

Learning intention: To use real data and a frequency table to work out averages and spread.

Resources: Notebooks; coins

Description: Use this activity before attempting Question 8. Let learners work individually or in pairs. Give each learner a coin. Learners spin the coin and record the number of 'throws' until a head appears. Depending on the size of the class, this could be repeated several times. Gather the class results in a frequency table. If no coins are available, use this table:

Throws	1	2	3	4	5	6	7	8
Frequency	23	13	5	3	3	0	2	1

If no coins are available, but you still want to use your own data, there are 'virtual' coins available on the internet. Alternatively you could use the random number generator on a calculator: even number = heads, odd number = tails.

Ask learners 'What is the average number of throws before a head appears?' They should now be familiar with three averages, the mode, the median and the mean. Ask learners to calculate each type of average. Look for possible errors in their methods.

The mode in the example above is 1 because it has the highest frequency. The median in the example is 2. It is between the 25th and 26th numbers as there were 50 throws. Make sure learners understand how to find the median from a frequency table. (This will help with Learner's Book Exercise 16.6, Question 8 later.)

The mean in the example is $113 \div 50 = 2.26$. Make sure learners understand how to calculate this using the frequency. They need to multiply each entry in the 'Throws' row by its frequency, add those values and then divide by the total of the frequencies [50]. (Common misconceptions are shown at the start of this section.)

Ask learners to choose an average to represent the data. The mean, in this case, is not the best choice. It is larger than the other two because of the two 7s and the 8. The mode or the median is a better choice. Learners should be able to justify choosing either of these.

- The mode is the most likely number of throws to produce a head. Learners might be surprised that it is only 1. Some learners may use their knowledge of probability from Unit 13 to realise there is an equal chance of a head or a tail.

- The median takes account of all the values. Unlike the mean, it is not unduly affected by a few exceptionally high values.

Learners should also be able to calculate the range. In the example it is $8 - 1 = 7$. Learners should appreciate that the range is not an average but a measure of spread.

It is the only measure of spread they need to know about in Stage 8.

> **Differentiation ideas:** If learners need more practice, set a similar activity. Ask learners to throw a fair dice and record how many throws they need to get a 6. Analyse the results in a similar way. In this case the range will probably be greater but the mode may be less appropriate for representing the data.

Plenary idea

Five teachers (3–5 minutes)

Resources: Mini whiteboards or notebooks

Description: Copy or display on the board:

You are told that the heights of five teachers are 1.55 m, 1.55 m, 1.62 m, 1.68 m and 2.05 m. This data gives a mode of 1.55 m, a median of 1.62 m and a mean of 1.69 m.

a Which average do you think is the most representative of the data?

b Explain why the other two averages are less representative than your choice.

> **Assessment ideas:** Allow peer marking. Ask learners to exchange books with a partner and read their answers. Discuss as a pair whether or not the written answers agree. If not, can they discuss and then agree on the best choice? If they can't agree, discuss as a class the reasons to choose one average rather than the others.

Guidance on selected *Thinking and working mathematically* questions

Conjecturing and Convincing

Learner's Book Exercise 16.6, Question 8

If you used Main teaching idea 'Heads?' from this Teacher's Resource then Question 8 will seem easier for learners. In this question, learners will use the mode, median, mean and range to support different conclusions from data. They need to remember to use the frequency when working out the three averages. If your class contains learners who find this difficult, you could just ask them to show that Marcus could be correct, not Zara or Arun.

Once all learners have finished, discuss the answers as a class. Learners should have said that Marcus could be correct if the mode was used. Team A scored five goals in five matches but team B only scored one goal in six matches. If all learners have understood this, they should be able to answer the rest of the question.

If learners mention the number 4 in their argument, they will need your help. Alternatively, you could ask a successful learner to explain what the frequency shows. Once learners have got the correct answers to part **a**, part **b** should be straightforward.

Homework ideas

As Section 16.6 will probably take more than one lesson, you can select questions from Workbook Exercise 16.6 at the end of each lesson. Only set questions that can be answered using skills and knowledge gained from that lesson. You can help learners to mark their homework at the start of the next lesson. This means you can address any problems before moving on.

You could ask learners to make a poster containing everything they think they need to remember for the end-of-unit test. The following lesson, it is important to share the posters in class, perhaps spread out over a few desks for everyone to look at. Discuss the different posters as a class. When the class agree that a point is important, that key point could be copied onto the board (by you or a learner). Agree on as many key points as possible. Learners could then improve their individual poster if necessary. Learners could store their poster at home as a possible revision tool towards mid-term or end-of-year exams.

Assessment idea

Give one copy of Resource sheet 16.6 Key words to each learner (you can download this resource from Cambridge GO). Learners should write in an example or an explanation (a basic definition) for each key word they have seen in Section 16. This should highlight any key words that need reinforcing. The understanding of these words is important for learners to succeed in exams.

Once completed, you could give them the answers. Alternatively, you could put learners into pairs or small groups to look at the key words box in each section and also the Glossary. Discuss with learners which of their explanations or examples show understanding and which need to be clearer.

If learners have been filling in a copy of Resource sheet 16.6 Keywords since the start of Unit 16, this assessment should be easier for them.